iPhone
The Missing Manual

Fourth Edition

iPhone: The Missing Manual, Fourth Edition   BY DAVID POGUE

Published by O'Reilly Media, Inc., 1005 Gravenstein Highway North, Sebastopol, CA 95472.

O'Reilly books may be purchased for educational, business, or sales promotional use. Online editions are also available for most titles (*safari.oreilly.com*). For more information, contact our corporate/institutional sales department: 800.998.9938 or *corporate@oreilly.com*.

Executive Editor: Chris Nelson

Copy Editor: Julie Van Keuren

Indexers: David Pogue, Matt Gibstein

Cover Designers: Monica Kamsvaag and Phil Simpson

Interior Designer: Phil Simpson (based on a design by Ron Bilodeau)

Print History:

August 2010:   Fourth Edition.

ISBN: 978-1-449-39365-6

[C]   [08/10]

Contents

The Missing Credits

 **David Pogue** (author) is the weekly tech columnist for *The New York Times,* an Emmy-winning correspondent for *CBS News Sunday Morning,* a weekly CNBC contributor, and the creator of the Missing Manual series. He's the author or coauthor of 51 books, including 25 in this series, six in the "For Dummies" line (including *Macs, Magic, Opera,* and *Classical Music*), two novels, and *The World According to Twitter.* In his other life, David is a former Broadway show conductor, a piano player, and a magician. He lives in Connecticut with his three awesome children.

Links to his columns and weekly videos await at *www.davidpogue.com.* He welcomes feedback about his books by email at *david@pogueman.com.*

Julie Van Keuren (copy editor) is a freelance editor, writer, and desktop publisher who runs her "little media empire" from her home in Billings, Montana. In her spare time she enjoys swimming, biking, running, and (hey, why not?) triathlons. She and her husband, M.H., have two sons, Dexter and Michael. *Email: little_media@yahoo.com.*

Rich Koster (technical reviewer). The iPhone was Rich's first cellphone as well as his first iPod, but it soon became his faithful electronic companion. As he got deeper into it, he began corresponding with David Pogue, sharing tips, tricks, and observations; eventually, David asked him to be the beta reader for this book's previous editions—and hired him as the tech editor for this one. Rich is a husband, a father, and creator of the Disney Echo at *DisneyEcho. emuck.com*—which he runs from his iPhone every day!

Acknowledgments

The Missing Manual series is a joint venture between the dream team introduced on these pages and O'Reilly Media. I'm grateful to all of them, especially to designer Phil Simpson and prose queen Julie Van Keuren, who have become my Missing Manual core team.

A few other friends did massive favors for this edition of this book. My fellow Times columnist Jude Biersdorfer wrote the earlier editions' chapters on iTunes, syncing, and accessories, and of course did a brilliant, witty job.

With boundless enthuisiasm, my summer intern Matt Gibstein became a master of Photoshop, InDesign, and the crazed Pogue production process in a matter of days. His work on the graphics, the index, and hunting down a lot of tweaky answers made the book's on-time publication possible. And Apple's Greg Joswiak, Natalie Kerris, Teresa Brewer, and Steve Sinclair donated valuable technical answers to my cause.

Thanks to David Rogelberg for believing in the idea, and above all, to my family. They make these books—and everything else—possible.

—*David Pogue*

The Missing Manual Series

Missing Manual books are superbly written guides to computer products that don't come with printed manuals (which is just about all of them). Each book features a handcrafted index; cross-references to specific page numbers (not just "See Chapter 14"); and RepKover, a detached-spine binding that lets the book lie perfectly flat without the assistance of weights or cinder blocks. Recent and upcoming titles:

Access 2010: The Missing Manual by Matthew MacDonald

AppleScript: The Missing Manual by Adam Goldstein

AppleWorks 6: The Missing Manual by Jim Elferdink and David Reynolds

Buying a Home: The Missing Manual by Nancy Conner

CSS: The Missing Manual by David Sawyer McFarland

Creating Web Sites: The Missing Manual by Matthew MacDonald

David Pogue's Digital Photography: The Missing Manual by David Pogue

Dreamweaver CS5: The Missing Manual by David Sawyer McFarland

eBay: The Missing Manual by Nancy Conner

Excel 2010: The Missing Manual by Matthew MacDonald

Facebook: The Missing Manual, 2nd Edition by E.A. Vander Veer

FileMaker Pro 11: The Missing Manual by Susan Prosser and Stuart Gripman

Flash CS5: The Missing Manual by Chris Grover

FrontPage 2003: The Missing Manual by Jessica Mantaro

Google Apps: The Missing Manual by Nancy Conner

The Internet: The Missing Manual by David Pogue and J.D. Biersdorfer

iMovie '09 & iDVD: The Missing Manual by David Pogue and Aaron Miller

iPad: The Missing Manual by J.D. Biersdorfer

iPhone App Development: The Missing Manual by Craig Hockenberry

iPhoto '09: The Missing Manual by David Pogue and J.D. Biersdorfer

iPod: The Missing Manual, 9th Edition by J.D. Biersdorfer

iWork '09: The Missing Manual by Josh Clark

JavaScript: The Missing Manual by David Sawyer McFarland

Living Green: The Missing Manual by Nancy Conner

Mac OS X Snow Leopard: The Missing Manual by David Pogue

Microsoft Project 2010: The Missing Manual by Bonnie Biafore

Netbooks: The Missing Manual by J.D. Biersdorfer

Office 2010: The Missing Manual by Nancy Conner and Matthew MacDonald

Office 2008 for Macintosh: The Missing Manual by Jim Elferdink

Palm Pre: The Missing Manual by Ed Baig

PCs: The Missing Manual by Andy Rathbone

Personal Investing: The Missing Manual by Bonnie Biafore, Amy E. Buttell, and Carol Fabbri

Photoshop CS5: The Missing Manual by Lesa Snider

Photoshop Elements 7: The Missing Manual by Barbara Brundage

Photoshop Elements 6 for Mac: The Missing Manual by Barbara Brundage

PowerPoint 2007: The Missing Manual by E.A. Vander Veer

QuickBase: The Missing Manual by Nancy Conner

QuickBooks 2009: The Missing Manual by Bonnie Biafore

Quicken 2009: The Missing Manual by Bonnie Biafore

Switching to the Mac: The Missing Manual, Snow Leopard Edition by David Pogue

Wikipedia: The Missing Manual by John Broughton

Windows XP Home Edition: The Missing Manual, 2nd Edition by David Pogue

Windows XP Pro: The Missing Manual, 2nd Edition by David Pogue, Craig Zacker, and Linda Zacker

Windows Vista: The Missing Manual by David Pogue

Windows 7: The Missing Manual by David Pogue

Word 2007: The Missing Manual by Chris Grover

Your Body: The Missing Manual by Matthew MacDonald

Your Brain: The Missing Manual by Matthew MacDonald

Your Money: The Missing Manual by J.D. Roth

 Tip There are also mini Missing Manual eBooks on specialized topics like *iBooks and ePeriodicals on the iPad, Doing Business on Facebook, Creating iPhone Apps with Cocoa Touch, Word Processing in Pages '09, Sharing Keynote Slideshows, Creating Keynote Slideshows, Add Audio and Video to Your Site, Attract Visitors to Your Site,* **and** *Add Interactivity to Your Site.*

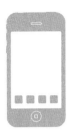

Introduction

How do you make the point that the iPhone has changed the world? The easy answer is "use statistics"—70 million sold, 250,000 downloadable programs on the iPhone App Store, 5 billion downloads… Trouble is, those statistics get stale almost before you've finished typing them.

Maybe it's better to talk about the aftermath. How since the iPhone came along, cell carriers (AT&T, Verizon, and so on) have opened up the calcified, conservative way they used to consider new cellphone designs. How every phone and its brother now have a touchscreen. How BlackBerry, Palm Pre, Google (Android) phones, and even Windows Mobile phones all have their own app stores. How, in essence, everybody wants to be the iPhone.

The thing is, they'll never quite catch up, because Apple is always moving, too. In June 2010, for example, it introduced the fourth iPhone model, the iPhone 4. It's slimmer, narrower, faster, cooler-looking. It also has a few new features, including a screen with better contrast and four times the sharpness, a better camera (with a flash), a second camera on the front for making free video calls, a longer-life battery, and so on.

More importantly, there's a new, free version of the iPhone's software, called iOS 4. (Why not "iPhone OS" anymore? Because the same operating system runs on the iPad and the iPod Touch. It's not just for iPhones anymore.)

iOS 4 adds all kinds of new features people have been pining for: multitasking (running more than one app at a time), folders for organizing all your apps, a 5X zoom in the camera, iBooks (an electronic book reader), a spelling checker, a desktop picture for your Home screens, and so on.

Why is it so important? Because you can run iOS 4 on *older* iPhone models (the 3G and the 3GS) without having to buy the iPhone 4. (Not all features work on the older models, though.) This book covers both the iPhone 4 and the iOS 4 software, even if you've installed it on an older phone.

About the iPhone

So what's the iPhone?

Well, it's a cellphone, obviously. But it's also a full-blown iPod, complete with a big, dazzling screen for watching TV shows and movies. And the iPhone is also the best pocket Internet viewer you've ever seen. It shows fully formatted email (with attachments, thank you) and displays entire Web pages with fonts and design intact. It's tricked out with a tilt sensor, a proximity sensor, a light sensor, WiFi, Bluetooth, GPS, a gyroscope (in the iPhone 4), and that amazing multitouch screen.

Furthermore, it's a calendar, an address book, a calculator, an alarm clock, a stopwatch, a stock tracker, a traffic reporter, an RSS reader, and a weather forecaster. It even stands in for a flashlight and, with the screen off, a pocket mirror.

But don't forget the App Store. Thanks to the hundreds of thousands of add-on programs that await there, the iPhone is also a fast, wicked-fun pocket computer. All those free or cheap programs can turn it into a medical reference, a musical keyboard, a time tracker, a remote control, a voice recorder, a tip calculator, an ebook reader, and so on. And whoa, those games! Hundreds of them, with smooth 3-D graphics and tilt control.

All of this sends the iPhone's utility and power through the roof. Calling it a phone is practically an insult.

(Apple probably should have called it an "iPod," but that name was taken.)

About This Book

By way of a printed guide to the iPhone, Apple provides only a fold-out leaflet. It's got a clever name—Finger Tips—but to learn your way around, you're expected to use an electronic PDF document. This PDF covers the basics well, but it's largely free of details, hacks, workarounds, tutorials, humor, and any acknowledgment of the iPhone's flaws. You can't mark your place, underline, or read it in the bathroom.

The purpose of this book, then, is to serve as the manual that should have accompanied the iPhone. (If you have an original iPhone, you really need one of this book's earlier editions. If you have an iPhone 3G or 3GS, this book assumes that you've installed the free iOS 4 software, described in Appendix A.)

Writing computer books can be an annoying job. You commit something to print, and then—bam—the software gets updated or revised, and suddenly your book is out of date.

That will certainly happen to this book. The iPhone is a *platform*. It's a computer, so Apple routinely updates and improves it by sending it new software bits. To picture where the iPhone will be five years from now, just look at how much better, sleeker, and more powerful today's iPod is than the original 2001 black-and-white brick.

Therefore, you should think of this book the way you think of the first iPhone: as a darned good start. To keep in touch with updates we make to it as developments unfold, drop in to the book's Errata/Changes page. (Go to *www. missingmanuals.com*, click this book's name, and then click View/Submit Errata.)

 Writing a book about the iPhone is a study in exasperation, because the darned thing is a moving target. Apple updates the iPhone's software fairly often, piping in new features, bug fixes, speed-ups, and so on.

This book covers the iPhone's 4.0.1 software. But eventually, there will be 4.0.2 software, 4.0.3, probably a 4.1, and so on. To keep current on the changes, check out the free "Missing CD" on this book's page at *www.missingmanuals.com*.

About the Outline

iPhone: The Missing Manual is divided into five parts, each containing several chapters:

- Part 1, **The iPhone as Phone,** covers everything related to phone calls: dialing, answering, voice control, voicemail, conference calling, text messaging, MMS, and the Contacts (address book) program. It's also where you can read about FaceTime, the iPhone 4's video-calling feature.

- Part 2, **Pix, Flix, & Apps,** is dedicated to the iPhone's built-in software programs, with a special emphasis on its multimedia abilities: playing music, podcasts, movies, TV shows, and photos; capturing still photos and videos; navigating with GPS; and so on. These chapters also cover app management: installing, organizing, and quitting apps—and, of course, the iPhone's special version of multitasking.

- Part 3, **The iPhone Online,** is a detailed exploration of the iPhone's third talent: its ability to get you onto the Internet, either over a WiFi hot spot connection or via AT&T's cellular network. It's all here: email, Web browsing, and *tethering* (that is, letting your phone serve as a glorified Internet antenna for your laptop).

- Part 4, **Connections,** describes the world beyond the iPhone itself—like the copy of iTunes on your Mac or PC that's responsible for filling up the iPhone with music, videos, and photos, and syncing the calendar, address book, and mail settings. These chapters also cover the iPhone's control panel, the Settings program; and how the iPhone syncs wirelessly with corporate networks using Microsoft Exchange ActiveSync—or with your own computers using Apple's MobileMe service.

 A couple of weeks after the iPhone 4 debuted in the summer of 2010, videos began appearing online, showing a peculiar quirk: If you hold the iPhone 4 so that the lower-left corner is pressed into your palm, you can see your signal-strength bars drop. You can actually see the bars disappearing. Sometimes, you drop the call as a result.

A cellphone that loses its signal when you pick it up? Well, *that* could be considered a drawback.

It doesn't happen to everyone. It doesn't happen everywhere. It's more likely if you're in a weak signal-strength area, and if you have sweaty palms. The problem seems to occur only when you're covering up the black gap in the stainless-steel band at the phone's lower-left edge.

Even more intriguing: Putting the phone in a case eliminates the problem. Even a "bumper"—like the $30 one that Apple sells—solves the problem. It's a thin, rubbery silicon band, available in a range of colors, that covers the metal edge entirely.

After an intense week of media hysteria, including a stinging "not recommended" review from Consumer Reports, Apple CEO Steve Jobs gave a short press conference. He showed several videos of other companies' smartphones that have exactly the same problem, insisting that signal weakening in certain grips is not just an iPhone issue.

He said the issue had been "blown out of proportion" but offered two short-term solutions: a free case or Apple bumper, or a full refund within 30 days of buying the phone.

These offers were good only through September 30, 2010; by then, Apple said it would have had time to study the problem and, presumably, to come up with a long-term solution (which might be extending the free-case offer).

This book went to press before that fateful day arrived. On this book's "Missing CD" page at *www.missingmanuals.com*, you'll find a free PDF supplement that reveals the exciting conclusion to the wild story of the iPhone 4 Death Grip.

In the meantime, if you experience the problem on your iPhone 4, you can avoid covering the black gap; you can put a piece of tape over it; you can use a case; or you can return the phone.

- Part 5, **Appendixes,** contains three reference chapters. Appendix A walks you through the setup process; Appendix B is a tour of accessories like chargers, car adapters, and carrying cases; and Appendix C is a master compendium of troubleshooting, maintenance, and battery information.

About→These→Arrows

Throughout this book, and throughout the Missing Manual series, you'll find sentences like this one: Tap Settings→Fetch New Data→Off. That's shorthand for a much longer instruction that directs you to open three nested screens in sequence, like this: "Tap the Settings button. On the next screen, tap Fetch New Data. On the screen after that, tap Off." (In this book, tappable things on the screen are printed in orange to make them stand out.)

Similarly, this kind of arrow shorthand helps to simplify the business of choosing commands in menus on your Mac or PC, like File→Print.

About MissingManuals.com

To get the most out of this book, visit www.missingmanuals.com. Click the Missing CD-ROMs link, and then click this book's title to reveal a neat, organized list of the shareware and freeware mentioned in this book.

The Web site also offers corrections and updates to the book; to see them, click the book's title, and then click View/Submit Errata. In fact, please submit corrections yourself! Each time we print more copies of this book, we'll make any confirmed corrections you've suggested. We'll also note such changes on the Web site, so you can mark important corrections into your own copy of the book, if you like. And we'll keep the book current as Apple releases more iPhone updates.

The Guided Tour

I f you'd never seen all the videos and photos of the iPhone, and you found it lying on someone's desk, you might not guess it was a phone (let alone an iPod/Web browser/alarm clock/stopwatch/voice recorder/musical instrument/compass). You can't see any antenna, mouthpiece, or earpiece—and, goodness knows, there are no number keys for dialing.

It's all there, though, hidden inside this sleek black-and-silver slab.

For the rest of this book, and for the rest of your life with the iPhone, you'll be expected to know what's meant by, for example, "the Home button" and "the Sleep switch." A guided tour, therefore, is in order. Keep hands and feet inside the tram at all times.

Sleep Switch (On/Off)

On the top-right edge of the iPhone, you'll find a silver metal button shaped like a dash. This, ladies and gents, is the Sleep switch.

It has several functions:

- **Sleep/Wake.** Tapping it once puts the iPhone to sleep—into Standby mode, ready for incoming calls but consuming very little power. Tapping it again turns on the screen so it's ready for action.

- **On/Off.** The same switch can also turn the iPhone off completely so it consumes no power at all; incoming calls get dumped into voicemail. You might turn the iPhone off whenever you're not going to use it for a few days.

  To turn the iPhone off, press the Sleep switch for 3 seconds. The screen changes to say slide to power off. Confirm your decision by placing a fingertip on the right-pointing red arrow and sliding to the right. The device shuts off completely.

Tip If you change your mind about turning the iPhone off, tap the Cancel button, or do nothing. If the iPhone decides you're not paying attention, it dismisses the slide to power off screen automatically.

To turn the iPhone back on, press the switch again for 1 second. The chromelike Apple logo appears as the phone boots up.

- **Answer call/Dump to voicemail.** When a call comes in, you can tap the Sleep button *once* to silence the ringing or vibrating. After four rings, the call goes to your voicemail.

  You can also tap it *twice* to dump the call to voicemail immediately. (Of course, because they didn't hear four rings, iPhone veterans will know you've blown them off. Bruised egos may result. Welcome to the new world of iPhone etiquette.)

- **Force restart.** The Sleep switch has one more function. If your iPhone is frozen, and no buttons work, and you can't even turn the thing off, this button is also involved in force-restarting the whole machine. Steps for this last-ditch procedure are on page 412.

Locked Mode

When you don't touch the screen for 1 minute, or when you put the iPhone to sleep, the phone *locks* itself. When it's locked, the screen isn't touch-sensitive. Fortunately, you can still take phone calls and control music playback.

Remember, this phone is all touchscreen, so it's much more prone to accidental button pushes than most phones. You wouldn't want to discover that your iPhone has been calling people or taking photos from the depths of your pocket or purse. Nor would you want it to dial a random number from your back pocket, a phenomenon that's earned the unfortunate name *butt-dialing*.

That's why the first thing you do after waking the iPhone is *unlocking* it. Fortunately, that's easy (and a lot of fun) to do: Place your fingertip on the gray arrow and slide it to the right, as indicated by the animation.

Tip The iPhone can demand a password each time it wakes up, if you like. See page 376. On the other hand, you can adjust how quickly the phone locks itself, or make it stop locking itself altogether; see page 376 again.

SIM Card Slot

On the edge of the phone, at the top (iPhone 3G and 3GS) or the right side (iPhone 4), there's a tiny pinhole next to what looks like a very thin slot cover. If you push an unfolded paper clip straight into the hole, the SIM card tray pops out.

So what's a SIM card?

It turns out that there are two major cellphone network types: *CDMA,* used by Verizon and Sprint, and *GSM,* used by AT&T, T-Mobile, and most other countries around the world. Your iPhone works only on GSM networks. (One huge reason that Apple chose AT&T as its exclusive carrier is that Apple wanted to design a phone that would work overseas.)

Every GSM phone stores your phone account info—details like your phone number and calling-plan details—on a tiny memory card known as a SIM card (Subscriber Identity Module). On

some phones, though not the iPhone, it even stores your address book.

What's cool is that, by removing the card and putting it into *another* GSM phone, you transplant the iPhone's brain. The other phone now knows your number and account details, which can be handy when your iPhone goes in for repair or battery replacement.

(The iPhone 4 uses a smaller type called a MicroSIM, which isn't compatible with nearly as many other phone models. But give it time.)

Apple thinks SIM cards are geeky and intimidating and that they should be invisible. That's why, unlike most GSM phones, your iPhone came with the card preinstalled and ready to go. Most people will never have any reason to open this tray, unless they just want to see what a SIM card looks like.

 Note: You can't use any other company's SIM card in the iPhone—it's not an "unlocked" GSM phone (at least, not officially; there are some unauthorized ways). Other recent AT&T cards work, but only after you first activate them. Insert the other card—it fits only one way, with the AT&T logo facing up—and then connect the iPhone to your computer and let the iTunes software walk you through the process.

If you were curious enough to open it up, you can close the tray simply by pushing it back into the phone until it clicks.

Headphone Jack

The tour continues with the top-left corner of the iPhone. Here's where you plug in the white earbuds that came with it.

This little hole is more than an ordinary 3.5-millimeter audio jack, however. It contains a secret fourth pin that conducts sound *into* the phone from the microphone on the earbuds' cord. Now you, too, can be one of those executives who walk down the street barking orders, apparently to nobody. The iPhone can stay in your pocket as you walk or drive. You hear the other person through your earbuds, and the mike on the cord picks up your voice.

The Screen

The touchscreen is your mouse, keyboard, dialing pad, and notepad. It's going to get fingerprinty and streaky.

But one of the best unsung features of the iPhone 3GS and iPhone 4 is the *oleophobic* screen. That may sound like an irrational fear of yodeling, but it's actually a coating that repels grease. You'll be amazed at how easily a single light wipe on your clothes restores the screen to its right-out-of-the-box crystal sheen.

You can also use the screen as a mirror when the iPhone is off.

 Note Geeks may enjoy knowing that the screen is 320 × 480 pixels on the iPhone 3G and 3Gs. But the iPhone 4, whose screen Apple calls the Retina display, packs in an astonishing 640 × 960 pixels. That's four times as sharp as the previous iPhones, and higher resolution than any phone on the market. It's really, *really* sharp, as you'll discover when you try to read text or make out the details of a map or photo.

But what about scratches? Fortunately, Apple learned its lesson on this one. The iPhone screen (and the iPhone 4's back panel, too) is made of optical-quality, chemically treated glass—not polycarbonate plastic like the iPod's screen. It's actually very difficult to scratch glass; try it on a windowpane someday.

If you're nervous about protecting your iPhone, you can always get a case for it (or a "bumper" for the iPhone 4—a silicone band that wraps around the metal edges). But in general, the iPhone is far more scratch-resistant than the iPod. Even many Apple employees carry the iPhone in their pockets without carrying cases.

Camouflaged behind the black glass above the earpiece, where you can't see them except with a bright flashlight, are two sensors. First, there's an ambient-light sensor that brightens the display when you're in sunlight and dims it in darker places. You can also adjust the brightness manually; see page 372.

Second, there's a proximity sensor. When something (like your head) is close to the sensor when you're using the phone functions, it shuts off the screen illumination and touch sensitivity. Try it out with your hand. (It works only in the phone application.) You save power and avoid tapping buttons with your cheekbone.

Screen Icons

Here's a roundup of the icons you may see in the status bar at the top of the iPhone screen, from left to right:

- ▪▪ll **Cell signal.** As on any cellphone, the number of bars indicates the strength of your cell signal, and thus the quality of your call audio and the likelihood of losing the connection. If there are zero bars, then the dreaded words "No service" appear here.

- E or 3G **Network type.** The E means your iPhone is connected to the Internet via AT&T's very slow EDGE cellular network. In general, if you have a cell signal, you also have an EDGE signal. (If you see this one ○, that means GPRS, better known as "the even older, even slower Internet network," is in operation instead.)

  If you see the 3G logo, though, get psyched; not only are you using an iPhone 3G, 3GS, or 4, but you're also in one of the cities where AT&T has installed a 3G network (much, much faster Internet).

- ✈ **Airplane mode.** If you see the airplane instead of signal and WiFi bars, then the iPhone is in Airplane mode (page 368).

- 🛜 **WiFi signal.** When you're connected to a wireless WiFi Internet hot spot (page 245), this indicator appears. The more "sound waves," the stronger the signal.

- 🔒 The iPhone is locked—meaning that the screen and most buttons don't work, to avoid accidental presses—whenever it goes to sleep. See page 7.

- **9:50 AM.** When the iPhone is unlocked, a digital clock replaces the lock symbol. To set the clock, see page 380.

- ▶ **Play indicator.** The iPhone is playing music. Before you respond, "Well, duh!" keep in mind that you may not be able to hear the music playing. For example, maybe the earbuds are plugged into the iPhone but aren't in your ears. So this icon is actually a handy reminder that you're running your battery down unnecessarily.

- ⏰ **Alarm.** You've got an alarm set. This reminder, too, can be valuable, especially when you intend to sleep late and don't *want* an alarm to go off. See page 229 for setting (and turning off) alarms.

- ✳ **Bluetooth connection.** The iPhone is connected wirelessly to a Bluetooth earpiece or a hands-free car system, as described on page 102. (If this symbol is gray, then it means that Bluetooth is turned on—and draining your battery—but that it's not connected to any other gear.)

- 🖳 **TTY symbol.** You've turned on Teletype mode, meaning that the iPhone can communicate with a Teletype machine. (That's a special machine that lets deaf people make phone calls by typing and reading text. It hooks up to the iPhone with a special cable that Apple sells from its Web site.)

- ☎ **Call forwarding.** You've told your iPhone to auto-forward any incoming calls to a different phone number (page 99). This icon is awfully handy—it explains at a glance why your iPhone never seems to get calls anymore.

- ▬ **VPN.** You corporate stud, you! You've managed to connect to your corporate network over a secure Internet connection, probably with the assistance of some highly paid system administrator—or by consulting page 364.

- ✳ **Syncing.** The iPhone is currently syncing with some Internet service.

- 🔋 **Battery meter.** When the iPhone is charging, the lightning bolt appears. Otherwise, the battery logo "empties out" from right to left to indicate how much charge remains. (On the iPhone 3GS and iPhone 4, you can even add a "% full" indicator to this gauge; see page 372.)

- **↗ Navigation active.** You're running a GPS navigation program in the background (yay, multitasking!).

  Why is a special icon necessary? Because those GPS apps slurp down battery power like a thirsty golden retriever. Apple wants to make sure you don't forget you're running it.

- **⊙ Rotation lock.** This icon reminds you that you've deliberately turned off the screen-rotation feature, where the screen image turns 90 degrees when you rotate the phone. Why would you want to? And how do you turn the rotation lock on or off? See page 17.

Home Button

Here it is: the one and only *real* button on the front of this phone. Push it to summon the Home screen, which is your gateway to everything the iPhone can do. (Details on the Home screen appear on page 28.)

Home button

Having a Home button is a wonderful thing. It means you can never get lost. No matter how deeply you burrow into the iPhone software, no matter how far off track you find yourself, one push of the Home button takes you all the way back to the beginning.

It sounds simple, but remember that the iPhone doesn't have an actual Back button or an End button. The Home button is the *only* way out of some screens.

As time goes on, Apple saddles the Home button with more and more functions. It's become Apple's only way to provide shortcuts for common features; that's what you get when you design a phone that only *has* one button. In iPhone Land, you can press the Home button one, two, or three times for different functions—or even hold it down for a moment. Here's the rundown.

One Press: Wake Up

Pressing the Home button once wakes the phone if it's in Standby mode. That's sometimes easier than finding the Sleep switch on the top edge.

Two Quick Presses: Task Switcher

If you press the Home button *twice quickly,* the screen dims, and the current image on it slides upward—to reveal the task switcher strip at the bottom. This feature is new in iOS 4, and was a *lonnng* time in the making. It's the key to the iPhone's new multitasking feature.

What you see here are icons of the four programs you've used most recently. Each time you swipe your finger to the left, you bring more icons into view, representing programs you opened less and less recently.

The point is that with a single tap, you can jump right back into a program you had open, without waiting for it to start up, show its welcome screen, and so on—and without having to scroll through 11 Home screens trying to find the icon of a favorite app.

In short, the task switcher permits, for the first time on the iPhone, a way to jump *directly* to another app, without a layover at the Home screen first.

This task switcher is the only visible element of iOS 4's new multitasking feature, which is described in delicious detail on page 188. Once you get used to it, that double-press of the Home button will become second nature—and your first choice for jumping among apps.

Note Multitasking works on the iPhone 3GS and the iPhone 4, but not on earlier models. If you have an original iPhone or the iPhone 3G, double-pressing the Home button doesn't open the task switcher.

Instead, it triggers your choice of shortcuts: to the Favorites speed-dial list, to the iPod controls, to the camera mode, or to the Spotlight search function. You choose which feature you want to dedicate the double-press to in Settings. For details, download the free PDF appendix to this chapter, "Redefining the Home Button Double-Press." It's available on this book's "Missing CD" page at *www. missingmanuals.com*.

Two Quick Presses, Part 2: The Widget Bar

Most of the time, you'll do the two-presses thing to open the task switcher so you can, well, switch tasks. But there are hidden gems awaiting.

If you summon the task switcher and then drag your finger to the right, the task switcher reveals a set of four hidden controls. These go by the name of widgets, meaning that they're not quite as full-blown as actual apps, but they still get their own icons. Here's what they do, left to right:

- **Rotation lock.** When you tap this button, the screen no longer rotates when you turn the phone 90 degrees. The idea is that sometimes, like when you're reading an ebook on your side in bed, you don't want the screen picture to turn; you want it to stay upright relative to your eyes, even though you're lying down. (A little ⟳ icon appears at the top of the screen to remind you why the usual rotating isn't happening.)

  The whole thing isn't quite as earth-shattering as it sounds—first, because it locks the image only one way: upright, in portrait orientation. You can't make it lock into widescreen mode. Furthermore, there aren't that many apps that rotate with the phone to begin with. But when that day comes when you want to read in bed sideways, your iPhone will be ready. (Tap the button a second time to turn rotating back on.)

- ◄◄, ▶, ►►. These controls govern music playback in whatever program is playing music in the background. They're exactly the same as the equivalent buttons in the iPod app itself (page 122)—but these are always two Home-button presses away, no matter what program you're in. You can skip a horrible song quickly and efficiently without having to interrupt what you're doing.

- **Music-app button.** Finally, the app icon here represents your iPhone's iPod app, or the Pandora Internet radio app, or whatever program is playing music in the background at the moment. Once again, the idea is to give you a quick shortcut when you want to switch albums, songs, or podcasts, so you don't have to meander back to the Home screen.

Three Presses: VoiceOver or White-on-Black

In Settings→General→Accessibility, you can set up a triple-press of the Home button (iPhone 4 or 3GS) to turn accessibility features on or off: VoiceOver (page 109) or white-on-black type (page 110). If you choose Ask, then a triple-click summons *three* buttons: VoiceOver, White on Black, and Zoom (page 111).

One Long Press: Voice Control

The Home button has one final trick: If you hold it down for about 3 seconds, you open up the *voice control* feature. Here, you can dial by speaking a name or number, or control music playback. Details on page 125.

 Tip The Home button is also part of the *force quit* sequence—a good troubleshooting technique when a particular program seems to be acting up. See page 412.

Silencer Switch, Volume Keys

Praise be to the gods of technology—this phone has a silencer switch (shown on page 8)! This tiny flipper, on the left edge at the top, means that no ringer or alert sound will humiliate you in a meeting, a movie, or church. To turn off the ringer, push the flipper toward the back of the phone. (On models prior to the iPhone 4, doing so exposes an orange dot, to remind you that you've turned on your silencer.)

Tip Even when silenced, the iPhone still makes noise in certain circumstances: when an alarm goes off; when you're playing iPod music; when you're using Find My iPhone (page 348); when you're using Voice Over (page 109); or, sometimes, when a game is playing. Also, the phone still vibrates when the silencer is engaged, although you can turn this feature off; see page 370.

No menus, no holding down keys, just instant silence. All cellphones should have this feature.

 Tip With practice, you can learn to tell if the ringer is on while the iPhone is still in your pocket. That's because when the ringer is *on,* the switch falls in a straight line with the volume keys. By swiping your thumb across these controls from front to back, you can feel whether the silencer switch is lined up or tilted away. (It's a lot harder to tell on the iPhone 4.)

Below the silencer, still on the left edge, are the volume controls—a single up/down rocker switch or, on the iPhone 4, separate metal + and – buttons. The volume controls work three different ways:

- **On a call,** these buttons adjust the speaker or earbud volume.

- **When you're listening to music,** they adjust the playback volume.

- **At all other times,** they adjust the volume of sound effects like the ringer and alarms.

Either way, a corresponding volume graphic appears on the screen to show you where you are on the volume scale.

The Bottom and the Back

On the bottom edge of the iPhone, Apple has parked three important components, none of which you'll ever have to bother with: the speakerphone speaker, the microphone, and, directly below the Home button, the 30-pin connector that charges and syncs the iPhone with your computer.

On the back of the iPhone, the camera lens appears in the upper-left corner. On the iPhone 3G and 3GS, the back is shiny hard plastic, in black or white; on the iPhone 4, it's the same hardened glass that's on the front. (For those scoring at home, Apple asserts that it's "aluminosilicate glass, chemically strengthened to be 30 times harder than plastic, more scratch resistant, and more durable than ever.")

And why are recent iPhone backs made of plastic or glass, and not metal, like the original iPhone? Because radio signals can't pass through metal. And there are a *lot* of radio signals in this phone. All told, there are 10 different radio transceivers inside: four each for the standard GSM frequencies; three for the three 3G frequencies; and one each for WiFi, Bluetooth, and GPS.

iPhone 4 Special Bits

A tour of the iPhone 4 includes a few extra stops.

- **On the back,** next to the camera lens, there's a flash—a tiny LED that provides illumination in low light, provided your subject isn't very far away. (It also can stay on when you're shooting video.)

- **On the top edge,** there's a tiny pinhole next to the headphone jack. This, believe it or not, is a microphone. It's the key to the iPhone 4's noise-cancellation feature. It listens to the sound of the world around you, and pumps in the opposite soundwaves to cancel out all that ambient noise. (It doesn't do anything for *you*—the noise cancellation affects only what the *other* guy hears, whomever you're talking to on the phone. Then again, you'll probably find that your end of the conversation sounds pretty good, too, since the sound chambers on the iPhone 4 were redesigned for better acoustics.)

- **On the front,** the iPhone 4 has a second camera. That tiny hole to the left of the earpiece speaker slot is, in fact, a front-facing camera. Its primary purpose is to let you conduct video chats using the FaceTime feature (page 79), but it's also handy for taking self-portraits or just checking to see if you have spinach in your teeth.

Just keep in mind that it's not nearly as good a camera as the one on the back. The front camera takes much lower-resolution shots (640 × 480 pixels), has no flash, and isn't as good in low light.

More on the iPhone's cameras in Chapter 6.

- **Around the edge,** that silver metal band is one of the iPhone 4's most famous features.

  Apple is so proud of it. This stainless-steel band is an Apple-concocted alloy, claimed to be five times as strong as steel. It's the primary structural component of the phone—everything else is attached to it.

  But this band is also part of the iPhone's antenna, and that's where the controversy begins; see page 4.

Top/left segments: Bluetooth, WiFi, GPS antennas

Right/bottom segments: voice and cellular data antennas

In the Box

Inside the minimalist box, you get the iPhone, its earbud/mike cord, and these items:

- **The charging/syncing cable.** When you connect your iPhone to your computer using this white USB cable, it simultaneously syncs and charges. (See Chapter 12.)

- **The AC adapter.** When you're traveling without a computer, you can plug the dock's USB cable into the included two-prong outlet adapter, so you can charge the iPhone directly from a wall socket.

 Note You may have noticed one standard cellphone feature that's *not* here: the battery compartment door.

The battery isn't user-replaceable. It's *rechargeable,* of course—it charges whenever it's connected via the USB cable—but after 300 or 400 charges, it will start to hold less juice. Eventually, you'll have to pay Apple to install a new battery (page 421). (Apple says the added bulk of a protective plastic battery compartment, a removable door and latch, and battery-retaining springs would have meant a much smaller battery—or a *much* thicker iPhone.)

- **Finger Tips.** Cute name for a cute fold-out leaflet of iPhone basics.

What you *won't* find in the box (because it wouldn't fit) is a CD containing the iTunes software. You're expected to have a copy of that on your computer already. In fact, you *must* have iTunes to use the iPhone (Chapter 12).

If you don't have iTunes on your computer, then you can download it from *www.apple.com/itunes*.

Seven Basic Finger Techniques

The iPhone isn't quite like any machine that came before it, and operating it isn't quite like using any other machine. You do everything on the touch-screen instead of with physical buttons. Here's what you need to know.

Tap

You'll do a lot of tapping on the iPhone's onscreen buttons. They're usually nice and big, giving your fleshy fingertip a fat target.

You can't use a fingernail or a pen tip; only skin contact works. (OK, you can also buy a special iPhone stylus. But a fingertip is cheaper and much harder to misplace.)

Drag

When you're zoomed into a map, Web page, email, or photo, you can scroll around just by sliding your finger across the glass in any direction—like a flick (described below), but slower and more controlled. It's a huge improvement over scroll bars, especially when you want to scroll diagonally.

Slide

In some situations, you'll be asked to confirm an action by *sliding* your finger across the screen. That's how you unlock the phone's buttons after it's been in your pocket, for example. It's ingenious, really; you may bump the touch screen when you reach into your pocket for something, but it's extremely unlikely that your knuckles will randomly *slide* it in just the right way.

You also have to swipe to confirm that you want to turn off the iPhone, to answer a call on a locked iPhone, or to shut off an alarm. Swiping like this is also a great shortcut for deleting an email or a text message.

Flick

A *flick* is a faster, less-controlled *slide.* You flick vertically to scroll lists on the iPhone. You'll discover—usually with some expletive like "Whoa!" or "Jeez!"— that scrolling a list in this way is a blast. The faster your flick, the faster the list spins downward or upward. But lists have a real-world sort of momentum; they slow down after a second or two, so you can see where you wound up.

At any point during the scrolling of the list, you can flick again (if you didn't go far enough) or tap to stop the scrolling (if you see the item you want to choose).

Pinch and Spread

In programs like Photos, Mail, Web, and Google Maps, you can zoom in on a photo, message, Web page, or map by *spreading*.

That's when you place two fingers (usually thumb and forefinger) on the glass and spread them. The image magically grows, as though it's printed on a sheet of rubber.

 Note The English language has failed Apple here. Moving your thumb and forefinger closer together has a perfect verb: *pinching*. But there's no word to describe moving them the opposite direction.

Apple uses the oxymoronic expression *pinch out* to describe that move (along with the redundant-sounding *pinch in*). In this book, the opposite of "pinching" is "spreading."

Once you've zoomed in like this, you can zoom out again by putting two fingers on the glass and pinching them together.

Double-Tap

Double-tapping is actually pretty rare on the iPhone, at least among the programs supplied by Apple. It's not like the Mac or Windows, where double-clicking the mouse always means "open." Because the iPhone's operating system is far more limited, you open something with *one* tap.

A double-tap, therefore, is reserved for three functions:

- In the Safari (the Web browser), Photos, and Google Maps programs, double-tapping zooms in on whatever you tap, magnifying it.

- In the same programs, as well as in Mail, double-tapping means "restore to original size" after you've zoomed in.

- When you're watching a video (or recording one on the iPhone 4), double-tapping switches the *aspect ratio* (video screen shape); see page 131.

Two-Finger Tap

This weird little gesture crops up in only one place: Google Maps. It means "zoom out." To perform it, tap once on the screen—with *two* fingers.

Charging the iPhone

The iPhone has a built-in, rechargeable battery that fills up a substantial chunk of its interior. How long one charge can drive your iPhone depends on what you're doing—music playback saps the battery least, Internet (*especially* 3G Internet) and video sap it the most. But one thing is for sure: Sooner or later, you'll have to recharge the iPhone. For most people, that's every other day or every night.

You recharge the iPhone by connecting the white USB cable that came with it. You can plug the far end into either of two places to supply power:

- **Your computer's USB jack.** In general, the iPhone charges even if your computer is asleep.

- **The AC adapter.** The little white two-prong cube that came with the iPhone connects to the end of the cradle's USB cable.

Unless the charge is *really* low, you can use the iPhone while it's charging. If the iPhone is unlocked, then the battery icon in the upper-right corner displays a lightning bolt to let you know that it's charging. If it's locked, pressing the Home button shows you a battery gauge big enough to see from space.

Battery Life Tips

The battery life of the iPhone is either terrific or terrible, depending on your point of view—and which model you have.

If you were an optimist, you'd point out that when these phones are using AT&T's 3G network, they get longer battery life than any other 3G phone. You'd also extol the iPhone 4's even better battery, which goes about 16 percent longer than the 3GS's.

If you were a pessimist, you'd observe that the 3G/3GS and 4 models get only 5 hours and 7 hours of talk time, respectively, compared with 8 hours on the original iPhone. And that if you're not careful, you might not even make it through a single day without needing a recharge.

So knowing how to scale back your iPhone's power appetite could come in extremely handy.

The biggest wolfers of electricity on your iPhone are its screen and its wireless features. Therefore, these ideas will help you squeeze more life out of each charge:

- **Dim the screen.** In bright light, the screen brightens (but uses more battery power). In dim light, it darkens.

> **Note** This works because of the ambient-light sensor that's hiding behind the glass above the earpiece. Apple says it experimented with having the light sensor active all the time, but it was weird to have the screen constantly dimming and brightening as you used it. So the sensor now samples the ambient light and adjusts the brightness only once—when you unlock the phone after waking it.

  You can use this information to your advantage. By covering up the sensor as you unlock the phone, you force it into a low-power, dim-screen setting (because the phone believes it's in a dark room). Or by holding it up to a light as you wake it, you get full brightness. In either case, you've saved all the taps and navigation it would have taken you to find the manual brightness slider in Settings.

- **Turn off 3G.** This is the biggie. If you don't see a **3G** icon on your iPhone's status bar, then you're not in a 3G hot spot (page 244), and you're not getting any benefit from the phone's battery-hungry 3G radio. By turning it off, you'll *double* the length of your battery. The iPhone 3G/3GS goes from 5 hours of talk time to 10; the iPhone 4 goes from 7 hours to 14!

To do so, from the Home screen, tap Settings→General→Network→ Enable 3G Off. Yes, this is sort of a hassle, but if you're anticipating a long day and you can't risk the battery dying halfway through, it might be worth doing. After all, most 3G phones don't even *let* you turn off their 3G circuitry.

 Tip Turning off 3G has another huge, huge benefit: It forces the phone to use AT&T's older, but much larger, non-3G cellular network. It's like switching from AT&T to Verizon on a per-call basis. Often, the result is that you can now place calls when you couldn't before. Next time you're getting a lot of dropped calls, remember this trick—and marvel.

- **Turn off WiFi.** If you're not in a wireless hot spot, you may as well stop the thing from using its radio. From the Home screen, tap Settings→Wi-Fi→Off.

  Or at the very least tell the iPhone to stop *searching* for WiFi networks it can connect to. Page 369 has the details.

- **Turn off cellular data.** This option is new in iOS 4. It turns off the cellular Internet features of your phone. You can still make calls, and you can still get online in a WiFi hot spot.

  This feature is designed for people who have signed up for one of AT&T's capped data plans (page 399), meaning you have to monitor how much Internet data you're using each month. If you discover that you've used up almost all of your data allotment for the month, and you don't want to go over your limit (and thereby trigger an overage charge), you can use this option to shut off all data. Now your phone is just a phone.

- **Turn off the phone, too.** In Airplane mode, you shut off both WiFi and the cellular radios, saving the most power of all. See page 368.

- **Turn off Bluetooth.** If you're not using a Bluetooth headset, then for heaven's sake shut down that Bluetooth radio. In Settings, tap General and turn off Bluetooth.

- **Turn off GPS.** If you won't be needing the iPhone to track your location, save it the power required to operate the GPS chip and the other location circuits. In Settings, tap General and turn off Location Services.

- **Turn off "push" data.** If your email, calendar, and address book are kept constantly synced with your Macs or PCs, then you've probably gotten yourself involved with Yahoo Mail, Microsoft Exchange (Chapter 14), or MobileMe (Chapter 13). It's pretty amazing to know that your iPhone is constantly kept current with the mother ship—but all that continual sniffing of the airwaves, looking for updates, costs you battery power. If you can do without the immediacy, then visit Settings→Mail, Contacts, Calendar→Fetch New Data; consider turning off Push and letting your iPhone check for new information, say, every 15, 30, or 60 minutes.

- **Turn off the screen.** On the iPhone 3GS and iPhone 4, you can actually turn off the screen, rendering it totally black and saving incredible amounts of battery power. Of course, you now have to learn the VoiceOver talking-buttons technology to navigate and operate the phone; see page 110.

Last battery tip: Beware of 3-D games and other add-on programs, which can be serious power hogs. And turn off EQ when playing your music (see page 392).

The Home Screen

The Home screen is the launching pad for every iPhone activity. It's what appears when you press the Home button. It's the immortal grid of colorful icons.

It's such an essential software landmark, in fact, that a quick tour might be helpful.

- **Icons.** Each icon represents one of your iPhone apps (programs): Calculator, Maps, Camera, and so on. Tap one to open that program.

  Your iPhone comes with about 20 icons preinstalled by Apple; you can't remove them. The real fun, of course, comes when you *add* to the starter set by downloading more apps from the App Store (Chapter 7).

- **Badges.** Every now and then, you'll see a tiny, round, red number "badge" on one of your app icons. It's telling you that something new awaits: new email, new text messages, new chat entries, new updates for the apps on your iPhone. It's saying, "Hey, you! Tap me!"

- **Home-page dots.** As you install more and more programs on your iPhone—and that will happen fast once you discover the App Store—you'll need more and more room for their icons.

The standard Home screen can't hold more than 20 icons. So where are all your games, video recorders, and tip calculators supposed to go?

Easy: The iPhone automatically makes room for them by creating *additional* Home screens. You can spread your new programs' icons across 11 such launch screens.

The little white dots are your map. Each represents one Home screen. If the third one is "lit up," then you're on the third Home screen.

To move among the screens, swipe horizontally—or tap to the right or left of the little dots to change screens.

And if you ever scroll too far away from the *first* Home screen, here's a handy shortcut: Press the Home button (yes, even though you're techni-cally already home). That takes you back to the first Home screen.

Tip The very first dot, at the far left, is actually a tiny magnifying glass. It represents the Spotlight (search) screen described on page 46. It's always waiting for you "to the left" of all the other Home screens.

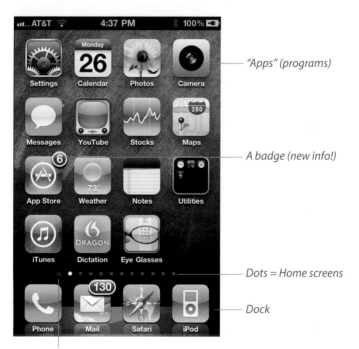

"Apps" (programs)

A badge (new info!)

Dots = Home screens

Dock

Spotlight screen

- **The Dock.** At the bottom of the Home screen, a row of four exalted icons sit on what looks like a polished glass tabletop. This is the Dock—a place to park the most important icons on your iPhone. These, presumably, are the ones you use the most often. That's why Apple starts you off with the Phone, Mail, Safari (Web), and iPod icons.

  What's so special about this row? As you flip among Home screens, this Dock never changes. You can never lose one of your four most cherished icons by straying from the first page, so they're always handy.

- **The background.** In iOS 4, you can replace the traditional black background (behind your app icons) with a photo. Now, a complicated, busy picture won't do you any favors—it will just make the icon names harder to read—so Apple provides a selection of handsome, relatively subdued wallpaper photos. But you can also choose one of your own photos.

  For instructions on changing the wallpaper, see page 148.

It's easy (and fun!) to rearrange the icons on your Home screens. Put the most frequently used icons on the first page, put similar apps into folders, reorganize your Dock. Full details are on page 177.

Typing, Editing, & Searching

2

The iPhone is amazing, all right. But as a pocket computer, it faces some fundamental limitations: It has no real keyboard and no real mouse. Which might be considered a drawback on a gadget that's capable of running hundreds of thousands of programs.

Fortunately, where there's a problem, there's software that can fix it. The modern iPhone virtual keyboard is smart in all kinds of ways—automatically predicting and correcting typos, for example. In iOS 4, you can even tap a mistyped word to see some suggestions for fixing it. This chapter covers every aspect of working with text on the iPhone: entering it, fixing it, and searching for it.

The Keyboard

Very few iPhone features have triggered as much angst, hope, and criticism as the onscreen keyboard. It's true, boys and girls: The iPhone has no physical keys. A virtual keyboard, therefore, is the only possible built-in system for typing text. Like it or not, you'll be doing a lot of typing on glass.

The keyboard appears automatically whenever you tap in a place where typing is possible: in an outgoing email or text message, in the Notes program, in the address bar of the Web browser, and so on.

Just tap the key you want. As your finger taps the glass, a "speech balloon" appears above your finger, showing an enlarged version of the key you actually hit (since your finger is now blocking your view of the keyboard).

In darker gray, surrounding the letters, you'll find these special keys:

- **Shift (⇧).** When you tap this key, it glows white to indicate that it's in effect. The next letter you type appears as a capital. Then the ⇧ key automatically returns to normal, meaning that the next letter will be lowercase.

- **Backspace (⊗).** This key actually has three speeds.

  Tap it once to delete the letter just before the blinking insertion point.

  Hold it down to "walk" backward, deleting as you go.

  If you *hold down the key long enough*, it starts deleting *words* rather than letters, one whole chunk at a time.

- **.?123**. Tap this button when you want to type numbers or punctuation. The keyboard changes to offer a palette of numbers and symbols. Tap the same key—which now says **ABC**—to return to the letters keyboard.

  Once you're on the numbers/symbols pad, a new dark gray button appears, labeled **#+=**. Tapping it summons a *third* keyboard layout, containing the less frequently used symbols, like brackets, the # and % symbols, bullets, and math symbols.

 Because the period is such a frequently used symbol, there's an awesome shortcut that doesn't require switching to the punctuation keyboard: At the end of a sentence, just tap the space bar *twice*. You get a period, a space, *and* a capitalized letter at the beginning of the next word. (This, too, can be turned off—see page 381—although it's hard to imagine why you'd want to.)

- **Return.** Tapping this key moves to the next line, just as on a real keyboard. (There's no Tab key or Enter key in iPhone Land.)

The Widescreen Keyboard

In some programs, you can turn the phone 90 degrees to type. When the keyboard stretches out the long way, the keys get a lot bigger. And it's a lot easier to type—even with two thumbs.

This glorious feature doesn't work in every program, alas. Fortunately, it works in some of the programs where you do the most typing: Mail, Messages (text messages), the Safari browser, Contacts, and Notes. (The screen also rotates in Camera, iPod, Calculator, and Stocks, though not for typing purposes.)

Making the Keyboard Work

Some people have no problem tapping those tiny virtual keys; others struggle for days. Either way, here are some tips:

- Don't be freaked out by the tiny, narrow keys. Apple *knows* your fingertip is fatter than that.

  So as you type, use the whole pad of your finger or thumb. Go ahead—tap as though you're trying to make a fingerprint. Don't try to tap with only a skinny part of your finger to match the skinny keys. You'll be surprised at how fast and accurate this method is. (Tap, don't press.)

- This may sound like New Age hooey, but *trust* the keyboard. Don't pause to check the result after each letter. Just plow on.

Tip Although you don't see it, the sizes of the keys on the iPhone keyboard are actually changing all the time. That is, the software enlarges the "landing area" of certain keys, based on probability.

For example, suppose you type *tim*. Now, the iPhone knows that no word in the language begins *timw* or *timr*—and so, invisibly, it enlarges the "landing area" of the E key, which greatly diminishes your chances of making a typo on that last letter. Cool.

- Start with one-finger typing. Two-thumb, BlackBerry-style typing comes later. You'll drive yourself crazy if you start out that way, although it's not bad when you're using the *widescreen* keyboard layout.

- Without cursor keys, how are you supposed to correct an error you made a few sentences ago? Easy—use the *Loupe.*

  Hold your fingertip down anywhere in the text until you see the magnified circle appear. Without lifting your finger, drag anywhere in the text; you'll see that the insertion point moves along with it. Release when the blue line is where you want to delete or add text, just as though you'd clicked there with a mouse.

Tip In the Safari address bar, you can skip the part about waiting for the Loupe to appear. Once you click into the address, start *dragging* to make it appear at once.

- Don't bother using the Shift key to capitalize a new sentence. The iPhone does that capitalizing automatically. (To turn this feature on or off, see page 381.)

Auto-Suggestions

If you make a mistake, don't reflexively go for the Backspace (⊗). Instead, just beneath the word you typed, you'll find the iPhone's proposed replacement. The software analyzes the letters *around* the one you typed and usually figures out what you really meant. For example, if you accidentally type *imsame*, the iPhone realizes that you meant *insane* and suggests that word.

To accept its suggestion, tap the space bar or any punctuation, like a period or question mark. To ignore the suggestion, tap it with your finger.

 Tip If you turn on Speak Auto-text (page 112), your iPhone 3GS or 4 will even *speak* the suggested word out loud. That way, you can keep your focus on the keyboard.

The suggestion feature can be especially useful when it comes to contractions, which are normally clumsy to type because you have to switch to the punctuation keyboard to find the apostrophe.

So you can save time by *deliberately* leaving out the apostrophe in contractions like *I'm, don't, can't,* and so on. Type *im, dont,* or *cant.* The iPhone proposes *I'm, don't,* or *can't,* so you can just tap the space bar to fix the word and continue.

The suggestion feature also kicks in when the iPhone thinks it knows how you intend to complete a *correctly* spelled word. For example, if you type *fathe,* the suggestion says *father.* This trick usually saves you only a letter or two, but that's better than nothing.

 Tip If you *accidentally* accept an autocorrect suggestion, tap the Backspace key. iOS 4 offers a word bubble that you can tap to reinstate what you'd originally typed.

Accented Characters

To produce an accented character (like é, ë, è, ê, and so on), keep your finger pressed on that key for one second. A palette of diacritical marks appears; slide onto the one you want, as you can see on the facing page.

Not all keys sprout this pop-up palette. Here's a list of the keys that produce alternative markings.

Key	Alternates
A	à á â ä æ ã å ā
C	ç ć č
E	è é ê ë ę ė ē
I	ī į í ì ï î i
L	ł
N	ń ñ
O	ō ø œ õ ó ò ö ô o
S	ß ś š
U	ū ú ù ü û
Y	ÿ
Z	ź ž ż
?	¿
'	' ' '
"	» « „ " "
-	—
$	€ £ ¥ ₩
&	§
0	°

How to Type Punctuation with One Touch

On the iPhone, the punctuation keys and alphabet keys appear on two differ-ent keyboard layouts. That's a *serious* hassle, because each time you want, say, a comma, it's an awkward, three-step dance: (1) Tap the **?123** key to get the punctuation layout. (2) Tap the comma. (3) Tap the **ABC** key or the space bar to return to the alphabet layout.

Imagine how excruciating it is to type, for example, "a P.O. Box in the U.S.A."! That's 34 finger taps and 10 mode changes!

Fortunately, there's a secret way to get a punctuation mark with only a *single* finger gesture.

The iPhone doesn't register most key presses until you *lift* your finger. But the Shift and Punctuation keys register their taps on the press *down* instead.

So here's what you can do, all in one motion:

❶ **Touch the .?123 key, but don't lift your finger.** The punctuation layout appears.

❷ **Slide your finger onto the period or comma key, and release.** The ABC layout returns automatically. You've typed a period or a comma with one finger touch instead of three.

> **Tip** If you're a two-thumbed typist, you can also hit the .?123 key with your left thumb, and then tap the punctuation key with your right. It even works on the #+= sub-punctuation layout, although you'll probably visit that screen less often.

In fact, you can type any of the punctuation symbols the same way. This technique makes a *huge* difference in the usability of the keyboard.

This same trick saves you a finger-press when capitalizing words, too. You can put your finger down on the ⇧ key and slide directly onto the letter you want to type in its uppercase version. Or, if you're a two-handed iPhone typist, you can work the Shift key like the one on your computer: Hold it down with your left thumb, type a letter with your right, and then release both.

How the Dictionary Works

The iPhone has an English dictionary (minus the definitions) built in. As you type, it compares what you've typed against the words in that dictionary (and against the names in your address book). If it finds a match or a partial match, it displays a suggestion just beneath what you've typed.

If you tap the space bar to accept the suggestion, wonderful.

If you don't—if you dismiss the suggestion and allow the "mistake" to stand—then the iPhone adds that word to a custom, dynamic dictionary, assuming that you've just typed some name, bit of slang, or terminology that wasn't in its dictionary originally. It dawns on the iPhone that maybe that's a legitimate word it doesn't know—and it adds it to the dictionary. From now on, in other words, it will accept that bizarre new word as a legitimate word—and, in fact, will even *suggest* it the next time you type something like it.

Words you've added to the dictionary actually *age*. If you stop using some custom term, the iPhone gradually learns to forget it. That's handy behavior if you never intended for that word to become part of the dictionary to begin with (that is, it was a mistake).

 If you feel you've really made a mess of your custom dictionary, and the iPhone keeps suggesting ridiculous alternate words, you can always start fresh. From the Home screen, tap Settings→General→Reset, and then tap Reset Keyboard Dictionary. Now the iPhone's dictionary is the way it was when it came from the factory, without any of the words it learned from you.

The Spelling Checker

Here's the world's friendliest typo-fixer, new in iOS 4. Apple calls it a spelling checker, but maybe that's stretching it.

The idea is that anytime the iPhone doesn't recognize something you've typed, it draws a dotted red underline beneath. Tap the word to see a pop-up balloon with three (and only three) alternate spellings. Often, one of them is what you wanted, and you can tap it to fix the mistake. (Equally often, not, and it's time to break out the Loupe and the keyboard.)

 Tip You can also invoke the spelling checker's suggestions even if you haven't made a typo. Tap just before the word; tap the insertion point; tap Replace. (You can see this effect on page 44.

International Typing

As the iPhone goes on sale around the world, it has to be equipped for non-English languages—and even non-Roman alphabets. Fortunately, it's ready.

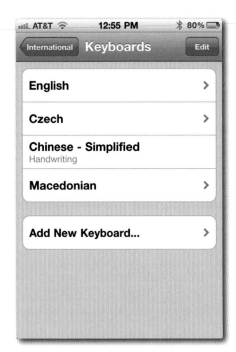

To prepare the iPhone for language switching, go to Settings→General→ International. Tap Language to set the iPhone's primary language (for menus, button labels, and so on).

To make other *keyboards* available, tap Keyboards, and then turn on the keyboard layouts you'll want available: Russian, Italian, whatever.

If you choose Japanese or Chinese, you're offered the chance to specify which *kind* of character input you want. For Japanese, you can choose a QWERTY layout or a Kana keypad. For Simplified or Traditional Chinese, you have a choice of the Pinyin input method (which uses a QWERTY layout) or handwriting recognition, where you draw your symbols onto the screen with your fingertip; a palette of potential interpretations appears to the right. (That's handy, since there are thousands of characters in Chinese, and you'd need a 65-inch iPhone to fit the keyboard.) Or hey—it's a free tic-tac-toe game!

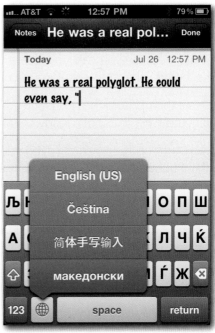

Now, when you arrive at any writing area in any program, you'll discover that a new icon has appeared on the keyboard: a tiny globe (⊕) next to the space bar. Each time you tap it, you rotate to the next keyboard you requested earlier. The new language's name appears briefly on the space bar to identify it.

Thanks to that ⊕ button, you can freely mix languages and alphabets within the same document, without having to duck back to some control panel to make the change. And thanks to the iPhone's virtual keyboard, the actual letters on the "keys" change in real time. (As an Apple PR rep puts it, "That's really hard to do on a BlackBerry.")

 Tip Here's an unsung new feature in iOS 4: If you, some United Nations translator, like to write in a lot of different languages, you no longer have to tap that ⊕ key over and over again to cycle through the keyboard layouts. Instead, hold your finger down on the ⊕ key. You get a convenient pop-up menu of the languages you've turned on, so you can jump directly to the one you want.

Connecting a Real Keyboard

This new iOS 4 feature barely merited an asterisk in Apple's marketing materials. But if you're any kind of wandering journalist, blogger, or writer, you might flip your lid over this: You can now type on a real, full-sized, plastic keyboard, and watch the text magically appear on the iPhone screen—wirelessly.

That's because you can now use a Bluetooth keyboard (the Apple Wireless Keyboard, for example) to type into your iPhone.

To set this up, from the Home screen, tap Settings→General→Bluetooth. Turn Bluetooth on, if it's not already.

Now turn on the wireless keyboard. After a moment, its name shows up on the iPhone screen in the Devices list; tap it. You'll know the pairing was successful, because when you tap in a spot where the on-screen keyboard would usually appear, well, it doesn't.

As you can probably imagine, typing is a lot easier and faster with a real keyboard than when you're trying to type on glass. As a bonus, the Apple keyboard's brightness, volume, and playback controls actually work to control the iPhone's brightness, volume, and playback.

 Tip The Apple keyboard's ⏏ key even works: It makes the iPhone's onscreen keyboard appear or disappear. Oh, and to switch languages, press ⌘-space bar on the wireless keyboard. You'll see the list of languages. Tap the space bar again to choose a different language.

When you're finished using the keyboard, turn it off. The iPhone goes back to normal.

There's another way to bypass the onscreen keyboard, too: Dictate. Using the free app called Dragon Dictation, you can actually speak what you want to type. Over an Internet connection, your words are turned into typed text in about 2 seconds. From there, one tap copies the results to a text message, an outgoing email, the clipboard for pasting somewhere, or Facebook or Twitter as an update.

Cut, Copy, Paste

After two years of customer whining and pining, Apple finally blessed the iPhone with Copy and Paste. You can grab a picture or text off a Web page and paste it into an email message, copy directions from email into Notes, paste a phone number from your address book into a text message, and so on.

Part of the problem, according to Apple, was the challenge of designing a way to select text and trigger Cut, Copy, and Paste functions—on a machine with no mouse and no menus! As on the Mac or PC, it takes three steps.

Step 1: Select the Text

Start by highlighting the text you want to cut or copy. Sounds simple, but there are two different ways to go about it:

- **Double-tap method.** Here's the quickest way. Double-tap the first word (or last word) that you want in the copied selection. That word is now highlighted, with blue dots at diagonal corners; drag these handles to expand the selection to include all the text you want to include. The little magnifying loupe helps you release the dot at just the right spot.

Double-tap…

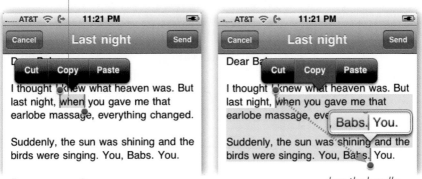

…drag the handle.

- **Insertion-point method.** This method involves more steps but offers a Select All option that you don't get with the double-tap.

    Tap in your text to place the blinking insertion point where you want it (below, left); then tap the insertion point itself to summon the selection buttons (middle). Tap Select All to copy everything in the text box or message. Or tap Select to get the two diagonal blue selection dots (right); drag the handles as already described.

> **Tip** On a Web page, you can't very well double-tap to select a word, because double-tapping means, "zoom in." So instead, *hold your finger down* on a word to produce the blue handles; the Loupe magnifies the proceedings to help you. (If you highlight the wrong word, keep your finger down and slide to the correct one; the highlighting goes with you.)
>
> However, if you're zoomed out to see the whole page, holding down your finger highlights the *entire block* of text (a paragraph or even a whole article) instead of one word. Now you can expand the selection to include a photo, if you like; that way, you can copy and paste the whole enchilada into an outgoing email message.

Tap the insertion point…   *tap Select…*

…then drag the blue handles to select text.

Step 2: Cut or Copy

At this point, you've highlighted the material you want, and the Cut and Copy buttons are staring you in the face. Tap Cut (to remove the selected text) or Copy (to leave it but place a duplicate on your invisible Clipboard). (The Replace button summons three alternate suggestions from the new iPhone spelling checker; see page 39.)

 Tip And what if you want to get rid of the text *without* copying it to the clipboard (because you want to preserve something you copied earlier, for example)? Easy: Just tape the Delete key!

Step 3: Paste

Finally, switch to a different spot in the text, even if it's in a different window (for example, a new email message) or a different program (for example, Calendar or Notes). Tap in any spot where you're allowed to type: Notes, email, text message, Safari's address bar, the Spotlight search box, a text box on a Web page, someone's Contacts screen, the top of the Calculator, even the phone-number display on the dialing keypad—just about anywhere. Tap the Paste button to paste what you cut or copied.

Ta-da! And to think that it took only two years.

(Possible Step 4: Undo)

Everyone makes mistakes, right? Fortunately, there's a secret Undo command, which can come in handy when you cut, copy, or paste something by mistake.

The trick is to *shake* the iPhone. The iPhone offers you an Undo button, which you can tap to confirm the backtracking. One finger touch instead of three.

In fact, you can even Undo the Undo. Just shake the phone again; now the screen offers you a Redo button. Fun! (Except when you shake the phone by accident and you get the "Nothing to Undo" message. But still.)

Spotlight: Global Search

Man, you will love this one.

The iPhone has a feature so fast, powerful, and useful, you'll wonder how the heck anyone survived without it: a global search feature called Spotlight. Just by typing a few letters, you can search almost the entire phone at once—or even the whole Web. Here's where it looks to find matches:

- **Contacts.** First names, last names, and company names.

- **Mail.** The To, From, and Subject lines of all accounts. (The iPhone doesn't try to search the text inside your email.)

- **Calendar.** Appointment names, meeting invitees, and locations (but not any notes attached to your appointments).

- **iPod.** Song, performer, and album names, plus the names of podcasts, videos, and audiobooks.

- **Notes.** The actual text of your notes.

- **Mail.** The header information (name, subject) of your email messages

- **Messages.** Yep, you can search your SMS text messages in iOS 4, too.

- **Your apps.** For frequent downloaders, this may be the juiciest function of all: Spotlight also searches the names of every single app on your iPhone. If you have dozens or hundreds installed, this is a much more efficient way to find one than trying to page through all the Home screens, eye-balling the icons as you go.

- **Search Web.** At the bottom of the list of search results, the Search Web button appears. Tap it to open Safari and begin an automatic search for the term you've typed, using Google or whatever search page you've specified in Settings.

- **Search Wikipedia.** At the *very* bottom of the list of search results, you get a Search Wikipedia option. As you could probably guess, tapping it opens up Wikipedia and performs a search for the term you've typed.

    These last two options are new in iOS 4. They might not *quite* seem to fit into the same categories as Mail, Apps, and so on. But once you get used to the idea that you've got quick Web search options right there in Spotlight, they can save you a few steps the next time you want to look something up online.

 It's worth noting that the Contacts, Mail, Calendar, iPod, and Notes programs have their *own* Search boxes (usually hidden until you scroll all the way to the top of their lists). Those individual Search functions are great when you're already *in* the program where you want to search. The Spotlight difference is that it searches all these apps at once.

How to Open Spotlight

The Spotlight screen is built into your Home screens (page 29)—at the far left.

Once you've pressed the Home button, you can either keep swiping your fin-ger to the right, or press the Home button again (and maybe a third time), until the Spotlight screen heaves into view.

(Truth is, that's an overly wordy description of what's usually a simple task. A slow double-press is usually all it takes.)

 If you have an iPhone 3G, you can designate the double-quick-press Home-button shortcut to mean "Open Spotlight," as described on page 379.

How to Search

The keyboard opens automatically (below, left). Begin typing to identify what you want to find and open. For example, if you were trying to find a file called *Pokémon Fantasy League,* typing just *pok* or *leag* would probably suffice. (Spotlight doesn't find text in the *middles* of words, though; it searches from the beginnings of words.)

A results list immediately appears below the search box, listing everything Spotlight can find containing what you've typed so far. (This is a live, interactive search; that is, Spotlight modifies the menu of search results *as you type.*)

They're neatly grouped by category; the beginning of each category is marked with an icon, and the light gray and medium gray backgrounds alternate to help you notice when a new category has begun.

 Tip If you drag your finger to scroll the list, the keyboard helpfully vanishes so you can see more of the list.

Contacts, apps, emails...

Pass your query on to the Web

If you see the icon of whatever you were hoping to dig up, just tap it to open it. The corresponding program (Contacts, Mail, iPod, the app you tapped, whatever) opens automatically.

How to Tweak Spotlight

You've just read about how Spotlight works fresh out of the box. But you can tailor its behavior to fit it to the kinds of things you look up most often. To open Spotlight's settings, start on the Home screen. Tap Settings→General→ Spotlight Search.

You can tweak Spotlight in two ways here:

- **Turn off categories.** The checkmarks identify the kinds of things that Spotlight tracks. If you find that Spotlight uses up precious screen space listing categories you don't use much, then tap to turn off their checkmarks. Now more of Spotlight's space-constrained screen is allotted to icon types you do care about.

- **Prioritize the categories.** This screen also lets you change the *order* of the category results; using the little ☰ grip strip at the right side, you can drag an individual list item up or down.

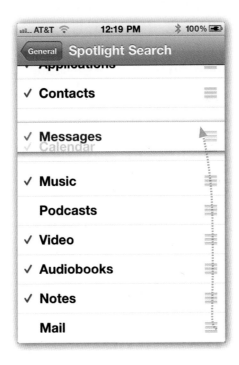

For example, the factory setting is for Contacts to appear first in the menu. But Contacts has its own search box, so it might make more sense to put Calendar or Applications at the top of the list so that it's quicker to do a schedule check or fire up a certain app. You'll have less scrolling to do once the results menu appears.

3

Phone Calls & FaceTime

As you probably know, using the iPhone in the U.S. means choosing AT&T Wireless as your cellphone carrier. If you're a Verizon, Sprint, or T-Mobile fan, too bad. AT&T (formerly Cingular) has the iPhone exclusively at least until 2012.

Why did Apple choose AT&T? For two reasons.

First, because Apple wanted a GSM carrier (page 8). Second, because of the way the cellphone world traditionally designs phones. It's the carrier, not the cellphone maker, that wears the pants, makes all the decisions, and wields veto power over any feature. That's why so much traditional cellphone software is so similar—and so terrible.

On this particular phone, however, Apple intended to make its own decisions, and so it required carte blanche to maneuver. AT&T agreed to let Apple do whatever it liked—without even knowing what the machine was going to be! AT&T was even willing to rework its voicemail system to accommodate Apple's Visual Voicemail idea (page 73).

In fact, to keep the iPhone under Apple's cloak of invisibility, AT&T engineering teams each received only a piece of it so that nobody knew what it all added up to. Apple even supplied AT&T with a bogus user interface to fake them out!

All right then: Suppose the "number of bars" logo in the upper-left corner of the iPhone's screen tells you that you've got cellular reception. You're ready to start a conversation.

Well, *almost* ready. The iPhone offers five ways to dial, but four of them require that you first be in the Phone *application*. The fifth way is dialing by voice, and it's available only on the iPhone 3GS and iPhone 4. The following pages cover all these methods.

Tip The iPhone's problems getting AT&T reception are now famous (see page 4). But if you find yourself dropping calls a lot (it happens a lot at airports and conferences because the airwaves are so crowded), consider *turning off the 3G feature* as described on page 374. You'll get slower Web pages, but also twice the battery life—and above all, it means that you're using an older, broader, less congested cellular network for your calls.

Dialing from the Phone App

To dial by tapping, open the Phone app like this:

❶ **Go Home, if you're not already there.** Press the Home button.

❷ **Tap the Phone icon.** It's usually at the bottom of the Home screen. (The tiny circled number in the corner of the Phone icon tells you how many missed calls and voicemail messages you have.)

Tip Of course, you can also double-press the Home button to open the task switcher. If you make calls often, the phone app's icon should be there waiting for you, as described on page 188. This shortcut skips the trip to the Home screen.

Now you've arrived in the Phone program. A new row of icons appears at the bottom, representing the four ways of dialing from here:

- **Favorites list.** Here's the iPhone's version of speed-dial keys: It lists the 50 people you think you call most frequently. Tap a name to make the call. (Details on building and editing this list begin below.)

- **Recents list.** Every call you've recently made, answered, missed, or dialed but hung up appears in this list. Missed callers' names appear in red lettering, which makes them easy to spot—and easy to call back.

  Tap a name or number to dial. Or tap the ⊙ button to view the details of a call—when, where, how long—and, if you like, to add this number to your Contacts list.

- **Contacts list.** This program also has an icon of its own on the Home screen; you don't have to drill down to it through the Phone button.

- **Keypad.** This dialing pad may be virtual, but the buttons are a *heck* of a lot bigger than they are on regular cellphones, making them easy to tap, even with fat fingers. You can punch in any number and then tap Call to place the call.

Once you've dialed, no matter which method you use, either hold the iPhone up to your head, put in the earbuds, turn on the speakerphone, or put on your Bluetooth earpiece—and start talking!

The few short paragraphs above, however, are only the Quick Start Guide. Here's a more detailed look at each of the four Phone-app modules.

The Favorites List

You may not wind up dialing much from Contacts. That's the master list, all right, but it's too unwieldy when you just want to call your spouse, your boss, or your lawyer. The iPhone doesn't have any physical speed-dial buttons, but it does have Favorites—a short, easy-to-scan list of the people you want to call most often.

You can add names to this list in either of two ways:

- **From the Contacts list.** Tap a name to open the Info screen, where you'll find a button called Add to Favorites. (This button appears only if there is, in fact, a phone number recorded for this person—as opposed to just an email address, for example.) If there's more than one phone number on the Info screen, you're asked to tap the one you want to add to Favorites.

- **From the Recents list.** Tap the button next to any name or number in the Recents list. If it's somebody who's already in your Contacts list, then you arrive at the Call Details screen, where one tap on Add to Favorites does what it says.

  If it's somebody who's not in Contacts yet, you'll have to *put* them there first. Tap Create New Contact, and then proceed as described on page 59. After you hit Save, you return to the Call Details screen so you can tap Add to Favorites.

The Favorites list holds 50 numbers. Once you've added 50, the Add to Favorites and **+** buttons disappear.

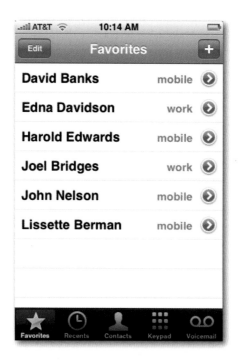

Reordering Favorites

Tapping that Edit button at the top of the Favorites list offers another handy feature, too: It lets you drag names up and down, so the most important people appear at the top of the list. Just use the right-side "grip strip" ≡ as a handle to move entire names up or down the list.

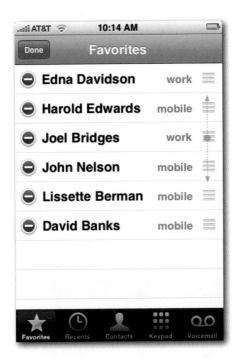

Deleting from Favorites

To delete somebody from your Favorites—the morning after a nasty political argument over drinks, for example—tap Edit. Then follow the usual iPhone deletion sequence: First tap the ⊖ button next to the unwanted entry, and then tap Remove to confirm.

The Recents List

Like any self-respecting cellphone, the iPhone maintains a list of everybody you've called or who's called you recently. The idea, of course, is to provide you with a quick way to call someone you've been talking to lately.

To see the list, tap Recents at the bottom of the Phone application. You see a list of the last 75 calls that you've received or placed from your iPhone, along with each person's name or number (depending on whether that name is in

Contacts or not), which phone number it is (mobile, home, work, or what-ever), city of the caller's home area code (for callers not in your Contacts), and the date of the call.

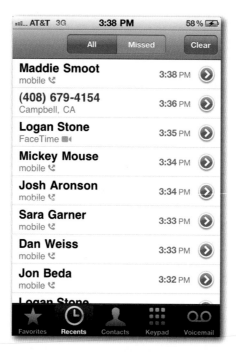

Here's what you need to know about the Recents list:

- Calls that you missed (or sent to voicemail) appear in red type. If you tap Missed at the top of the screen, you see *only* your missed calls. The color-coding and separate listings are designed to make it easy for you to return calls that you missed, or to try again to reach someone who didn't answer when you called.

- A tiny ☎ icon lets you know which calls you *made* (to differentiate them from calls you *answered*).

- To call someone back—regardless of whether you answered or dialed the call—tap that name or number in the list.

- Tap the ⊙ button next to any call to open the Call Details screen. At the top of the screen, you can see whether this was an Outgoing Call, an Incoming Call, or a Missed Call.

What else you see here depends on whether or not the other person is in your Contacts list.

If so, the Call Details screen displays the person's whole information card. A little table displays all of the incoming and outgoing calls to or from this person that day. A star denotes a phone number that's also in your Favorites list.

If the call *isn't* from someone in your Contacts, then you get to see a handy notation at the top of the Call Details screen: the city and state where the calling phone is registered.

• To save you scrolling, the Recents list thoughtfully combines consecutive calls to or from the same person. If some obsessive ex-lover has been calling you every 10 minutes for 4 hours, you'll see "Chris Meyerson (24)" in the Recents list. (Tap the ⊙ button to see the exact times of the calls.)

• To erase the entire list, thus ruling out the chance that a coworker or significant other might discover your illicit activities, tap Clear at the top of the screen. You'll be asked to confirm your decision. (There's no way to delete individual items in this list.)

The Contacts List

The Phone app offers four ways to dial—Favorites, Recents, Contacts, and Keypad—but the Contacts list is the source from which all other lists spring. That's probably why it's listed twice: once with its own button on the Home screen, and again at the bottom of the Phone application.

Contacts is your address book—your master phone book.

> **Tip** Your iPhone's own phone number appears at the very top of the Contacts list within the Phone module. (If you tap the Contacts icon on your Home screen instead, your phone number doesn't appear.) Drag down on the list to reveal its hiding place above the Search box.
>
> That's a much better place for it than deep at the end of a menu labyrinth, where it is on most phones.

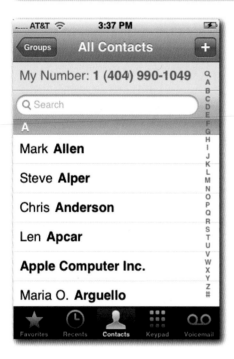 

If your social circle is longer than one screenful, then you can navigate this list in any of three ways.

First, you can savor the distinct pleasure of flicking through it (page 23).

Second, if you're in a hurry to get to the T's, use the A to Z index down the right edge of the screen. You can tap the last-name initial letter you want (R or W or whatever). Alternatively, you can drag your finger up or down the index. The list scrolls in real time.

Third, you can use the Search box at the very top of the list, above the A's. (If you don't see it, tap the tiny ⚲ icon at the top of the A to Z index on the right side of the screen, or just flick the list downward.)

Tap inside the Search box to make the keyboard appear. As you type, Contacts pares down the list, hiding everyone whose first, last, or company name doesn't match what you've typed so far. It's a really fast way to pluck one name out of a haystack.

(To restore the full list, clear the Search box by tapping the ⊗ at its right end.)

In any case, when you see the name you want, tap it to open its "card," filled with phone numbers and other info. Tap the number you want to dial.

 Tip Your iPhone excels at syncing with existing address books. It can slurp in the addresses from the Mac or PC, for example (Chapter 12), and from a corporate Exchange server (page 14), and from a MobileMe account (Chapter 13).

If you can't seem to find someone in the list, you may be looking in the wrong list. Tap Groups at the top-left corner, in that case, to return to the list of accounts. Tap All Contacts to view a single, unified list of everyone your phone knows about.

Adding to the Contacts List

Every cellphone has a Contacts list, of course, but the beauty of the iPhone is that you don't have to type in the phone numbers one at a time. Instead, the iPhone sucks in the entire phone book from your Mac or PC, MobileMe, and/or an Exchange server at work.

 Tip Actually, it can slurp in your phone list from the SIM card of an older GSM cellphone, too. See page 386.

It's infinitely easier to edit your address book on the computer, where you have an actual keyboard and mouse. The iPhone also makes it very easy to add someone's contact information when they call, email, or send a text message to your phone, thanks to a prominent Add to Contacts button.

But if, in a pinch, on the road, at gunpoint, you have to add, edit, or remove a contact manually, here's how to do it.

Start by making sure you've selected the right account, as described on the previous page. You don't want to add the person to the wrong account.

On the Contacts screen, tap the **+** button. You arrive at the New Contact screen, which teems with empty boxes. It's been redesigned in iOS 4; you can now type in all this person's details on a single screen, without having to keep ducking back and forth to the main "card" screen.

 Many computer address book programs, including Mac OS X's Address Book, also let you place your contacts into *groups*—subsets like Book Club or Fantasy League Guys. You can't create or delete groups on the iPhone, but at least the groups from your Mac or PC get synced over to the iPhone. To see them, tap Groups at the top of the Contacts list.

If you do use the Groups feature, then remember to tap the group name you want *before* you create a new contact. That's how you put someone into an existing group. (If not, tap All Contacts instead.)

And now, a few tips and tricks for the data-entry process:

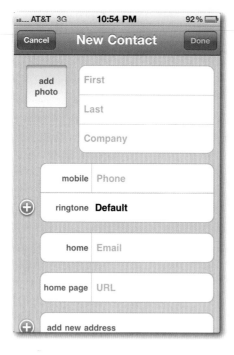
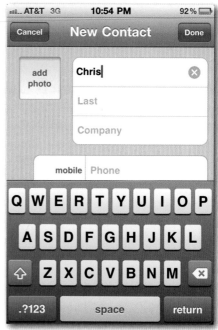

- **The keyboard opens automatically** when you tap in a box. And the iPhone capitalizes the first letter of each name for you.

 Tip If you know somebody has AT&T like you, add "(AT&T)" after the last name. That way, when he calls, you'll know that the call is free (like all AT&T-to-AT&T calls).

- **Phone numbers are special.** When you enter a phone number, the iPhone adds parentheses and hyphens for you. (You can even enter text phone numbers like 800-GO-BROWNS; the iPhone converts them to digits when it dials.)

If you need to insert a pause—for dialing access numbers, extension numbers, or voicemail passwords—type #, which introduces a 2-second pause in the dialing. You can type several to create longer pauses.

To change the label for a number ("mobile," "home," "work," etc.), tap the label that's there now. The Label screen offers a choice of mobile, home, work, main, fax, and so on. There's even a label called iPhone, so you and your buddy can gloat together.

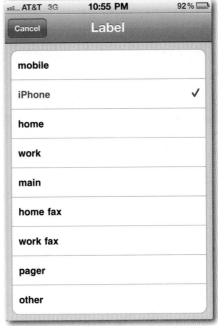

- **Infinite Expand-O Fields mean you'll never run out of room.** This might take some explanation.

  Almost every field (empty box) on a Contacts card is infinitely expanding. That is, the instant you start filling in a field, another, new, empty box appears right below it, so you can immediately add *another* phone number, email address, URL, address, or whatever. (The only non-expanding fields are First, Last, Company, and Ringtone.)

  For example, when you start creating a "card" for someone, the phone-number box is labeled mobile. If you start entering a phone number into the field next to it, a new, *second* empty phone-number box appears just below it (labeled iPhone—Apple's wishful thinking!), so you'll have a place to enter a second phone number for this person. When you do that, a *third* box appears. And so on.

  There's always one empty field, so you can never run out of places to add more phone numbers, addresses, and so on. (Don't worry—the perpetual empty box doesn't appear once you're finished editing the person's "card.")

- **You can add a photo of the person, if you like.** Tap Add Photo. If you have a photo of the person already, tap Choose Photo. You're taken to your photo collection, where you can find a good headshot (Chapter 6).

  Alternatively, tap Take Photo to activate the iPhone's built-in camera. Frame the person, and then tap the green camera button to snap the shot.

  In either case, you wind up with the Move and Scale screen (facing page, right). Here, you can frame up the photo so that the person's face is nicely sized and centered. Spread two fingers to enlarge the photo; drag your finger to move the image within the frame. Tap Choose to commit the photo to the address book's memory. (Back on the Info screen where you started, a miniature version of the photo now appears. Tap edit if you want to change the photo, take a new one, adjust the Move and Scale screen, or get rid of the photo altogether.)

From now on, this photo will pop up whenever the person calls.

- **Choose a ringtone.** The word "Default" in the Ringtone box lets you know that when this person calls, you'll hear your standard ringing sound. But you can, if you like, choose a different ringtone for each person in your address book. The idea is that you'll know by the sound of the ring who's calling.

 Note It's one ringtone per person, not per phone number. Of course, if you really want one ringtone for your buddy's cellphone and another for his home phone, you can always create a different Contacts "card" for each one.

To choose a ringtone, tap Default (or the word ringtone next to it). On the next screen, tap the sound you want, and then tap Save to return to the Info screen where you started.

- **You can add new fields of your own.** Very cool: If you tap Add Field at the bottom of the screen, then you go down the rabbit hole into Field Land, where you can add any of 12 additional info bits about the person whose card you're editing: Prefix (like Mr. or Mrs.), Suffix (like M.D. or Esq.), Nickname, Job Title, an Instant Message address, a phonetic pronunciation for people with weird names, and so on.

  When you tap one of these labels, you return to the Info screen, where you'll see that the iPhone has inserted the new, empty field in the most intelligent spot. For example, if you add a Phonetic First Name, that box appears just below the First name box. The keyboard opens, so you can fill in the blank.

- **Link and unlink Unified Contacts.** As noted earlier, your phone can sync up with different accounts. Your Contacts app might list three different sets of names and numbers: one stored on your phone, one from a MobileMe account, and a third from your corporate Exchange server at work. In the old days, therefore, certain names might show up in the All Contacts list two or three times—not an optimal situation.

  In iOS 4, as a favor to you, the iPhone displays each person's name only once in that master All Contacts list. If you tap that name, you open up the new Unified Info screen for that person. It includes *all* the details from *all* of the underlying cards from that person.

 Note The iPhone combines cards in the All Contacts list only if the first and last names are exactly the same. If there's a difference in name, suffix, prefix, or middle name, no unifying takes place. Remember, too, that you see the unification only if you view the All Contacts list (page 59).

To see which cards the iPhone is combining for you, scroll to the bottom of the card. There, the Linked Cards section shows you which cards have been unified.

Here, you can tap a listing to open the corresponding card in the corresponding account. You can also unlink one of the cards (tap Edit, then ⊖, then Unlink). For that matter, you can manually link a card, too; Tap Edit, tap Link Contact, and then choose a contact to link to this unified card—even if the name isn't a perfect match.

It's OK to link Joe Carnelia's card with Joseph Carnelia's card—they're probably the same person. But don't link up *different* people's cards. Remember, the whole point is to make the iPhone combine all their phone numbers, all their email addresses, and so on, onto a single card— which could get confusing fast.

Clearly, this stuff gets complex. But in general, the iPhone tries to do the right thing. For example, if you edit the information on the Unified card, you're actually changing that information only on the card in the corresponding account. (Unless you *add* information to the Unified Info card. In that case, the new data tidbit is added to *all* of the underlying source-account cards.)

 To delete any info bit from a Contacts "card," tap the ⊖ button next to it, and then tap the red Delete button to confirm.

Home info   *Unified info*   *Work info*

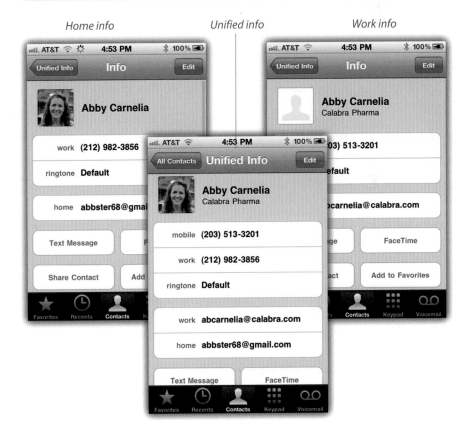

Adding a Contact on the Fly

There's actually another way to add someone to your Contacts list—a faster, on-the-fly method that's more typical of cellphones. Start by bringing the phone number up on the screen:

- Tap Home, then Phone, then Keypad. Dial the number, and then tap the **+1** button.

- You can also add a number that's in your Recents (recent calls) list, storing it in Contacts for future use. Tap the ⊘ button next to the name.

In both cases, finish up by tapping Create New Contact (to enter this person's name for the first time) or Add to Existing Contact (to add a new phone number to the card of someone who's already in your list). Off you go to the Contacts editing screen shown on page 59.

Editing Someone

To make corrections or changes, tap the person's name in the Contacts list. In the upper-right corner of the Info card, tap Edit.

You return to the screens already described, where you can make whatever changes you like. To edit a phone number, for example, tap it and change away. To delete a number (or any other info bit), tap the ⊖ button next to it, and then tap Delete to confirm.

Deleting Someone

Truth is, you'll probably *add* people to your address book far more often than you'll *delete* them. After all, you meet new people all the time—but you delete people primarily when they die, move away, or break up with you.

To zap someone, tap the name in the Contacts list and then tap Edit. Scroll down, tap Delete Contact (facing page, left), and confirm by tapping Delete Contact again.

Sharing a Contact

There's a lot of work involved in entering someone's contact information. It would be thoughtful, therefore, if you could spare the next guy all that effort—by sending a fully formed electronic business card to him. It can be yours, or anyone's in your Contacts list.

To do that, open the contact's "card," scroll to the bottom, and tap Share Contact. Now you're offered a choice of Email or MMS (facing page, right).

Tap your choice, address the message (to an email address or, for MMS, a cell-phone number), and send it. The recipient, assuming she has a half-decent smartphone or address-book program on the receiving end, can install that person's information with a single tap on the attachment.

> **Tip** Ever meet someone at a party or conference, and wish you could just exchange business cards electronically, iPhone to iPhone? You can, using the free app Bump. If you both have this app, adding your address-book cards to each other's Contacts lists is as easy as literally bumping your iPhone-holding fists together. Wirelessly. Without having to type anything at all.

The Keypad

The fourth way to place a call is to tap Keypad at the bottom of the screen. The standard iPhone dialing pad appears. It's just like the number pad on a normal cellphone, except that the "keys" are much bigger and you can't feel them.

To make a call, tap out (or paste) the phone number—use the ⊗ key to back-space if you make a mistake—and then tap the green Call button.

You can also use the keypad to enter a phone number into your Contacts list, thanks to the little +👤 icon in the corner. See page 66 for details.

Voice Dialing

The iPhone may have been the last one to show up at the smartphone party with voice dialing, but at least it's here now. If you have an iPhone 3GS or iPhone 4, you can now call somebody just by saying "call Chris at home" or "dial 225-3210." (Voice dialing doesn't work on older iPhone models.)

Voice dialing is a big deal on any phone, because it lets you keep your eyes on the road while you're driving. (Yes, yes, cellphone use in the car is dangerous and, in some states, illegal. And studies have shown that it's the act of talking on the phone—not just holding a phone up to your head—that causes distraction-related accidents. But we all know people do it anyway.)

On the iPhone, though, it's an even bigger deal, because it means that you can now place a phone call with only *a single button press.* Without voice dialing, you have to wake the phone, unlock it, tap your way to the Phone app, tap the list you want, tap a number, and then tap Dial—a lot of steps.

To dial by voice, *hold down the Home button* for 3 seconds. (If you're wearing the earbuds, hold down the center button; if you have a Bluetooth earpiece, hold down the Call button.)

 Tip The hold-down-the-button thing works even when the phone is asleep and locked! This tip makes it extraordinarily easy to place calls quickly. (If you're worried about the security of this option, you can turn it off; see page 377.)

You hear a crisp double-beep, and then the Voice Control screen appears. The wavy line in the center reflects what the iPhone is "hearing" at the moment; you'll see it respond to your voice.

The words flying across the background are meant to help you learn the Voice Control feature. They're cues to the commands the phone understands.

Many have to do with iPod playback and are described on page 125. For calling purposes, there are only two commands to know: "Call" and "Dial." They're interchangeable, but you have to follow each with one of two utterances:

- **A name from your Contacts list.** For maximum efficiency, say the first *and* last names, along with which number you want: "work" (or "at work"), "home" (or "at home"), "mobile," and so on.

Note The iPhone doesn't recognize "cell" or "cellphone," however.

You might say, therefore, "Call Chris Patterson at home," or "Dial Esmerelda at work." (Saying only the first name is OK if there's nobody else in your Contacts list with that name.)

If you don't specify a last name and which phone number you want, then the little talking iPhone lady asks you which one you meant—"Chris Patterson: Home? Work? Or mobile?"—and you have to speak the answer.

 Tip You don't actually have to say "call" or "dial" in *English*. The iPhone recognizes the equivalent words in 32 different languages. Collect them all!

- **A phone number.** You can also speak the digits of a phone number. For example, "Call four six six, oh seven two seven."

 Note You have to say every digit separately. None of this "eighty-two hundred" or "forty-two, forty-three" stuff. (There's only one exception: You're allowed to say "eight hundred" for 800 numbers.)

The iPhone syntho-lady always repeats what she thinks she heard—she might confirm, for example, "Chris Patterson, home"—and then dials.

Voice dialing usually works, but there will be plenty of times when the iPhone mishears you. Noisy backgrounds, accents, and similarity of Contact name spellings can confuse it. If the confirmation is incorrect, you have about a second to interrupt the dialing by saying "no," "wrong," "not that," "not that one," or (believe it or not) "nope." The iPhone lady hangs up so you can try again.

Other times, you'll hear "no match found" even when you know there is a match. Try again, or just say "cancel" and give up.

 Note In iOS 4, you can now say, "What time is it?" (Actually, what's new is that the phone will *answer* you.)

Answering Calls

When someone calls your iPhone, you'll know it; three out of your five senses are alerted. Depending on how you've set up your iPhone, you'll *hear* a ring, *feel* vibration, and *see* the caller's name and photo fill that giant iPhone screen. (Smell and taste will have to wait until iOS 5.0.)

 Note For details on choosing a ring sound (ringtone) and Vibrate mode, see page 371. And for info on the silencer switch, see page 18.

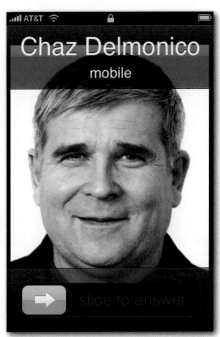

How you answer depends on what's happening at the time:

- **If you're using the iPhone,** tap the green Answer button. Tap End Call when you both have said enough.

- **If the iPhone is asleep or locked,** the screen lights up and says, "slide to answer." If you slide your finger as indicated by the arrow, you simultaneously unlock the phone and answer the call.

- **If you're wearing earbuds,** the music nicely fades out and then pauses; you hear the ring both through the phone's speaker and through your earbuds. Answer by squeezing the clicker on the right earbud cord or by using either of the methods described above.

When the call is over, you can click again to hang up—or just wait until the other guy hangs up. Either way, the music fades in again and resumes from precisely the spot where you were so rudely interrupted.

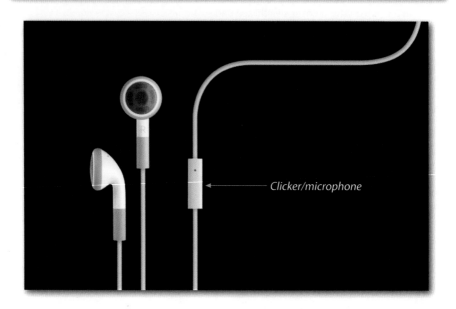

Clicker/microphone

Multitasking

Don't forget, by the way, that the iPhone is a multitasking master. Once you're on the phone, you can dive into any other program—to check your calendar, for example—without interrupting the call.

If you're in either a 3G area or a WiFi hot spot (Chapter 9), you can even surf the Web, check your email, or use other Internet functions of the iPhone without interrupting your call. (If you have only Edge service, you won't be able to get online until the call is complete.)

Silencing the Ring

Sometimes, you need a moment before you can answer the call; maybe you need to exit a meeting or put in the earbuds, for example. In that case, you can stop the ringing and vibrating by pressing one of the physical buttons on the edges (the Sleep/Wake button or either volume key). The caller still hears the phone ringing, and you can still answer it within the first four rings, but at least the sound won't be annoying those around you.

(This assumes, of course, that you haven't just flipped the silencer switch.)

Not Answering Calls

And what if you're listening to a *really* good song, or you see that the call comes from someone you *really* don't want to deal with right now?

In that case, you have two choices. First, you can just ignore it. If you wait long enough (four rings), the call will go to voicemail (even if you silence the ringing/vibrating as described above).

Second, you can dump it to voicemail *immediately* (instead of waiting for the four rings). How you do that depends on the setup:

- **If you're using the iPhone,** tap the Ignore button on the screen.

- **If the iPhone is asleep or locked,** tap the Sleep button twice fast.

- **If you're wearing the earbuds,** squeeze the microphone clicker for 2 seconds.

Of course, if your callers know you have an iPhone, they'll also know that you've deliberately dumped them into voicemail—because they won't hear all four rings.

Fun with Phone Calls

Whenever you're on a call, the iPhone makes it pitifully easy to perform stunts like turning on the speakerphone, putting someone on hold, taking a second call, and so on. Each of these is a one-tap function.

Here are the six options that appear on the screen whenever you're on a call.

Mute

Tap this button to mute your own microphone, so the other guy can't hear you. (You can still hear him, though.) Now you have a chance to yell upstairs, to clear the phlegm from your throat, or to do anything else you'd rather the other party not hear. Tap again to unmute.

Keypad

Sometimes, you have to input touch tones, which is generally a perk only of phones with physical dialing keys. For example, that's usually how you operate home answering machines when you call in for messages, and it's often required by automated banking, reservations, and similar systems.

Tap this button to produce the traditional iPhone dialing pad, illustrated on page 68. Each digit you touch generates the proper touch tone for the computer on the other end to hear.

When you're finished, tap Hide Keypad to return to the dialing-functions screen, or tap End Call if your conversation is complete.

Speaker

Tap this button to turn on the iPhone's built-in speakerphone—a great hands-free option when you're caught without your earbuds or Bluetooth headset. (In fact, the speakerphone doesn't work if the earbuds are plugged in or if a Bluetooth headset is connected.)

When you tap the button, it turns blue to indicate that the speaker is activated. Now you can put the iPhone down on a table or counter and have a conversation with both hands free. Tap Speaker again to channel the sound back into the built-in earpiece.

Tip Remember that the speaker is on the bottom edge of the phone. If you're having trouble hearing it, and the volume is all the way up, consider pointing the speaker toward you, or even cupping one hand around the bottom to direct the sound.

Add Call (Conference Calling)

The iPhone is all about software, baby, and that's nowhere more apparent than in its facility for handling multiple calls at once.

The simplicity and reliability of this feature put other cellphones to shame. Never again, in attempting to answer a second call, will you have to tell the first person, "If I lose you, I'll call you back."

Suppose you're on a call. Here are some of the tricks you can do:

- **Make an outgoing call.** Tap Add Call. The iPhone puts the first person on hold—neither of you can hear the other—and returns you to the Phone program and its various phone-number lists. You can now make a second call just the way you made the first. The top of the screen makes clear that the first person is still on hold as you talk to the second.

- **Receive an incoming call.** If a second call comes in while you're on the phone, you see the name or number (and photo, if any) of the new caller. You can tap either Ignore (meaning, "Send to voicemail; I'm busy now"), Hold Call + Answer (the first call is put on hold while you take the second), or End Call + Answer (ditch the first call).

Whenever you're on two calls at once, the top of the screen identifies both other parties. Two new buttons appear, too:

- **Swap** lets you flip back and forth between the two calls. At the top of the screen, you see the names or numbers of your callers. One says HOLD (the one who's on hold, of course) and the other bears a white telephone icon, which lets you know whom you're actually speaking to.

  Think how many TV and movie comedies have relied on the old "Whoops, I hit the wrong call waiting button and now I'm bad-mouthing somebody directly to his face instead of behind his back!" gag. That can't happen on the iPhone.

  You can swap calls by tapping Swap or by tapping the HOLD person's name or number.

- **Merge Calls** combines the two calls so all three of you can converse at once. Now the top of the screen announces, "Bill O'Reilly & Al Franken" (or whatever the names of your callers are), and then changes to say "Conference."

If you tap the ⊙ button, then you see the names or numbers of everyone in your conference call (as shown on the facing page). You can drop one of the calls by tapping its ⊖ button (and then End Call to confirm), or choose Private to have a person-to-person private chat with one participant. (Tap Merge Calls to return to the conference call.)

> **Note** If a call comes in while you're already talking to someone, tap Hold Call + Answer. Then tap Merge Calls if you want to add the newcomer to the party.

This business of combining calls into one doesn't have to stop at two. At any time, you can tap Add Call, dial a third number, and then tap Merge to combine it with your first two. And then a fourth call, and a fifth. With you, that makes six people on the call.

Then your problem isn't technological, it's social, as you try to conduct a meaningful conversation without interrupting one another.

Just remember that if you're on the phone with five people at once, you're using up your monthly AT&T minutes five times as fast. Better save those conference calls for weekends!

FaceTime

Tap this button to switch from your current phone call into a face-to-face video call, using the new FaceTime feature described on page 79.

(This feature requires that both you and the other guy have iPhone 4 models, and that you're both in WiFi hot spots; Apple puts a FaceTime button here on the screen even when those conditions aren't met, which is a little confusing.)

Hold

When you tap this button, you put the call on hold. Neither you nor the other guy can hear anything. Tap again to resume the conversation.

 If you're scratching your head because you can't see the Hold button on your iPhone 4, you're right; Apple replaced it with the FaceTime button. But you can still trigger the Hold function—by holding down the Mute button for a couple of seconds.

Contacts

This button opens the address book program, so that you can look up a number or place another call.

Overseas Calling

The iPhone is a *quad-band GSM* phone, which is a fancy way of saying it also works in any of the 200 countries of the world (including all of Europe) that have GSM phone networks. Cool!

But AT&T's international roaming charges will cost you anywhere from 60 cents to $5 per minute. Not so cool!

If you, a person in Oprah's tax bracket, are fine with that, then all you have to do is remember to call AT&T before you travel. Ask that they turn on the international roaming feature. (They can do that remotely. It's a security step.)

Then off you go. Now you can dial local numbers in the countries you visit, and receive calls from the U.S. from people who dial your regular number, with the greatest of ease. You can even specify which overseas cell carrier you want to carry your calls, since there may be more than one that's made roaming agreements with AT&T.

See page 369 for details on specifying the overseas carrier. And see *www.wireless.att.com/learn/international/long-distance* for details on this roaming stuff. (Beware of the *data* charges—they're even higher than the voice charges. Bills of $4,000 aren't unusual following three-week trips abroad! See page 375.)

If you're *not* interested in paying those massive roaming charges, however, you might want to consider simply renting a cellphone when you get to the country you're visiting.

 Note The iPhone can even add the proper country codes automatically when you dial U.S. numbers; see page 388.

As for calling overseas numbers *from* the U.S., the scheme is simple:

- **North America (Canada, Puerto Rico, Caribbean).** Dial 1, the area code, and the number, just like any other long-distance call.

- **Other countries.** Dial 011, the country code, the city or area code, and the local number. How do you know the country code? Let Google be your friend.

 Tip Instead of dialing 011, you can just hold down the 0 key. That produces the + symbol, which means 011 to the AT&T switchboard.

These calls, too, will cost you. If you do much overseas calling, therefore, consider cutting the overseas-calling rates down to the bone by using Jajah.com. It's a Web service that cleverly uses the Internet to conduct your call—for 3 cents a minute to most countries, vs. 11 cents using the phone company.

You don't have to sign up for anything. Just go to *www.jajah.com* on your iPhone. Fill in your phone number and your overseas friend's number, and then click Call.

In a moment, your phone will ring—and you'll hear your friend saying hello. *Neither of you* actually placed the call—Jajah called both of you and connected the calls—so you save all kinds of money. Happy chatting!

 Note Or here's another possibility: Download a voice-over-Internet program like Skype or Line2 from the iPhone App Store. (Similar: Fring and TruCall.)

Whenever you're in a WiFi hot spot, Skype lets you make free calls to any of the 300 million other people who have Skype. Both Skype and Line2 let you call regular telephone numbers, overseas, for about 2.1 cents a minute. And Line2 makes free calls to regular phone numbers in the U.S. when you're in an overseas WiFi spot. Sweet!

FaceTime

The iPhone 4, as you're probably aware, has two cameras—one on the back and one on the front. And that can mean only one thing: video calling has arrived.

The iPhone is not the first phone that can make video calls. But it's the first one that can make *good* video calls, reliably, with no sign up or setup, with a single tap. The picture and audio are generally rock-solid, with very little delay, and it works the first time and every time. Now Grandma can see the baby, or you can help someone shop from afar, or you can supervise brain surgery even from thousands of miles away. (If you're a brain surgeon, of course.)

However, you can enjoy these "Jetsons" fantasies only if you and your calling partner both have iPhone 4s, and only when you're both in strong WiFi hot spots. In time, other software companies may create FaceTime-compatible programs for other gadgets and computers. And Apple implies that in 2011, you'll be able to make such calls over the cellular airwaves, not just over WiFi.

In any case, FaceTime could not be easier to fire up. You can try it in either of two situations:

- **When you're already on a phone call with someone.** This is a good technique when you want to ask first if the other guy *wants* to do video, or when you've been chatting and suddenly there's some *reason* to do video. In any case, there's nothing to it: Just tap the FaceTime icon that's right on the screen when you pull the phone away from your face.

- **From scratch.** You can also start up a videochat without placing a phone call first. Once you and your loved one (or your minion) have become accustomed to FaceTime, you may want to skip the initial phone-call part, especially since it costs you AT&T minutes. You can also use FaceTime even when you can't get an AT&T signal.

    Of course, if you're not already on a call, the iPhone doesn't yet know whom you want to call. So you have to tell it.

Open your Contacts app, tap the person's name, and then tap the FaceTime button. Or, from within the Phone app, call up your Favorites or Recents list. Tap the blue ⊙ button next to a name to open the Contacts card; tap FaceTime.

At this point, the other guy receives an audio and video message inviting him to a chat. If he taps Accept, then you're on.

You're on each other's screens, seeing and hearing each other in real time. (You appear on your own screen, too, in a little inset window. Consider it spinach-in-your-teeth protection.)

Once the chat has begun, here's some of the fun you can have:

- **Rotate the screen.** FaceTime works in either portrait (upright) or landscape (widescreen) view; just turn your phone 90 degrees. (Of course, if your calling partner doesn't *also* turn her phone, she'll see your picture all squished and tiny, with big black areas filling the rest of the screen.)

 Tip: The Rotation Lock button described on page 17 works in FaceTime, too. That is, you can stop the picture from rotating when you turn the phone—as long as you're happy with full-time upright (portrait) orientation.

- **Show what's in front of you.** Sometimes, *you* are not the important thing; sometimes, you'll want to show your friend what you're looking at. That is, you'll want to turn on the camera on the *back* of the iPhone, the one pointing away from you, to show off the baby, the artwork, or the broken engine part.

That's easy enough; just tap the (icon) icon on your screen. The iPhone switches from the front camera to the back camera. Now you and your callee can both see what you're seeing. (It's a lot less awkward than using a laptop for this purpose, because the laptop's camera always faces away from you—so you can't see what you're showing.)

Tap the (icon) icon again to return to the front camera.

- **Snap a commemorative photo.** You can immortalize a chat by using the screenshot keystroke (Sleep + Home) described on page 160. You'll wind up with a still photo of your videochat in progress, safely nestled in your Photos app.

- **Mute the audio.** Tap the 🎤 icon to silence the audio that you're sending. Great when you need to yell at the kids.

- **Mute the video.** When you leave the FaceTime app for any reason (press the Home button and then open a different program, if you like), the other guy's screen goes black. He can't see what you're doing when you leave the FaceTime screen. He can still hear you, though.

  This feature was designed to let you check your calendar, look something up on the Web, or whatever, while you're still videochatting. But it's also a great trick when you need to adjust your clothing, pick your nose, or otherwise shield your activity from whomever's on the other end.

  In the meantime, the call is, technically, still in progress—and a green banner at the top of the Home screen reminds you of that. Tap there, on the green bar, to return to the video call.

When you and your buddy have had quite enough, tap the End button to terminate the call. (Although it's easy to jump from phone call to videochat, there's no way to go the other direction.)

And marvel that you were alive to see the day.

Voicemail, Texting, & Other Phone Tricks

4

O nce you've savored the exhilaration of making phone calls on the iPhone, you're ready to graduate to some of its fancier tricks: voicemail, text messages, AT&T features like Caller ID and Call Forwarding, and a Bluetooth headset or car kit.

Visual Voicemail

On the iPhone, you don't *dial in* to check for answering-machine messages people have left for you. You don't enter a password. You don't sit through some Ambien-addled recorded lady saying, "You have...17...messages. To hear your messages, press 1. When you have finished, you may hang up...."

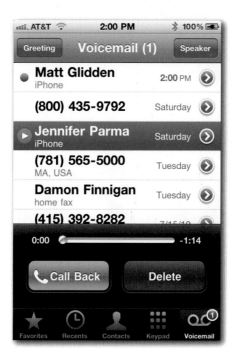

Instead, whenever somebody leaves you a message, the phone wakes up, and a notice on the screen lets you know who the message is from. You also hear a sound, unless you've turned that option off in Settings or turned on the silencer switch (page 18).

That's your cue to tap Home→Phone→Voicemail. There you see all your messages in a tidy chronological list. (The list shows the callers' names if they're in your Contacts list; otherwise it shows their numbers.) You can listen to them in any order—you're not forced to listen to three long-winded friends before discovering that there's an urgent message from your boss. It's a game-changer.

Setup

To access your voicemail, tap Phone on the Home screen, and then tap Voicemail on the Phone screen.

The very first time you visit this screen, the iPhone prompts you to make up a numeric password for your voicemail account—don't worry, you'll never have to enter it again—and to record a "Leave me a message" greeting.

You have two options for the outgoing greeting.

- **Default.** If you're microphone-shy, or if you're famous and you don't want stalkers and fans calling just to hear your famous voice, then use this option. It's a prerecorded, somewhat uptight female voice that says, "Your call has been forwarded to an automatic voice message system. 212-661-7837 is not available." *Beep!*

- **Custom.** This option lets you record your own voice saying, for example, "You've reached my iPhone. You may begin drooling at the tone." Tap Record, hold the iPhone to your head, say your line, and then tap Stop.

  Check how it sounds by tapping Play.

Then just wait for your fans to start leaving you messages!

Using Visual Voicemail

In the voicemail list, a blue dot ● indicates a message you haven't yet played.

 Tip You can work through your messages even when you're out of AT&T cellular range—on a plane, for example—because the recordings are stored on the iPhone itself.

There are only two tricky things to learn about Visual Voicemail:

- **Tap a message's name twice to play it.** That's a deviation from the usual iPhone Way, where just *one* tap does the trick. In Visual Voicemail, tapping a message just selects it and activates the Call Back and Delete buttons at the bottom of the screen. You have to tap *twice* to start playback.

- **Turn on Speaker Phone first.** As the name Visual Voicemail suggests, you're *looking* at your voicemail list—which means you're *not* holding the phone up to your head. The first time people try using Visual Voicemail, therefore, they generally hear nothing!

  That's a good argument for hitting the Speaker button *before* tapping messages that you want to play back. That way, you can hear the playback *and* continue looking over the list. (Of course, if privacy is an issue, you can also double-tap a message and then quickly whip the phone up to your ear.)

 Note If you're listening through the earbuds or a Bluetooth earpiece or car kit, of course, you hear the message playing back through *that*. If you really want to listen through the iPhone's speaker instead, tap Audio, and then Speaker Phone. (You switch back the same way.)

Everything else about Visual Voicemail is straightforward. The buttons do exactly what they say:

- **Delete.** The Voicemail list scrolls with a flick of your finger, but you still might want to keep the list manageable by deleting old messages. To do that, tap a message and then tap Delete. The message disappears instantly. (You're not asked to confirm.)

 The iPhone hangs on to old messages for 30 days—even ones you've deleted. To listen to deleted messages that are still on the phone, scroll to the bottom of the list and tap Deleted Messages.

On the Deleted screen, you can Undelete a message that you actually don't want to lose yet (that is, move it back to the Voicemail screen) or tap Clear All to erase these messages for good.

- **Call Back.** Tap a message and then tap Call Back to return the call. Very cool—you never even encounter the person's phone number.

- **Rewind, Fast Forward.** Drag the little white ball in the scroll bar (beneath the list) to skip backward or forward in the message. It's a great way to replay something you didn't catch the first time.

- **Greeting.** Tap this button (upper-left corner) to record your voicemail greeting.

- **Call Details.** Tap the ⊙ button to open the Info screen for the message that was left for you. Here you'll find out the date and time of the message.

If it was left by somebody who's in your Contacts list, you can see *which* of that person's phone numbers the call came from (indicated in blue type), plus a blue ★ if that number is in your Favorites list. Oh, and you can add this person to your Favorites list at this point by tapping Add to Favorites.

If the caller's number isn't in Contacts, then you're shown the city and state where that person's phone is registered. And you'll be offered a Create New Contact button and an Add to Existing Contact button, so you can store it for future reference.

In both cases, you also have the option to return the call (right from the Info screen) or fire off a text message.

Dialing in for Messages

Gross and pre-iPhonish though it may sound, you can also dial in for your messages from another phone. (Hey, it could happen.)

To do that, dial your iPhone's number. Wait for the voicemail system to answer.

As your own voicemail greeting plays, dial *, your voicemail password, and then #. You hear the Uptight AT&T Lady announce the first "skipped" message (actually the first unplayed message), and then she'll start playing them for you.

After you hear each message, she'll offer you the following options (but you don't have to wait for her to announce them):

- To delete the message, press 7.

- To save it, press 9.

- To replay it, press 4.

- To hear the date, time, and number the message came from, press 5. (You don't hear the lady give you these last two options until you press "zero for more options"—but they work anytime you press them.)

 Tip If this whole Visual Voicemail thing freaks you out, you can also dial in for messages the old-fashioned way, right from the iPhone. Open the keypad and hold down the 1 key, just as though it's a speed-dial key on any normal phone.

After a moment, the phone connects to AT&T; you're asked for your password, and then the messages begin to play back, just as described above.

Text Messages (SMS)

"Texting," as the young whippersnappers call it, was *huge* in Asia and Europe before it began catching on in the United States. These days, however, it's increasingly popular, especially among teenagers and twentysomethings.

SMS stands for Short Messaging Service. An SMS text message is a very short note (under 160 characters—a sentence or two) that you shoot from one cellphone to another. What's so great about it?

- Like a phone call, it's immediate. You get the message off your chest right now.

- As with email, the recipient doesn't have to answer immediately. The message waits for him even when his phone is turned off.

- Unlike a phone call, it's nondisruptive. You can send someone a text message without worrying that he's in a movie, a meeting, or anywhere else where talking and holding a phone up to the head would be frowned upon. (And the other person can answer nondisruptively, too, by sending a text message *back*.)

- You have a written record of the exchange. There's no mistaking what the person meant. (Well, at least not because of sound quality. Whether or not you can understand the texting shorthand culture that's evolved from people using no-keyboard cellphones to type English words—"C U 2mrO," and so on—is another matter entirely.)

The basic iPhone plans don't come with any text messages. You can pay $5 a month for 200 messages, or pay more for more. Remember that you use up one of those 200 each time you send *or receive* a message.

And by the way, *picture and video messages* (known as MMS, or multimedia messaging service) count as regular text messages.

Receiving a Text Message

When you get an SMS, the iPhone plays a quick marimba riff and displays the name or number of the sender *and* the message, in a translucent message rectangle. If you're using the iPhone at the time, you can tap Close (to keep doing what you were doing) or Reply (to open the message).

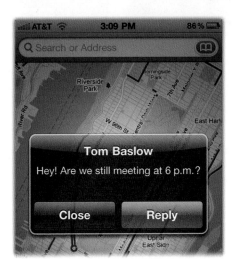

Otherwise, if the iPhone was asleep, it wakes up and displays the message right on its Unlock screen (below, left). You have to unlock the phone and then open the Messages program manually. Tap the very first icon in the upper-left corner of the Home screen.

 Tip The Messages icon on the Home screen bears a little circled number "badge," letting you know how many new text messages are waiting for you.

Either way, the look of Messages might surprise you. It resembles iChat, Apple's chat program for Mac, in which incoming text messages and your replies are displayed as though they're cartoon speech balloons (above, right).

 Tip The last 50 exchanges appear here. If you want to see even older ones, scroll to the very top and tap Load Earlier Messages.

To respond to the message, tap in the text box at the bottom of the screen. The iPhone keyboard appears. Type away, and then tap Send. Assuming your phone has cellular coverage, the message gets sent off immediately.

Tip Links that people send you in text messages actually work. For example, if someone sends you a Web address, tap it with your finger to open it in Safari. If someone sends a street address, tap it to open it in Google Maps. And if someone sends a phone number, tap it to dial.

And if your buddy replies, then the balloon-chat continues, scrolling up the screen. Don't forget to turn the iPhone 90 degrees for a bigger, wider keyboard!

 Tip If all this fussy typing is driving you nuts, you can always tap the big fat Call button to conclude the transaction by voice.

The Text List

What's cool is that the iPhone retains all these exchanges. You can review them or resume them at any time by tapping Messages on the Home screen. A list of text message conversations appears; a blue dot indicates conversations that contain new messages.

Tip If you've sent a message to a certain group of people, you can pre-address a new note to the same group by tapping the old message's row here.

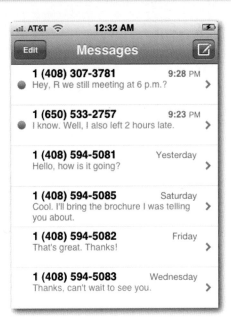

The truth is, these listings represent *people,* not conversations. For example, if you had a text message exchange with Chris last week, a quick way to send a new text message (on a totally different subject) to Chris is to open that "conversation" and simply send a "reply." The iPhone saves you the administrative work of creating a new message, choosing a recipient, and so on.

 Tip Hey, you can search text messages now! At the very top of the list, there's a Search box. You can actually find text inside your message collection.

If having these old exchanges hanging around presents a security (or marital) risk, you can delete one in either of two ways:

- **From the Text Messages list:** *Swipe* away the conversation. Just swipe your finger horizontally across the conversation's name (either direction). That makes the Delete confirmation button appear immediately.

- **From within a conversation's speech-balloons screen:** Tap Edit to open the message-deletion screen. Here you can delete all the exchanges simultaneously (tap Clear All) or vaporize only particularly incriminating messages. To do that, tap the round ✅ buttons for the individual balloons you want to nuke; then tap Delete (2) (or whatever number the button says). Tap Done.

 Note Interestingly, you can also *forward* some messages you've selected in this way. When you tap the Forward button, a new outgoing text message appears, ready for you to specify the new recipient.

Sending a New Message

If you want to text somebody you've texted before, the quickest way, as noted above, is simply to resume one of the "conversations" already listed in the Text Messages list.

But options to fire off text messages lurk all over the iPhone. A few examples:

- **In the Messages program.** From the Home screen, tap Messages. The iPhone opens the list of messages you've received. Tap the ☑ button at the top-right corner to open a new text message window.

    Address it by typing a few letters of the recipient's name and then choosing from the list of matches. Or tap the ✚ button, which opens your Contacts list. Tap the person you want to text.

Note Your *entire* Contacts list appears here, even ones with no cellphone numbers. But you can't text somebody who doesn't have a cellphone number.

- **In the Contacts, Recents, or Favorites lists.** Tap a person's name in Contacts, or ⊙ next to a listing in Recents or Favorites, to open the Info screen; tap Text Message. In other words, sending a text message to anyone whose cellphone number lives in your iPhone is only two taps away.

- **From Photos or Voice Memos.** Whenever you see a 🖅 (Share) button—when you're looking at a photo or a video in Photos, for example, or when you tap the ☰ button in Voice Memos—the usual list of sending options appears. It usually includes Email, MobileMe—and MMS. Tapping MMS sends you back to Messages, where the photo, video, or audio file is ready to send. (More on multimedia messages shortly.)

You can now tap that ➕ button again to add *another* recipient for this same message (or tap the **?123** button to type in a phone number). Lather, rinse, repeat as necessary; they'll all get the same message.

In any case, the skinny little text message composition screen is waiting for you now. You're ready to type and send!

New Options in iOS 4

You might not think that an act as simple as sending a text message would come with a bunch of options, but you'd be wrong. If you tap Settings→Messages, you'll stumble upon two new text-messaging options in iOS 4:

- **Group Messaging.** Suppose you're sending a message to three friends named A, B, and C (they had very unimaginative parents). When they reply to your message, the responses will appear in a Messages thread that's dedicated to this particular group (facing page, left). It works only if *all* of you have turned on Group Messaging. (Note to the paranoid: It also means that everyone sees everyone else's phone numbers.)

- **Character Count.** If a message is longer than 160 characters, the iPhone breaks it up into multiple messages. That's convenient, sure. But if your cellphone plan permits only a fixed number of messages a month, you could wind up sending (and spending) more than you intended.

  The new Character Count feature can save you. When it's on, after your typing wraps to a second line, a little counter appears just above the Send button ("71/160," for example, as shown here at right). It tracks how many characters remain within your 160-character limit for one message.

- **Show Subject Field.** If email messages can have Subject lines, why not text messages? Now, on certain newfangled phones (like yours), they can; the message arrives with a little dividing line between the subject and the body, offering your recipient a hint as to what it's about.

 Note It's OK to leave the Subject line blank. But if you leave the *body* blank, the message won't send. (Incidentally, when you do fill in the subject line, what you're sending is a multimedia (MMS) message, rather than a plain old text message.)

Picture, Audio, or Video Messages

Man, we waited long enough for this. It was absolutely bizarre that, for all its other superpowers, the iPhone could not send photos to other cellphones, let alone audio clips or video clips. This feature—called MMS (multimedia messaging service) was on every cellphone on earth, even the $20 starter phones. But not on the iPhone.

Fortunately, MMS is here now. To send a photo or (on the iPhone 3GS or iPhone 4) a video, tap the ◉ icon next to the box where you type your text messages (shown on the next page at right). Two buttons appear: Take Photo or Video or Choose Existing.

(On the iPhone 3G, the first button says Take Photo instead.)

If you want to transmit a photo or video that's already on your phone, then tap Choose Existing; your Photos app opens automatically, showing all your photos and videos. Tap the one you want and then tap Choose. If you choose Take Photo or Video instead, then your Camera app opens so you can take a new picture or snag a video clip.

In any case, you now return to your SMS conversation in progress—but now that photo or video appears inside the Send box. Type a caption or comment, if you like. Then tap Send to fire it off to your buddy.

Capturing Text-Message Goodies

In general, text messages are fleeting; most people have no idea how they might capture them and save them forever. Copy and Paste helps with that. (So does the amazing Google Voice service, but that's another conversation.)

Some of the stuff *in* those text messages is easy to capture, though. For example, if you're on the receiving end of an MMS photo or video, tap the small preview in the speech bubble. It opens at full-screen size so you can have a better look at it—and if it's a video, there's even a ▶ button so you can play it.

Either way, if the picture or video is good enough to preserve, tap the  button. You're offered a Save Image or Save Video button; tap to add the photo or video to your iPhone's collection.

If someone sends you contact information (name and address, for example), you can add it to your Address Book. Just tap inside that bubble, and then tap either Create New Contact or Add to Existing Contact.

Free Text Messaging

Text messaging is awesome. Paying for text messaging, not so much.

Fortunately, there are all kinds of sneaky ways to do text messaging for free. Yes, you read that right: free. Here are a couple of examples:

Solution #1: TextFree Unlimited. It's an app from the App Store that gives your iPhone its own phone number just for free text or picture messages, so you can send and receive all you want without paying a cent.

Solution #2: Sign up for a free Google Voice account. It has a million great features. But one of the best is that it lets you send and receive free text messages. You can do that from your computer (an amazingly useful feature, actually) at *voice.google.com*, or using the pseudo-app for your iPhone (in Safari, visit *m.google.com/voice* to see it).

Chat Programs

The iPhone doesn't **come** with any chat programs, like AIM (AOL Instant Messenger), Yahoo Messenger, or MSN Messenger. But installing one yourself—like AIM, below—is simple, as described in Chapter 7.

If you're a hard-core chatter, though, what you really want is an all-in-one app like IM+ or Beejive IM. You get a single app that can conduct chats with people on just about every chat network known to man: GTalk, Yahoo, MSN/Live Messenger, AIM, iChat, ICQ, MySpace, Twitter, Facebook, Jabber, and Skype.

Call Waiting

Call waiting has been around for years. With a call-waiting feature, when you're on one phone call, you hear a beep indicating that someone else is calling in. You can tap the Flash key on your phone—if you know which one it is—to answer the second call while you put the first one on hold.

Some people don't use call waiting because it's rude to both callers. Others don't use it because they have no idea what the Flash key is.

On the iPhone, when a second call comes in, the phone rings (and/or vibrates) as usual, and the screen displays the name or number of the caller, just as it always does. Buttons on the screen offer you three choices:

- **Ignore.** The incoming call goes straight to voicemail. Your first caller has no idea that anything's happened.

- **Hold Call + Answer.** This button gives you the traditional call-waiting effect. You say, "Can you hold on a sec? I've got another call," to the first caller. The iPhone puts her on hold, and you connect to the second caller.

  At this point, you can jump back and forth between the two calls, or you can merge them into a conference call, just as described on page 75.

- **End Call + Answer.** Tapping this button hangs up on the first call and takes the second one.

If call waiting seems a bit disruptive all the way around, you can turn it off (the switch is in Settings→Phone→Call Waiting). When call waiting is turned off, incoming calls go straight to voicemail when you're on the phone.

Call Forwarding

Here's a pretty cool feature you may not have even known you had. It lets you route all calls made to your iPhone number to a *different* number. How is this useful? Let us count the ways:

- When you're home. You can have your cellphone's calls ring your home number so you can use any extension in the house, and so you don't miss any calls while the iPhone is turned off or charging.

- When you send your iPhone to Apple for battery replacement, you can forward the calls you would have missed to your home or work phone number.

- When you're overseas, you can forward the number to one of the Web-based services that answers your voicemail and sends it to you as an email attachment (like GrandCentral.com or CallWave.com).

- When you're going to be in a place with little or no AT&T cell coverage (Alaska, say), you can have your calls forwarded to your hotel or a friend's cellphone. (Forwarded calls eat up your allotment of minutes, though.)

You have to turn on call forwarding while you're still in an area with AT&T coverage. Start at the Home screen. Tap Settings→Phone→Call Forwarding, turn call forwarding on, and then tap in the new phone number. That's all there is to it—your iPhone will no longer ring.

At least not until you turn the same switch off again.

Caller ID

Caller ID is another classic cellphone feature. It's the one that displays the phone number of the incoming call (and sometimes the name of the caller).

The only thing worth noting about the iPhone's own implementation of caller ID is that you can prevent *your* number from appearing when you call *other* people's phones. From the Home screen, tap Settings→Phone→Show MyCaller ID, and then tap the On/Off switch.

Bluetooth Earpieces and Car Kits

The iPhone has more antennas than an ant colony: seven for the cellular networks, one for WiFi hot spots, one for GPS, and one for Bluetooth.

Bluetooth is a short-range wireless *cable elimination* technology. It's designed to untether you from equipment that would ordinarily require a cord. Bluetooth crops up in computers (print from a laptop to a Bluetooth printer), in game consoles (like Sony's wireless PlayStation controller), and above all, in cellphones.

There are all kinds of things Bluetooth *can* do in cellphones, like transmitting cameraphone photos to computers, wirelessly syncing your address book from a computer, or letting the phone in your pocket serve as a wireless

Internet antenna for your laptop. But most people use the iPhone's Bluetooth primarily for hands-free calling.

To be precise, it works with those tiny wireless Bluetooth earpieces, of the sort you see clipped to people's ears, as well as with cars with Bluetooth phone systems. If your car has one of these "car kits" (Acura, Prius, and many other models include them), you hear the other person's voice through your stereo speakers, and there's a microphone built into your steering wheel or rearview mirror. You keep your hands on the wheel the whole time.

 This discussion covers *monaural* **Bluetooth earpieces intended for phone calls. But the iPhone can also handle Bluetooth** *stereo* **headphones, intended for music. Details are on page 127.**

Pairing with a Bluetooth Earpiece

So far, Bluetooth hands-free systems have been embraced primarily just by the world's geeks for one simple reason: It's *way* too complicated to pair the earpiece (or car) with the phone.

So what's pairing? That's the system of "marrying" a phone to a Bluetooth earpiece, so that each works only with the other. If you didn't do this pairing, then some other guy passing on the sidewalk might hear your conversation through *his* earpiece. And you probably wouldn't like that.

The pairing process is different for every cellphone and every Bluetooth earpiece. Usually it involves a sequence like this:

❶ **On the earpiece, turn on Bluetooth. Make the earpiece discoverable.** *Discoverable* just means that your phone can "see" it. You'll have to consult the earpiece's instructions to learn how to do so.

❷ **On the iPhone, tap Home→Settings→General→Bluetooth. Turn Bluetooth to On.** The iPhone immediately begins searching for nearby Bluetooth equipment. If all goes well, you'll see the name of your earpiece show up on the screen.

❸ **Tap the earpiece's name. Type in the passcode, if necessary.** The *passcode* is a number, usually four or six digits, that must be typed into the phone within about a minute. You have to enter this only once, during the initial pairing process. The idea is to prevent some evildoer sitting nearby in the airport waiting lounge, for example, to secretly pair *his* earpiece with *your* iPhone.

The user's manual for your earpiece should tell you what the passcode is (if one is even required).

When you're using a Bluetooth earpiece, you *dial* using the iPhone itself (unless you're using voice dialing, of course). You generally use the iPhone's own volume controls, too. You generally press a button on the earpiece itself to answer an incoming call, to swap call waiting calls, and to end a call.

If you're having any problems making a particular earpiece work, Google it. Type "iPhone Motorola H800 earpiece," for example. Chances are good that you'll find a writeup by somebody who's worked through the setup and made it work.

Car Kits

The iPhone works beautifully with Bluetooth car kits, too. The pairing procedure generally goes exactly as described above: You make the car discoverable, enter the passcode on the iPhone, and then make the connection.

Once you're paired up, you can answer an incoming call by pressing a button on your steering wheel, for example. You make calls either from the iPhone or, in some cars, by dialing the number on the car's own touchscreen.

 Note When Bluetooth is turned on but the earpiece isn't, or when the earpiece isn't nearby, the ✷ icon appears in gray. And when it's connected and working right, the earpiece's battery gauge appears on the iPhone's status bar.

Of course, studies show that it's the act of driving while conversing that causes accidents—not actually holding a phone. So the hands-free system is less for safety than for convenience and compliance with state laws.

Custom Ringtones

The iPhone comes with 25 creative and intriguing ringing sounds, from an old car horn to a peppy marimba lick. Page 371 shows you how to choose the one you want to hear when your phone rings. You can also buy ready-made pop-music ringtones from the wireless iTunes Store (page 135).

But where's the fun in that? Surely you don't want to walk around listening to the same ringtones as the millions of *other* iPhone owners.

Fortunately, you can also make up *custom* ring sounds, either to use as your main iPhone ring or to assign to individual callers in your Contacts list. This section covers the two official ways of going about it—carving 30-second ringtone snippets out of pop songs and recording your own in GarageBand on a Mac—and points you to the two sneakier ways.

iTunes Ringtones

Apple began selling custom ringtones from its iTunes Store in 2007. Using simple audio tools in the latest version of the iTunes program, you can buy a song for $1, choose a 30-second chunk, pay $1 more for the ringtone, and sync the result to your iPhone.

(Now, if paying a second dollar to use 30 seconds of a song you *already own* strikes you as a bit of a rip-off, you're not alone. But look at the bright side: That's a lot cheaper than most ringtones. Pop-song ringtones from T-Mobile and Sprint cost $2.50 apiece; from Verizon, they're $3. You don't get to customize them, choose the start and end points, adjust the looping, and so on.)

Unfortunately, not all iTunes songs can become ringtones—only the ones whose rights-cleared-by-the-lawyers status is designated by a bell icon. To see that icon, add the Ringtones *column* to the iTunes list by right-clicking or Control-clicking any column name and then choosing Ringtones from the pop-up menu. You can see the Ringtones column (and some bell icons) here.

When you see a purchased song in your iTunes list that bears the lucky bell, click the bell itself. The *Ringtone Editor,* which looks like a horizontal strip of sound waves, appears at the bottom of the window.

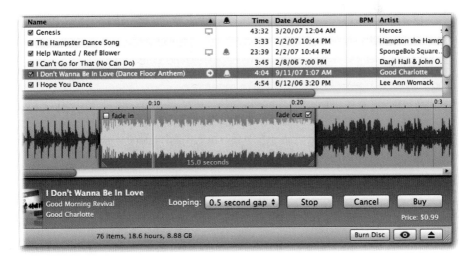

Your ringtone can be up to 30 seconds long. Start, therefore, by dragging the blue, highlighted rectangle around until it's sitting on the portion of the song you want to serve as your ringtone. At any time, you can...

- Click Preview to hear what the ring will sound like.

- Adjust the length of the ring snippet by dragging its lower corners.

- Control how much of a silent gap you want between repetitions of the ring, using the Looping pop-up menu.

- Turn off the fade-in or fade-out by turning off the corresponding checkboxes.

- Freeze the ringtone in its current condition and sync it to your iPhone by clicking Buy. Your cost: $1.

After your next sync with your iPhone, you'll find a new section, called Custom, in the list of available ringtones (Settings→Sounds). It's the list of the new ringtones you've bought—or built, as described next.

GarageBand Ringtones

If you have a Macintosh, then you can also create your own ringtones without paying anything to anyone—by using GarageBand, the music-editing program that comes on every new Mac (version '08 or later).

Start by building the ringtone itself. You can use GarageBand's Loops (prerecorded instrumental snippets designed to sound good together), for example, or sound you've recorded with a microphone. (There's nothing like the prerecorded sound of your spouse's voice barking out from the phone: "HONEY! PICK UP! IT'S ME!" every time your beloved calls.)

If you're not especially paranoid about record-company lawyers, you can also import any song at all into GarageBand—an MP3, AIFF, MIDI, or non-copy-protected AAC file, for example—and adapt a piece of it into a ringtone. That's one way for conscientious objectors to escape the $1-per-ringtone surcharge.

In any case, once you have your audio laid out in GarageBand tracks, press the letter C key. That turns on the *Cycle strip*—the yellow bar in the ruler shown on the facing page. Drag the endpoints of this Cycle strip to determine the length of your ringtone (up to 40 seconds long).

One feature that's blatantly missing on the iPhone is a "vibrate, *then* ring" option. That's where, when a call comes in, the phone first vibrates silently to get your attention and begins to ring out loud only if you still haven't responded after, say, 10 seconds.

GarageBand offers the solution: Create a ringtone that's silent for the first 10 seconds (drag the Cycle strip to the left of the music) and only *then* plays a sound. Then set your iPhone to vibrate and ring. When a call comes in, the phone plays the ringtone immediately as it vibrates—but you won't hear anything until after the silent portion of the ringtone has been "played."

Press the space bar to start and stop playback as you fiddle with your masterpiece.

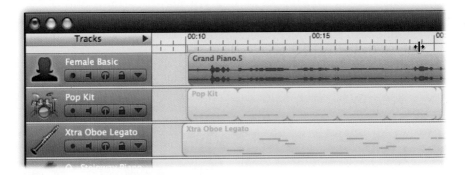

When everything sounds good, choose Share→Send Ringtone to iTunes. Next time you set up your iPhone sync, click the Ringtones tab in iTunes and schedule your newly minted ringtone for transfer to the phone.

There are two other, less official ways to create ringtones. One method lets you snag a piece of any not-copy-protected song in your iTunes library. The process takes several steps, but it's free and doesn't require special software. Details are in the free PDF appendix on this book's "Missing CD" at *www.missingmanuals.com*.

The other is to use a program like Ringtone Recorder Pro, a $1 download from the App Store. It emails you a ringtone (for subsequent syncing from iTunes) from anything you can record with your iPhone's microphone—voices, music, any audio—which is a very cool idea.

Nike + iPhone

Here's what you might consider an unlikely partnership: Apple + Nike. For $20, you can buy a tiny Nike/Apple transmitter that you slip into a special socket in specially marked Nike running shoes.

 Tip Pssst—you don't actually need the shoes. Online, you can buy a cheap little Velcro pouch that fastens the transmitter to any old shoe. Or just stick the transmitter in your sock.

Then, as you run, you could listen to your workout playlists; in the background, the software displays your time, distance, pace, and calories burned. It even talks to you—for example, letting you know when you were halfway and near the end of the run. After each run or walk, you can upload the data to *Nikeplus.com* to track your progress, slice and dice your statistics, compare workouts with other people, or even challenge them to a virtual race.

(Don't buy the $30 Sport Kit by mistake. It includes another part—a snap-on iPod receiver—which the iPhone doesn't need.)

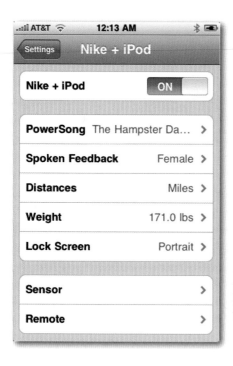

To get started, you have to unlock the dormant Nike feature. From the Home screen, tap Settings. Scroll wayyyy down the list until you see the cluster of settings for your individual apps; one of them is Nike + iPod. Tap to turn this feature On. Now the whole screen of Nike + iPod settings appears:

- **PowerSong.** A *PowerSong* is one particularly motivating tune that you can summon (by tapping PowerSong) as your willpower to keep running begins to fade. ("I Will Survive," perhaps?) Tap here to open your master iPod song list, where you can choose the song you want.

- **Spoken Feedback.** As you run, a voice periodically reports your progress. Here's where you specify the gender of that voice (the male one is Lance Armstrong) or turn it off altogether.

- **Distances.** Specify your favorite units: miles or kilometers.

- **Weight.** Input your body weight. (The software needs this detail to calculate how many calories you're burning.)

- **Lock Screen.** As you run and jiggle, you don't want the screen display to keep flipping between horizontal and vertical orientations. Don't worry; it won't, because on this screen, you specify how you want the Nike display frozen. You can choose Portrait, Landscape Left, or Landscape Right.

- **Sensor, Remote.** Use these two options to "pair" your iPhone with your shoe sensor and your optional Nike remote control, respectively.

Now find and tap the Nike + iPod icon on your Home screen. On the Workouts screen, tap the sort of run you want: Basic (just run), Time (a fixed time), Distance, or Calorie (run till you've burned off a certain number of calories).

Once you begin running, the screen tracks your progress stats: distance, elapsed time, pace (minutes per mile), and calories burned. A green progress bar shows you how much of the run you've completed. At any time, you can tap PowerSong (to play your motivational fave) or End Workout (you wuss!), whereupon you see a Summary screen.

 Tip If necessary, you can duck into another program on your iPhone while you're running. (Email-aholics, you know who you are.) When you press the Home button, the Nike app recedes into the background; a red "Touch to return to workout" strip appears at the top of your Home screen and whatever app you open.

When the workout is over, you can tap History to see a summary of your runs, or My Workouts to save canned run-type/music combinations.

Next time you sync your iPhone with iTunes, you'll see a new Nike + iPod tab at the top, where your workout summary appears. A checkbox lets you know that your workout data will get transmitted to Nikeplus.com automatically. Go there to study your stats and track your progress!

 Tip Truth is, you really don't need to invest in all of this Nike + iPod stuff just to track your workouts. The App Store (Chapter 7) is full of programs that do pretty much the same thing. RunKeeper, for example, uses the iPhone's own up-and-down motion as you run (rather than a transmitter in your shoe) to track your footsteps. Like Nike, it has a companion Web site—not as polished or complete as Apple/Nike's, of course—that tracks your stats and progress. It even taps into the iPhone's GPS to know where you ran—and shows you a map of your path on the Web.

Best of all, these apps work with any iPhone, not just the 3GS and 4.

Talking Buttons—and Accessibility

If you were told the iPhone was one of the easiest phones in the world for a blind person to use, you might spew your coffee. The thing has no physical keys at all! How would a blind person use it?

You won't believe the lengths to which Apple has gone to make the iPhone usable for the blind (iPhone 3GS and 4); you can literally turn the screen off and operate *everything*—do your email, surf the Web, adjust settings, run apps—by tapping and letting the phone speak what you're touching, in whatever language your iPhone uses. It's pretty amazing.

You can also magnify the screen, reverse black for white (for better-contrast reading), or convert stereo music to mono (great if you're deaf in one ear).

Here's a rundown. To turn on any of the features described here, go to the Home screen and tap Settings→General→Accessibility.

 Tip You can turn the iPhone's accessibility features on and off with a triple-click on the Home button. See page 18 for details.

VoiceOver

VoiceOver is the option that makes the iPhone speak everything you touch— even the little status gauges at the top of the screen.

On the VoiceOver settings pane, tap the On/Off switch to turn VoiceOver on. You can also adjust the Speaking Rate of the synthesized voice.

Now you're ready to start using the iPhone in VoiceOver mode. There's a lot to learn, and practice makes perfect, but here's the overview:

- **Tap something to hear it.** Tap icons, words, even status icons at the top; as you go, the voice tells you what you're tapping. "Messages." "Calendar." "Mail—14 new items." "45 percent battery power." You can tap the dots on the Home screen, and you'll hear, "Page 3 of 9."

  Once you've tapped a screen element, you can also flick your finger left or right—anywhere on the screen—to "walk" through everything on the screen, left to right, top to bottom.

Tip A little black rectangle appears around whatever the voice is identifying. That's for the benefit of sighted people who might be helping you.

- **Double-tap the screen to "tap" it.** Ordinarily, you tap something on the screen to open it. But since single-tapping now means "speak this," you need a new way to open everything. So: To open something you've just heard identified, double-tap *anywhere on the screen*. (You don't have to wait for the voice to finish talking.)

Tip Or do a *split tap*. Tap something to hear what it is—and with that finger still down, tap somewhere else with a different finger to open it.

There are all kinds of other special gestures in VoiceOver. Make the voice stop speaking with a *two-finger tap;* read everything, in sequence, from the top of the screen with a *two-finger upward flick;* scroll one page at a time with a *three-finger flick up or down;* go to the next or previous screen (Home, Stocks, and so on) with a *three-finger flick left or right;* and more.

Or try a *three-finger triple tap;* it blacks out the screen, giving you total privacy as well as a heck of a battery boost. (Repeat to turn the screen back on.)

If you rely on VoiceOver for using your iPhone, then you should download the free PDF appendix to this chapter from this book's "Missing CD" page at *www.missingmanuals.com*.

 Tip VoiceOver is especially great at reading your iBooks e-books out loud. Details on page 242.

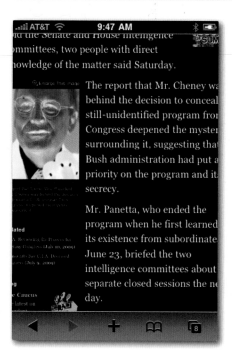

White on Black

By reversing the screen's colors black for white, like a film negative, you create a higher-contrast effect that some people find is easier on the eyes. To try it out, go to Settings→General→Accessibility and turn on White on Black. (The colors reverse, too—blue for yellow, and so on—an interesting effect, to say the least.)

Zooming

The iPhone may be a neat little computer, but it's a neat *little* computer; it has the smallest screen of any laptop on the market. Every now and then, you might need a little help reading small text or inspecting those tiny graphics.

If you turn on Zoom (in Settings→General→Accessibility), then you can magnify the screen whenever it's convenient, up to 500 percent. Of course, the screen image is now too big to fit the physical glass of the iPhone, so you'll need a way to scroll around on your jumbo virtual screen. Here's the scheme:

- **Turn zooming on or off** by tapping the screen with three fingers.

  (That's why you can't use Zoom while VoiceOver is also turned on; the three-finger tap has a different function in each.) The screen is now 200 percent of original size.

- **Pan around the virtual giant screen** by dragging or flicking with three fingers.

> **Tip** Once you begin a three-finger drag, you can lift two of your fingers. You can slide the remaining finger close to any screen border to continue scrolling in that direction—faster the closer you are to the edge.

- **Zoom in more or less** by double-tap/dragging with three fingers. It's like double-tapping, except that you leave your fingers down on the second tap—and drag them upward to zoom in more (up to 500 percent), or down to zoom out again.

> **Tip** Once again, you can lift two of your three fingers after the dragging has begun. That way, it's easier to see what you're doing.

Mono Audio

If you're deaf in one ear, then listening to any music that's a stereo mix can be frustrating; you might be missing half the orchestration or the vocals. When you turn on the Mono Audio option in Settings→General→Accessibility, the iPhone mixes everything down so that the left and right channels contain the same monaural playback. Now you can hear the entire mix in one ear.

 Tip This is also a great feature when you're sharing an earbud with a friend, or when one of your earbuds is broken.

Speak Auto-text

You know how the iPhone suggests a word as you type (page 35)? This option in Settings→General→Accessibility makes the iPhone speak each suggestion. That effect has two benefits: First, you don't have to take your eyes off the keyboard, which is great for speed and concentration. Second, if you're zoomed in, you may not be able to see the suggested word appear under your typed text—but now you still know what the suggestion is.

5 The iPhone as iPod

O f the iPhone's Big Three talents—phone, Internet, and iPod—its iPoddishness may be the most successful. This function, after all, is the only one that doesn't require the participation of AT&T and its network. It works even on planes and in subways. And of all the iPhone functions, this one gets the most impressive battery life (30 hours of music playback on the 3GS, or 40 hours on the iPhone 4).

This chapter assumes that you've already loaded some music or video onto your iPhone, as described in Chapter 12.

To enter iPod Land, press the Home button and then tap the orange iPod icon at the lower-right corner of the screen.

Tip A reminder: There's another way to get to the iPod mode. Just double-press the Home button. That opens the task switcher at the bottom of the screen. One swipe to the right, and you're viewing the iPod playback controls, along with the icon for the iPod app itself.

List Land

The iPod program begins with lists—lots of lists. The first four icons at the bottom of the screen represent your starter lists, as follows:

Playlists

A *playlist* is a group of songs you've placed together, in a sequence that makes sense to you. One might consist of party tunes; another might hold romantic dinnertime music; a third might be drum-heavy workout cuts.

In the olden days, you could create playlists only in the iTunes software, as described on page 310. After you sync the iPhone with your computer, the playlists appear here. In iOS 4, however, you can create playlists right on the phone, as described on the next page.

Using Playlists

Scroll the Playlist list by dragging your finger or by flicking. To see what songs or videos are in a playlist, tap its name. (The > symbol in an iPod menu always means "Tap to see what's in this list.")

 Tip Here's a universal iPhone convention: Anywhere you're asked to *drill down* from one list to another—from a playlist to the songs inside, for example—you can backtrack by tapping the blue button at the upper-left corner of the screen. Its name changes to tell you what screen you came from (Playlists, for example).

You now arrive at a Playlist details screen, where your tracks are listed for your inspection. To start playing a song or video once you see it in the playlist list, tap it.

Tap Edit, if you like, to drag the songs into a new sequence or delete some of them. Tap Clear if you want to choose a different set of songs within this playlist name, or Delete to get rid of the playlist altogether. (Tapping Shuffle starts them playing right now, in a random order.)

Creating Playlists on the Phone

The single "On-the-Go" playlist concept of iPhones gone by is gone. Now you can make as many new playlists as you want, right on the iPhone. Whatever playlists you create (or edit) here will wind up back on your computer, in iTunes, the next time you sync.

Here's how to make a playlist. In the iPod app, on the Playlists screen, tap Add Playlist. Type a name for your new playlist (below, left), and then tap Save.

Now you're shown an alphabetical master list of songs. Tap each song that you want to add to the new playlist (you don't have to tap the **+** button itself). Tap Done when you've added all the songs you want.

You arrive at the details screen for this playlist (above, center), where you can inspect or edit your handiwork. Tap Edit to rearrange the playlist songs or delete some (above, right). Or tap Playlist to back out to the list of playlists, where your newly minted playlist is nestled in the list.

Artists, Songs, Videos

The other icons across the bottom of the iPod screen go like this:

- **Artists.** This list identifies all the bands, orchestras, or singers in your collection. Even if you have only one song from a certain performer, it shows up here.

    Once again, you drill down to the list of individual songs or videos by tapping an artist's name. At that point, tap any song or video to begin playing it.

- **Songs.** Here's an alphabetical list of every song on your iPhone. Scroll or flick through it, or use the index at the right side of the screen to jump to a letter of the alphabet, or scroll all the way to the top and type a song name, album name, podcast name, or band's name into the Search box. Tap anything to begin playing it.

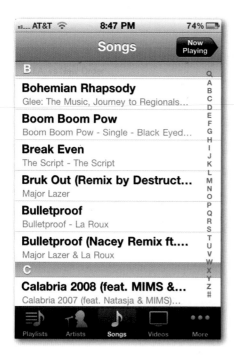 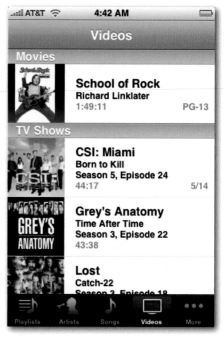

- **Videos.** Tap this icon for one-stop browsing of all the video material on your phone, organized by category: Movies, TV Shows, Music Videos, and Podcasts—video podcasts, that is. (You see only one listing for each podcaster, along with the number of episodes you've got). A handy thumbnail photo next to each video gives you a hint as to what's in it, and you also see the total playing time of each one.

You can probably guess, at this point, how you start one playing: by tapping its name. But don't forget to rotate the iPhone 90 degrees; all videos play in landscape orientation (the wide way).

 Tip At the bottom of any of these lists, you'll see the total number of items *in* that list: "76 Songs," for example. At the top of the screen, you may see the Now Playing button, which opens up the playback screen of whatever's playing.

Best of all, if you *drag downward* on any list—Music, Videos, Podcasts, whatever— you'll see that a Search box has been hiding from you, up off the top of the screen. It lets you search your audio/video stash by name (title, band, or album).

Other Lists

Those four lists—Playlists, Artists, Songs, Videos—are only suggestions. On a *real* iPod, of course, you can slice and dice your music collection in all kinds of other listy ways: by Album, Genre, Composer, and so on.

You can do that on the iPhone, too; there just isn't room across the bottom row to hold more than four list icons at a time.

To view some of the most useful secondary lists, tap the fifth and final icon, labeled More. The More screen appears, listing a bunch of other ways to view your collection:

- **Albums.** That's right, it's a list of all the CDs from which your music collection is derived, complete with miniature pictures of the album art. Tap an album's name to see a list of songs that came from it; tap a song to start playing it.

- **Audiobooks.** One of the great pricey joys of life is listening to digital "books on tape" that you've bought from Audible.com (page 309). They show up in this list. (Audiobooks you've ripped from CDs don't show up here—only ones you've downloaded from Audible.)

 Tip In a hurry? You can speed up the playback or audiobooks (or podcasts) without making the narrator sound like a chipmunk—or slow the narrator down if he's talking too fast. Page 124 has the details.

- **Compilations.** A *compilation* is one of those albums that's been put together from many different performers. You know: "Zither Hits of the 1600s," "Kazoo Classics," and so on. You're supposed to turn on the Compilation checkbox manually, in iTunes, to identify songs that belong together in this way. Once you've done that, all songs that belong to compilations you've created show up in this list.

- **Composers.** Here's your whole music collection sorted by composer—a crumb the iPod/iPhone creators have thrown to classical-music fans.

- **Genres.** Tap this item to sort your collection by musical genre: Pop, Rock, World, Podcast, Gospel, or whatever.

- **Podcasts.** Here are all your podcasts (page 308), listed by creator. A blue dot indicates that you haven't yet listened to some of the podcasts by a certain podcaster. Similarly, if you tap a podcast's name to drill down, you'll see the individual episodes, once again marked by blue "you haven't heard me yet" dots.

- **iTunes U.** Here are the lectures, lab reports, movies, and other educational materials supplied to the world by universities. You can find and subscribe to them using iTunes.

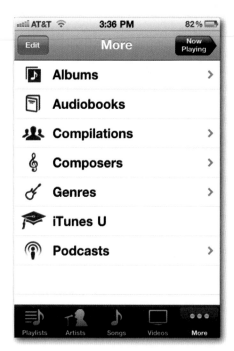 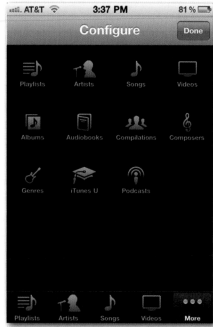

Customizing List Land

Now you know how to sort your collection by every conceivable criterion. But what if you're a huge podcast nut? Are you really expected to open up the More screen (shown at left on the facing page) every time you want to see your list of podcasts? Or what if you frequently want access to your audiobooks or composer list?

Fortunately, you can add the icons of these lists to the bottom of the main iPod screen, where the four starter categories now appear (Playlists, Artists, Songs, Videos). That is, you can replace or rearrange the icons that show up here so the lists you use most frequently are easier to open.

To renovate the four starter icons, tap More and then Edit (upper-left corner). You arrive at the Configure screen (facing page, right).

Here's the complete list of music-and-video sorting lists: Albums, Podcasts, Audiobooks, Genres, Composers, Compilations, Playlists, Artists, Songs, and Videos.

To replace one of the four starter icons at the bottom, use a finger to drag an icon from the top half of the screen downward, directly onto the *existing* icon you want to replace. It lights up to show the success of your drag.

When you release your finger, you'll see that the new icon has replaced the old one. Tap Done in the upper-right corner.

Oh, and while you're on the Edit screen: You can take this opportunity to *rearrange* the first four icons at the bottom. Drag them around with your finger. Fun for the whole family!

Cover Flow

Anytime you're using the iPhone's iPod personality, whether you're playing music or just flipping through your lists, you can rotate the iPhone 90 degrees in either direction—so it's in landscape orientation—to turn on Cover Flow. *Nothing* gets oohs and ahhs from an admiring crowd like Cover Flow.

In Cover Flow, the screen goes dark for a moment—and then it reappears, showing 2-inch-tall album covers, floating on a black background. Push or flick with your fingers to make them fly and flip over in 3-D space, as though they're CDs in a record-store rack.

If you tap one (or tap ❸ in the lower-right corner), the album flips around so you can see the "back" of it, containing a list of songs from that album. Tap a song to start playing it; tap the **||** in the lower-left corner to pause. Tap the back (or the ❷ button) again to flip the album cover back to the front and continue browsing.

To turn off Cover Flow, rotate the iPhone upright again.

So what, exactly, is Cover Flow for? You could argue that it's a unique way to browse your collection, to seek inspiration in your collection without having to stare at scrolling lists of text.

But you could also argue that it's just Apple's engineers showing off.

The Now Playing Screen (Music)

Whenever a song is playing, the Now Playing screen appears, filled with information and controls for your playback pleasure.

For example:

- **Return arrow.** At the top-left corner of the screen, the fat, left-pointing arrow means, "Return to the list whence this song came." It takes you back to the list of songs in this album, playlist, or whatever.

- **Song info.** Center top: the artist name, track name, and album name. Nothing to tap here, folks. Move along.

- **Album list.** At the top-*right* corner, there's a ≣ icon that seems to say "list." Tap it to view a list of the other songs on *this* song's album.

Tip You can double-tap the big album art picture to open the track list, too. It's a bigger target.

Return to list

Songs on this album

Swipe this way to return to the list

Volume slider

This track-listing screen offers three enjoyable activities. You can jump directly to another cut by tapping its name. You can check out the durations of the songs in this album.

And you can *rate* a song, ranking it from one to five stars, by tapping its name and then tapping one of the five dots at the top of the screen. If you tap dot number 3, for example, then the first three dots all turn into stars. You've just given that song three stars. When you next sync your iPhone with your computer, the ratings you've applied magically show up on the same songs in iTunes.

To return to the Now Playing screen, tap the upper-right icon once again. (Once you tap, that icon looks like the album cover.) Or, for a bigger target, double-tap any blank part of the screen.

- **Album art.** Most of the screen is filled with a bright, colorful shot of the original CD's album art. (If none is available—if you're listening to a song *you* wrote, for example—you see a big gray generic musical-note picture. You can drag or paste in an album-art graphic—one you found on the Web, for example—in iTunes.)

Controlling Playback (Music)

Once you're on the Now Playing screen, a few controls await your fingertip—some obvious and some not so obvious.

- **Play/Pause button.** The Pause button looks like this **II** when the music is playing. If you do pause the music, then the button turns into the Play button (▶).

 If you're wearing the earbuds, pinching the microphone clicker serves the same purpose: It's a Play/Pause control.

Incidentally, when you plug in headphones, the iPhone's built-in speaker turns off, but when you unplug the headphones, your music pauses instead of switching abruptly back to the speaker. You may have to unlock the iPhone and navigate to the iPod program to resume playback.

Hidden controls

- **Previous, Next ().** These buttons work exactly as they do on an iPod. That is, tap ◀◀ to skip to the beginning of this song (or, if you're already at the beginning, to the previous song). Tap ▶▶ to skip to the next song.

 Tip If you're wearing the earbuds, you can pinch the clicker *twice* to skip to the next song.

If you hold down one of these buttons instead of tapping, then you re-wind or fast-forward. It's rather cool, actually—you get to hear the music speeding by as you keep your finger down, without turning the singer into a chipmunk. The rewinding or fast-forwarding accelerates if you keep holding down the button.

- **Volume.** You can drag the round, white handle of this scroll bar (bottom of the screen) to adjust the volume—or you can use the volume keys on the left side of the phone.

 Tip If you use your iPhone for its iPod features a lot, don't miss the task switcher (page 188). It's the row of icons that appears when you double-press the Home button. If you swipe it to the right, you summon a playback-control bar from within any iPhone program, so you don't have to go to the iPod app just to change tracks or pause the music.

Of course, you probably didn't need a handsome full-color book to tell you what those basic playback controls are for. But there are also four *secret* controls that don't appear until you tap anywhere on an empty part of the screen (for example, on the album cover):

- **Loop button.** If you *really* love a certain album or playlist, you can command the iPhone to play it over and over again, beginning to end. Just tap the Loop button (🔁) so it turns blue (🔁).

 Tip Tap the Loop button a second time to endlessly loop *just this song.*

A tiny "1" icon appears on the blue loop graphic, like this 🔂, to let you know that you've entered this mode. Tap a third time to turn off looping.

- **Scroll slider.** This slider (top of the screen) reveals three useful statistics: how much of the song you've heard, in minutes and seconds (at the left end), how much time remains (at the right end), and which slot this song occupies in the current playlist or album.

To operate the slider, drag the tiny round handle with your finger. (Tapping directly on the spot you want to hear doesn't work.)

- **Genius button (❈).** Tap the ❈ button to create a Genius playlist based on the song you're listening to. You can read more about Genius playlists on page 133; for now, it's enough to know that, although Apple is cagey about the specifics, a Genius playlist is a semi-randomized, auto-created playlist of songs from your library that "sound great" together. (Basically, it seems to clump songs by their degree of rockiness: soft-rock songs, harder rock, and so on.)

  - **Shuffle button.** Ordinarily, the iPhone plays the songs in an album sequentially, from beginning to end. But if you love surprises, tap the ✖ button so it turns blue. Now you'll hear the songs on the album in random order.

To hide the slider and the Loop, Genius, and Shuffle buttons, tap an empty part of the screen once again.

By the way, there's nothing to stop you from turning on Shuffle *and* Loop, meaning that you'll hear the songs on the album played endlessly, but never in the same order twice.

 Tip Shake the whole iPhone to shuffle—that is, to start playing another random song.

Special Podcast/Audiobook Controls

When you're listening to a podcast or an audiobook, tapping any empty part of the screen during playback produces, once again, that ordinarily hidden strip of controls. This time, though, three new buttons replace the Loop, Genius, and Shuffle buttons described above:

- **Email (✉).** This button opens up an outgoing email message containing a link to the podcast's original spot in the iTunes store, so you can share the goodness.

- **30-second repeat (↺).** Does what it says. Perfect when you've just been interrupted by an inquiry from a spouse, boss, or highway patrolman.

- **Playback speed (½x, 1x, or 2x).** This feature may be God's gift to the audiobook or podcast fan: It changes how fast people are talking.

Get through a podcast or audiobook faster when you're stuck with a slow droner; slow it down if it's a New York mile-a-minute chatterer. Each time you tap this button, the playback cycles through to the next speed.

 Tip Along with the special podcast controls, you also get superimposed white text on the album art when you tap the screen. It displays a description of the episode, if the creators of the podcast bothered to supply it.

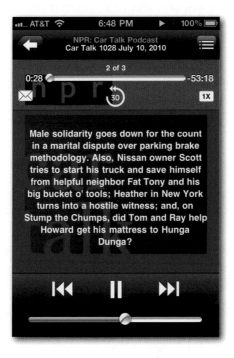

Voice Control

On the iPhone 3GS and iPhone 4, you can also control the iPod's playback by voice, just by speaking into the iPhone's microphone (as though you're using the phone) or into the earbuds cord. Playback is the *other* control your voice has over the iPhone. (Phone dialing is the first, as described in Chapter 3).

The beauty of voice control is that you don't have to be in the iPod mode to do it. You can be in any app. And you don't even have to look at the iPhone to do it. Why, in theory, you could even be driving (although you'd never be fiddling with your phone in the car, right?).

To issue a playback command, hold down the Home button (or the center earbuds button, if you're wearing those) for 3 seconds, or until you hear the happy double-beep of success. Now the blue Voice Control screen appears (shown on page 68), complete with animated words flying across to remind you of the sorts of commands the iPhone understands. They include:

- **"Play" or "Play music."** Starts the iPod a-playing. It resumes with whatever you were listening to most recently.

- **"Pause" or "Pause music."** Does what you'd think.

- **"Previous song" or "Next song."** Skips to the previous or next song in your playlist or album.

- **"Play [album, artist, or playlist]."** When you're in the mood for U2, say, "Play U2." If you want your Jogging Toonz playlist, say, "Play Jogging Toonz." If you want a certain album, say, "Play 'Abbey Road'" (or whatever).

  The little digital iPhone voice lady tells you what she thinks you want her to do—"Playing 'Abbey Road'"—and then the music begins. If she got it wrong—and she does fairly often—you can either press the Home button again and start over or just use your finger to tap what you want.

- **"Shuffle."** Skips to a random new song.

- **"What's playing?" or "What song is this?" or "Who is this song by?" or "Who sings this song?"** The iPhone voice lady tells you what you're listening to: "Now playing 'Barbie Girl' by Aqua."

- **"Genius" or "Play more songs like this" (or just "Play more like this").** All these commands do the same thing: They use the Genius feature (page 133) to choose a different song that's musically *similar* to the one you were just listening to (roughly the same tempo and rockiness).

- **"Cancel."** If you summoned the Voice Control screen but now you've changed your mind—maybe the song you were hating just got to a good part—say "Cancel" to go back to what you were doing.

Multi(music)tasking

Once you're playing music, it keeps right on playing, even if you press the Home button and move on to do some other work on the iPhone. After all, the only thing more pleasurable than surfing the Web is surfing it to a Beach Boys soundtrack.

A tiny ▶ icon at the top of the screen reminds you that music is still playing. That's handy if the earbuds are plugged in but you're not wearing them.

 Tip Even with the screen off, you can still adjust the music volume (use the buttons on the left side of the phone), pause the music (pinch the earbud clicker once), or advance to the next song (pinch it twice).

Music is playing

Or if you've got something else to do—like jogging, driving, or performing surgery—tap the Sleep/Wake switch to turn off the screen. The music keeps playing, but you'll save battery power.

When a phone call comes in, the music fades, and you hear your chosen ring-tone—through your earbuds, if you're wearing them. Squeeze the clicker on the earbud cord, or tap the Sleep/Wake switch, to answer the call. When the call ends, the music fades back in, right where it left off.

Bluetooth Stereo Headphones

Bluetooth wireless stereo is a wicked-cool feature that snuck onto the marketplace a few years ago, but practically nobody noticed. That's probably (a) because you had to buy *both* a special set of headphones or speakers capable of receiving Bluetooth stereo signals *and* a Bluetooth transmitter to snap onto your music player, and (b) because the real name for this feature is *Bluetooth A2DP profile.* Yuck.

If you have an iPhone, there's one less thing to buy. You still have to buy some wireless headphones, but at least you don't have to buy the transmitter; it's built right into the iPhone 3G, 3GS, and 4.

Shop for your headphones carefully. You want to make sure the box specifically says "A2DP." (There are lots of Bluetooth *headsets,* used for making office phone calls and so on, that do not play *music* over Bluetooth.) Motorola, Altec Lansing, and Plantronics sell several A2DP headphones, for example. There are also Bluetooth A2DP stereo speakers that broadcast your iPhone's music from as far as 20 or 30 feet away.

Once you've bought your 'phones, you have to introduce them to the iPhone—a process called *pairing*.

From the Home screen, tap Settings→General→Bluetooth. Turn Bluetooth on; you see the Searching ✳ animation as the iPhone wirelessly hunts for your headphones.

Grab them, turn them on, and start the pairing procedure, as described in the manual. Usually, that means holding down a certain button until a tiny light starts flashing. At that point, the headphones' name appears on the iPhone's screen.

> **Tip** If the headphones or speakers require a one-time passcode—it's usually 000, but check the manual—the iPhone's keyboard appears automatically, so you can type it in.

A couple of seconds later, it says Connected; at this point, any sound that the iPhone would ordinarily play through its speakers or earbuds now plays through the headphones. Not just music—which, in general, sounds amazing—but chirps, game sounds, and so on.

Furthermore, the Bluetooth symbol now appears at the bottom of the Now Playing screen. When you tap it, the iPhone lets you choose whether to play its sounds through the wireless headphones or through the speaker (or headphones or dock connector, whichever is currently hooked up) as usual.

 Tip For best results, switch the audio back to the iPhone's built-in sources *before* you turn off your headphones. Otherwise, the iPhone can get confused and play nothing at all.

Once you're playing music through your headphones, the iPhone's own volume controls don't do anything; use the controls on the headphones themselves.

If your headset has a microphone, too, you can even answer and make phone calls wirelessly. (There's an Answer button right on the headphones.)

Using Bluetooth wireless stereo does eat up your battery charge faster. But come on: listening to your music without wires, with the iPhone still in your pocket or bag? How cool is that?

Controlling Playback (Video)

Having a bunch of sliders and buttons on the screen doesn't inconvenience you much when you're listening to music. The action is in your ears, not on the screen.

But when you're playing video, *anything* else on the screen is distracting, so Apple hides the video playback controls. Tap the screen once to make them appear, and again to make them disappear.

Here's what they do:

- **Done.** Tap this blue button, in the top-left corner, to stop playback and return to the master list of videos.

- **Scroll slider.** This progress indicator (top of the screen) is exactly like the one you see when you're playing music. You see the elapsed time, remaining time, and a white, round handle that you can drag to jump forward or back in the video.

- **Zoom/Unzoom.** In the top-right corner, a little or button appears. Tap it to adjust the zoom level of the video, as described on the facing page.

- **Play/Pause (▶/II).** These buttons (and the earbud clicker) do the same thing to video as they do to music: alternate playing and pausing.

- **Previous, Next (I◀◀, ▶▶I).** Hold down your finger to rewind or fast-forward the video. The longer you hold, the faster the zipping. (When you fast-forward, you even get to hear the sped-up audio, at least for the first few seconds.)

If you're watching a movie from the iTunes Store, you may be surprised to discover that it comes with predefined chapter markers, just like a DVD. Internally, it's divided up into scenes. You can tap the I◀◀ or ▶▶I button to skip to the previous or next chapter marker—a great way to navigate a long movie quickly.

Tip If you're wearing the earbuds, you can pinch the clicker *twice* to skip to the next chapter, or *three times* to go back a chapter.

- **Volume.** You can drag the round, white handle of this scroll bar (bottom of the screen) to adjust the volume—or you can use the volume keys on the left side of the phone.

- **Language ().** You won't see this button often. But when you do, it summons subtitle and alternate-language soundtrack options, just like a DVD player.

Tip To delete a video, swipe across its name in the Videos list; tap Delete to confirm. (You still have a copy on your computer, of course.) The iPhone no longer offers to delete a video after it plays it to the end, like it did in the early days.

Zoom/Unzoom

The iPhone's screen is bright, vibrant, and stunningly sharp. (The 3G and 3GS have 320 × 480 pixels, crammed so tightly that there are 160 of them per inch; the iPhone 4 is four times as sharp.) It's not, however, the right shape for videos.

Standard TV shows are squarish, not rectangular. So when you watch TV shows, you get black letterbox columns on either side of the picture.

Movies have the opposite problem. They're *too* wide for the iPhone screen. So when you watch movies, you wind up with *horizontal* letterbox bars above and below the picture.

Some people are fine with that. After all, HDTV sets have the same problem. At least when letterbox bars are onscreen, you know you're seeing the complete composition of the scene the director intended.

Other people can't stand letterbox bars. You're already watching on a pretty small screen; why sacrifice some of that precious area to black bars?

Fortunately, the iPhone gives you a choice. If you double-tap the video as it plays, you zoom in, magnifying the image so it fills the entire screen. Or, if the playback controls are visible, you can also tap  or ▓.

Of course, now, you're not seeing the entire original composition. You lose the top and bottom of TV scenes, or the left and right edges of movie scenes.

Fortunately, if this effect chops off something important—some text, for example—the original letterbox view is just another double-tap away.

Familiar iPod Features

In certain respects, the iPhone is *not* a traditional iPod. It doesn't have a click wheel, it doesn't come with any games, and it doesn't offer disk mode (where the iPod acts as a hard drive for transporting computer files).

 Tip OK, OK—there actually *is* a way to simulate iPod disk mode on the iPhone. Just download an app like PhoneView or iPhone Drive. You can find them on this book's "Missing CD" page at *www.missingmanuals.com*.

It does have a long list of traditional iPod features, though. You just have to know where to find them.

Volume Limiter

It's now established fact: Listening to a lot of loud music through earphones can damage your hearing. Pump it up today, pay for it tomorrow.

MP3 players can be sinister that way, because in noisy places like planes and city streets, people turn up the volume much louder than they would in a quiet place, and they don't even realize how high they've cranked it.

That's why Apple created the password-protected volume limiter. It lets parents program their children's iPods (and now iPhones) to max out at a certain volume level that can be surpassed only with the password; see page 393.

Sound Check

This feature smooths out the master volume levels of tracks from different albums, helping to compensate for differences in their recording levels. It doesn't deprive you of peaks and valleys in the music volume, of course—it affects only the baseline level. You turn it on or off in Settings (page 392).

Equalization

Like any good music player, the iPhone offers an EQ function: a long list of presets, each of which affects your music differently by boosting or throttling back various frequencies. One might bring out the bass to goose up your hip-hop tunes; another might emphasize the midrange for clearer vocals; and so on. To turn the EQ on or off, or to choose a different preset, see page 392.

Lyrics

If you've pasted lyrics for a song into iTunes on your computer (or used one of the free automated lyric-fetching programs—search "iTunes lyrics" in Google), you can make them appear on the iPhone screen during playback just by tapping the album art on the playback screen. (Scroll with a flick.)

TV Output

When you crave a bigger screen than 3½ inches, you can play your iPhone's videos on a regular TV set. All you need is Apple's Composite AV Cable or Component AV Cable ($50 each), depending on the kind of TV you have.

The Genius Playlist

Apple's Genius playlist feature supposedly analyzes all of your music, and then, at the click of a button, creates a playlist containing other songs from your library that "sound great" with one particular "seed" song.

If you've use this feature in iTunes on your Mac or PC, and you've built up a Genius playlist or two, you'll find those playlists on your iPhone, too. But you can also make a Genius playlist right on the phone.

To do that, start playing a song that you want to be the "seed"—the one you want the playlist to sound the most like. Then tap the ❋ button on the Now Playing screen (page 123-124). The Genius screen appears, displaying the songs it's proposing for your new instant Genius playlist. (That is, *if* you have enough music on the machine. If you don't have quite a lot of music, you may get the "This song does not have enough related songs" error message. Tap OK and then try a different song.)

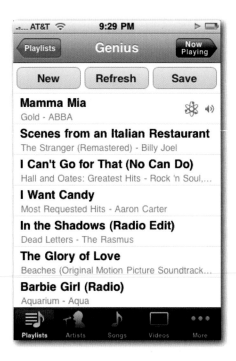

If the suggestions look fine, then tap Save. The new playlist now appears among your others on the Playlists screen, named after your seed song, bearing the ❋ logo to remind you that the phone created that wicked mix.

Next time you sync, this playlist will return to the mothership—iTunes—on your computer. Ordinarily, you can delete a Genius playlist just like any other—but once it's been sent home to iTunes, you can delete it *only* from your Mac or PC.

If you spot a song you can't stand, then tap Refresh to make the iPhone try again with a different assortment (based on the seed song). Or tap New to choose a different seed song and start all over.

The Wireless iTunes Store

It's freaky but true: The iPhone lets you shop Apple's iTunes Store, browsing, buying, and downloading songs wirelessly. Any songs you buy (from 80 cents to $1.30 each) get autosynced back to your computer's copy of iTunes when you get home. Whenever you hear somebody mention a buy-worthy song, for example, you can have it within a minute.

In the bad old days, you could shop the store only when you were on a WiFi network. Now, however, you can also buy songs over AT&T's cellular network, for instant gratification that the you of 1995 never would have believed.

To begin, tap iTunes on the Home screen. The icons at the bottom of the screen include Music, Videos, Ringtones, and Search.

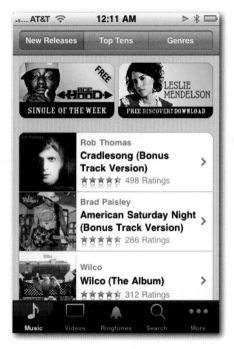 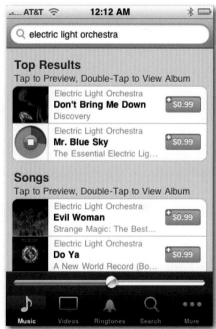

When you tap Music, Videos, or Ringtones, the top of the screen offers further drilling-down buttons like New Releases, Top Tens (meaning "most popular"), and Genres; under Videos, you get Movies, TV Shows, and Music Videos.

(Beneath the Music list: a Redeem button, which you can tap if you've been given an iTunes gift certificate or promo code, and your current credit balance.)

Tip: In theory, you can even buy *videos* on the cellular network (and not just WiFi hot spots). In practice, you're limited to certain music videos. If you try to buy a TV show or movie, an error message says: "This item is over 10MB." Which is AT&T's way of saying, "We don't want you jamming up our precious cellular network with your hefty video downloads, bucko."

Note, by the way, that you can *rent* movies from the store instead of buying them outright. You pay only $3, $4, or $5 to rent (vs. $10 to $16 to buy). But once you start watching, you have only 24 hours to finish; after that, the movie deletes itself from your phone. (On the other hand, if you sync *before* the expiration moment, the movie transfers itself to iTunes on your Mac or PC.)

To search for something in particular, tap Search. The keyboard appears. Type the name of a song, movie, show, performer, or album. At any time, you can stop typing and tap the name of a match to see its details.

All these tools eventually take you to a list of songs. Tap a song's name to hear an instant 30-second preview (tap again to stop). Tap the price button to buy the song, show, or album (and tap BUY NOW to confirm). Enter your iTunes account password, if you're asked.

 Tip: See the tiny **+** symbol on the price button? It indicates that the song is not copy-protected. You're free to copy it to as many Macs, PCs, and music players as you like. (For best results, don't distribute them to buddies or the Internet, however, unless you like legal trouble.)

At this point, your iPhone downloads the music or video you bought.

If you tap More at the bottom of the screen, you get these options:

- **Podcasts.** Browse for thousands of free, and delightful, podcasts (commercial and homemade downloadable "radio shows" and "TV shows").

- **Audiobooks.** This means you, Audible.com subscribers. Wondered where all your books were? Here they are.

- **iTunes U.** Instant access to free, professionally audio-recorded university lectures. It's intended for college kids, of course, but there's all kinds of good stuff here for anyone.

- **Downloads.** Shows you a progress bar for anything you've started to download. Also shows you anything that's queued up to download but hasn't started yet.

 Tip If you tap Edit, you'll see that you can replace any of the four iTunes Store bottom-row icons with one of the More buttons (Audiobooks, Downloads, iTunesU, or Podcasts). The procedure is exactly like the one described on page 119.

Now you've done it: downloaded one of the store's 10 million songs, 1 million podcasts, 3,000 TV shows, or 3,000 movies directly to your phone. Next time you sync, that song will swim *upstream* to your Mac or PC, where it will be safely backed up in iTunes. (If you lost your connection before the iPhone was finished downloading, your Mac or PC will finish the job automatically. Cool.)

 Tip In many Starbucks shops and a few other places (hotels, bookstores, and so on), your iPhone (and laptop) get a free WiFi connection to iTunes. Cool.

When you're in a Starbucks, another slick feature awaits: On the iPhone, a Starbucks button appears at the bottom of the screen automatically, leading to a Now Playing display that identifies what's playing in the store right now.

6 Taking Photos, Shooting Video

This chapter is all about the iPhone's ability to display photos copied over from your computer, to take new pictures with its built-in camera, and (on the 3GS and 4 models) to capture videos.

You've probably never seen pictures and movies look this good on a pocket gadget. The iPhone screen is bright, the colors are vivid, and the super-high pixel density makes every shot of your life look cracklin' sharp.

The camera on the iPhone 4 has been significantly improved from the one on the earlier iPhones. The photos *can* look every bit as good as what you'd get from a dedicated camera—but not always. With moving subjects, it's pretty obvious that you used a cameraphone. Even so, when life's little photo ops crop up, some camera is better than no camera.

Opening Photos

In Chapter 12, you can read about how to choose which photos you want copied to your iPhone. After the sync is done, you can drill down to a certain set of photos as follows.

 Tip In iOS 4, the Photos app has been made fully rotational. That is, you can turn the phone 90 degrees. Whether you're viewing a list, a screen full of thumbnails, or an individual photo, the image on the screen rotates, too, for easier admiring.

❶ On the Home screen, tap Photos.

The Photo Albums screen appears. First on the list is Camera Roll, which means "Pictures you've taken with the iPhone."

Next is Photo Library, which means *all* the photos you've selected to copy from your Mac or PC.

After that is the list of *albums* you've brought over from the computer. (An album is the photo equivalent of a playlist. It's a subset of photos, in a sequence you've selected.)

❷ **Tap one of the rolls or albums.**

Now the screen fills with 20 postage-stamp-sized thumbnails of the photos in this roll or album. You can scroll this list by flicking.

❸ **Tap the photo you want to see.**

It fills the screen, in all its glory.

 Tip If you hold your finger down on the photo, a Copy button appears. That's the first step if you want to paste an individual photo into an email message, an MMS (picture or video) message to another phone, and so on.

Faces and Places

The Albums list may not be the only way to burrow into your photo collection. If you use iPhoto or Aperture (Apple's photo-editing programs for the Mac), a special treat awaits you: You can browse your photos according to who's in them or where they were taken. This is the intriguing world of what Apple calls *Faces* and *Places* data.

- **Faces.** Both iPhoto and Aperture have features that let you identify, by name, the people whose faces are in your photos. Once you've given the software a running start, it can find those people in the rest of your photo collection automatically. That's handy every now and then—when you need a photo of your kid for a school project, for example.

- **Places.** The iPhone can also show you, on a map, where you took your pictures. Not all your photos—just the ones that you or your camera has geotagged (flagged with invisible latitude and longitude coordinates for reference later). You can read about geotagging on page 165; for now, it's enough to note that you can now see the locations of your geotagged photos right on a map, represented by pushpins.

In theory, all the pictures you take with the iPhone itself show up in Places, because the iPhone geotags every picture you take (unless you've turned off the Camera location feature in Settings→General→Location Services).

If any of your photos do, in fact, have face or geotagging information stored with them, then additional buttons show up at the bottom of the Photos screen. Tap *Faces* (below, left) to see a list of the people you identified in iPhoto or Aperture; tap *Places* (below, right) to see a map with pushpins showing where you took the photos. From here, you can drill down; tap a face to see thumbnails of all the pictures that person is in (even if they come from all different albums); tap a pushpin to see a little flag telling you how many photos were taken there, and then tap the ⊙ button to see the thumbnails of those shots.

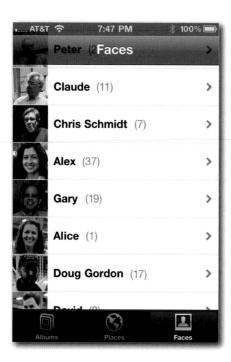 

Flicking, Rotating, Zooming, Panning

Once a photo is open at full size, you have your chance to perform the four most famous and most dazzling tricks of the iPhone: flicking, rotating, zooming, and panning a photo.

- **Flicking** right to left is how you advance to the next picture or movie in the batch. (Flick from left to right to view the *previous* photo.)

- **Rotating** is what you do when a horizontal photo or video appears on the upright iPhone, which makes the photo look small and fills most of the screen with blackness.

  Just turn the iPhone 90 degrees in either direction. Like magic, the photo itself rotates and enlarges to fill its new, wider canvas. No taps required. (This doesn't work when the phone is flat on its back—on a table, for example. It has to be more or less upright.)

  This trick also works the other way—that is, you can also make a *vertical* photo or video fit better when you're holding the iPhone horizontally. Just rotate the iPhone upright.

- **Zooming** a photo means magnifying it, and it's a blast. One quick way is to double-tap the photo; the iPhone zooms in on the portion you tapped, doubling its size.

Another way is to use the two-finger spread technique (page 24). That technique gives you more control over what gets magnified and by how much.

(Remember, the iPhone doesn't actually store the giganto 12-megapixel originals of pictures you took with your fancy digital camera—only scaled-down, iPhone-appropriate versions—so you can't zoom in more than about three times the original size.)

Once you've spread a photo bigger, you can then pinch the screen to scale it down again. Or just double-tap a zoomed photo to restore its original size. (You don't have to restore a photo to original size before advancing to the next one, though; if you flick enough times, you'll pull the next photo onto the screen.)

- **Panning** means moving a photo around on the screen after you've zoomed in. Just drag your finger to do that; no scroll bars are necessary.

 When the iPhone is rotated, all the controls and gestures reorient themselves. For example, flicking right to left still brings on the next photo, even if you're now holding the iPhone the wide way.

Deleting Photos

If some photo no longer meets your exacting standards, you can delete it. But this action is trickier than you may think.

- **If you took the picture using the iPhone,** no sweat. Open the photo; tap the 🗑 button. When you tap Delete Photo, that picture is gone.

- **If the photo was synced to the iPhone from your computer,** well, that's life. The iPhone remains a *mirror* of what's on the computer. In other words, you can't delete the photo right on the phone. Delete it from the original album on your computer (which does *not* mean deleting it from the computer altogether). The next time you sync the iPhone, the photo disappears from it, too.

Photo Controls

If you tap the screen once, some useful controls appear. They remain on the screen for only a couple of seconds, so as not to ruin the majesty of your photo, so act now.

- **Album name.** You can return to the thumbnails page by tapping the screen once, which summons the playback controls, and then tapping the album name in the upper-left corner.

- **Photo number.** The top of the screen says, "88 of 405," for example, meaning that this is the 88th photo out of 405 in the set.

- **Share icon.** Tap the  button in the lower left if you want to do something more with this photo than just stare at it. You can use it as your iPhone's wallpaper, send it by email, use it as somebody's headshot in your Contacts list, send it to another cellphone, or post it on the Web (if you have a MobileMe account). All four of these options are described in the next sections.

Photo number

Album name —— The Year O' Adventure   **95 of 172**

.ıl.. AT&T   12:07 AM   50%

Share ——

Previous   Next

- **Previous/Next arrows.** These white arrows are provided for the benefit of people who haven't quite figured out that they can *flick* to summon the previous or next photo.

Slideshows

You can turn any album, or the Camera Roll itself, into a slideshow by tapping the ▶ button (shown in the center shot on page 140).

A slideshow is a great way to show off your photos and videos. You can specify how many seconds each photo hangs around, and what kind of visual transition effect you want between photos, by opening Settings→Photos. You can even turn on looping or random shuffling of photos there, too.

While the slideshow is going on, avoid touching the screen—that stops the show. And remember that you must let each video play to its conclusion if you want the show to continue. But feel free to turn the iPhone 90 degrees to accommodate landscape-orientation photos as they come up; the slideshow keeps right on going.

 Tip What kind of slideshow would it be without background music? On the Home screen, tap iPod and start a song playing. Yank out the earbuds so the music comes from the speaker. Now return to Photos and start the slideshow—with music!

Copying/Sending/Deleting in Batches

You can select batches of photos at once, which is great for sending several pictures in a single email (up to five); for pasting them as a group into another program; for pasting them into an outgoing MMS message; or for deleting a bunch of pictures in one fell swoop.

The fun begins on the page of thumbnails that appears when you tap an album, a face, a Place thumbtack, or Camera Roll. Tap the ➦ button.

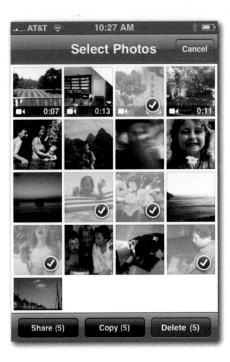

A new button row sprouts across the bottom. First, however, tap the thumbnails of the photos or videos you want to manipulate. With each tap, a checkmark appears, meaning, "OK, this one will be included." (Tap again to remove the checkmark.)

Now you can tap one of the bottom-row buttons:

- **Share.** When you tap Share (5) (or whatever the number of selected photos or videos happens to be), you're offered a new choice of buttons: either Email or MMS (page 150).

- **Copy.** Tapping this one copies the indicated number of photos to the invisible iPhone clipboard. Now you can switch to another program—like Messages or Mail—and paste the selected photos or videos. (You may be able to paste them into non-Apple apps, too.)

- **Delete.** Here's where you can delete a bunch of photos at once. (Here again, you can delete only photos or videos you've taken *with the iPhone*—not ones you transferred from your computer.)

Photo Wallpaper

Wallpaper, in the world of iOS 4, can refer to the background photo that appears in either of two places: the Home screen (plastered behind your app icons) or the Unlock screen (which appears every time you wake the iPhone).

You can replace Apple's standard photos with one of your photos or with a different one of Apple's. You go at this task in either of two ways.

Start in Settings

From the Home screen, tap Settings→Wallpaper.

Now you see miniatures of the two places you can install wallpaper—a Lock screen and a Home screen (facing page, left). (Each shows what you've got installed there as wallpaper at the moment.) These aren't separate buttons; that is, this isn't the place to indicate which screen (Lock or Home) you're redecorating. Just tap once on the whole thing to move on.

When you tap that picture, you're shown a list of photo sources you can use as backgrounds. They include:

- **Wallpaper.** Apple has supplied 27 professional, presized photos and textures that you can use as your wallpaper until you get your own photographic skills in shape (facing page, right).

- **Camera Roll.** These are thumbnails of photos you've taken using the iPhone itself.

- **Albums.** If you've synced any sets of photos from your computer to the iPhone, they're listed here, too.

All of these pictures show up as thumbnail miniatures; tap one to see what it looks like at full size. If it looks good, tap Set. (In iOS 4, the Mona Lisa is no longer one of your choices. Leonardo da Vinci's lawyers must have sued.)

Now the iPhone wants to know which of the two places you want to use this wallpaper; tap Set Lock Screen, Set Home Screen, or Set Both (if you want the same picture in both places).

Start in the Photos App

The task of applying one of your own photos to your Home or Lock screen can also begin in the Photos app. Open one of your photos, as described in the previous pages. Tap the 🖻 button, and then tap Use as Wallpaper.

You're now offered the Move and Scale screen so you can fit your rectangular photo within the square wallpaper "frame." Pinch or spread to enlarge the shot; drag your finger on the screen to scroll and center it.

Finally, tap Set. Here again, you specify where you want to use this wallpaper; tap Set Lock Screen, Set Home Screen, or Set Both (if you want the same picture in both places).

Three Ways to Send Photos or Videos

You can send a photo or video by email, by picture message to another cellphone, or to a Web page—all right from the iPhone.

That's useful when you're out shopping and want to seek your spouse's opinion on something you're about to buy. It's handy when you want to remember the parking-garage section where you parked ("4 South"). It's great when you want to give your buddies a glimpse of whatever hell or heaven you're experiencing at the moment.

Start in the Photos app. Tap your way to the photo or video you want to send. Once it's on the screen before you, tap the 🖆 button. Now you have a bunch of options:

- **Email Photo (Email Video).** The iPhone automatically compresses, rotates, and attaches the photo or video clip to a new outgoing message. All you have to do is address it and hit Send.

At that point, you're asked how much you want the photo *scaled down* from its original size. Tap Small, Medium, Large, or Actual Size, using the megabyte indicator as a guide.

 Note This size choice doesn't appear when you're emailing low-resolution images, like a screenshot (an image you captured from the iPhone's own screen). The iPhone figures it's not big enough to cause anyone any trouble.

Why is this necessary? Because many email systems won't accept attachments larger than 5 megabytes; even four "actual size" photos taken with the iPhone 4 would be too big to send by email. The iPhone used to scale your photos down automatically, without offering any control over how much; be grateful that iOS 4 lets you choose. The Size button you tap controls how big the photo will be on the receiving end—and how long the message will take to send.

In general, when you send Small, the photo will arrive in the recipient's message window about the size of a brownie. A Medium image will fill the email window. Large will fill your recipient's computer screen. And Actual Size is intended for making printouts. It sends the full, multimegabyte originals (2048 × 1536 on the iPhone 3GS; 2592 × 1936 on the iPhone 4).

 Tip Using the steps on page 147, you can send up to five photos at once.

- **MMS.** You can also send a photo or video as a *picture or video message.* It winds up on the screen of the other guy's cellphone. (The geek name for this feature is MMS, for multimedia messaging service.)

  That's a delicious feature, almost handier than sending a photo by email. After all, your friends and relatives don't sit in front of their computers all day and all night (unless they're serious geeks).

  Tap MMS and then specify the phone number of the recipient (or choose someone from your Contacts list), type a little note, tap Send, and off it goes.

Tip Free photo-sharing sites like Flickr and Snapfish let you upload photos from your phone, too. For example, Flickr gives you a private email address for this purpose (visit *www.flickr.com/account/uploadbyemail* to find out what it is). The big ones, including Flickr, also offer special iPhone apps (from the App Store) that make uploading easier.

Keep in mind that this system isn't as good as syncing your camera shots back to your Mac or PC, because emailed photos get scaled down to a very low resolution compared with the originals..

- **MobileMe.** If you're paying $100 a year for one of Apple's MobileMe accounts, then a special treat awaits you: You can send photos from your iPhone directly to your online Web photo gallery, where they appear instantly, to the delight of your fans.

  There's some setup required; it's all covered in Chapter 13. Once that's all set up, though, you can tap the Send to MobileMe button that appears when you tap the 📧 button.

  You're offered the chance to type in a name and a description for your picture. If you scroll up, you'll find that the keyboard has been hiding a list of your the MobileMe Web galleries. Tap the album name you want.

When you tap Publish, the iPhone flings the photo on the screen straight up on that Web album, for all to enjoy. When the uploading is complete, the iPhone offers you buttons that let you take a look at the published items online—or send an email link to them to your adoring fans.

 Tip You can also post photos and videos to other people's MobileMe galleries, if they've turned on the option that permits such craziness. The process is different, however: You're supposed to email your photos and videos to the Web gallery's private address. Your buddies will have to supply that info.

Headshots for Contacts

If you're viewing a photo of somebody who's listed in Contacts, then you can use it (or part of it) as her headshot. After that, her photo appears on your screen every time she calls.

You can add a photo to a contact from either direction: starting with the photo, or starting with the person's "card" open in Contacts.

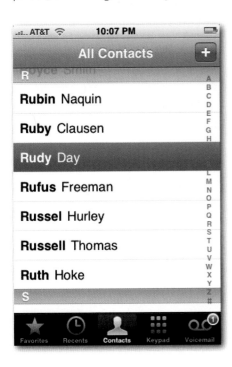

Starting with the Photo

In the Photos app, open a picture that you want to assign to someone in your address book. Tap the ⤴ button, and then tap Assign To Contact.

Your address book list pops up. Tap the right person's name.

Now you see a preview of what the photo will look like when that person calls. This is the Move and Scale screen. It works just as it does when you set wallpaper, as described earlier. But when choosing a headshot for a contact, it's even more important. You'll want to crop the photo and shift it in the frame so only *that person* is visible. It's a great way to isolate one person in a group shot, for example.

Start by enlarging the photo: Spread your thumb and forefinger against the glass. As you go, *shift* the photo's placement in the frame with a one-finger drag. When you've got the person correctly enlarged and centered, tap Set Photo.

Starting with the Contact

In iOS 4, you can also assign a photo to somebody's Contacts card right from the card itself; you don't have to begin the process from the photo.

Just open the card, tap Edit, and then tap Add Photo. Now you can hunt through your photo collection until you find a good one. Tap it, do your thing on the Move and Scale screen, and off you go.

Taking Still Photos

The little hole on the back of the iPhone, in the upper-left corner, is its camera.

On the iPhone 4, it's pretty impressive, at least for a cellphone cam. It has an LED flash, it takes very good 5-megapixel photos, and it does pretty well in low light. In bright light, it takes surprisingly clear, vivid, high-resolution photos.

The earlier iPhone models' cameras aren't quite as good—no flash, lower resolution (2048 × 1536 on the iPhone 3GS; 1600 × 1200 on the earlier models)—but they're still fine as long as your subject is sitting still and well lit. Action shots come out blurry, and dim-light shots come out rather grainy.

Now that you know what you're in for, here's how it works.

On the Home screen, tap Camera. During the 2 seconds that it takes the Camera program to warm up, you see a very cool shutter iris-opening effect.

Tip If you use the camera a lot, you should put the Camera icon on the Dock. That way, no matter what app you're in, accessing the camera is just one Home-button press away. Details are on page 179.

The first time you use the camera, you're asked if it's OK to *geotag* your shots (record where you were when you took them). Unless you're a burglar or you're having an affair, tap OK.

Now frame up the shot, using the iPhone screen as your viewfinder. (At 3½ inches, it's most likely the largest digital-camera viewfinder you've ever used.) You can turn it 90 degrees for a wider shot, if you like.

iPhone 3GS/iPhone 4 Goodies

If you have an iPhone 3GS or iPhone 4, then you have an additional step to consider. See the white box that appears briefly on the screen?

It's telling you where the iPhone thinks the most important part of the photo is. That's where it will focus; that's the area it examines to calculate the overall brightness of the photo (exposure); and that's the portion that will determine the overall *white balance* of the scene (that is, the color cast).

But often, dead-center is not the most important part of the photo. The cool thing is that you can *tap* somewhere else in the scene to move that white square—to make the camera recalculate the focus, exposure, and white balance.

Here's when you might want to do this tapping:

- **When the whole image looks too dark or too bright.** If you tap a *dark* part of the scene, you'll see the whole photo brighten up; if you tap a *bright* part, the whole photo will darken a bit. You're telling the camera, "Redo your calculations so *this* part has the best exposure; I don't really care if the rest of the picture gets brighter or darker."

Tap here; this spot is correctly exposed, but the rest is too dark.   *Tap here; everything brightens up accordingly.*

- **When the scene has a color cast.** If the photo looks, for example, a little bluish or yellowish, tap a different spot in the scene—the one you care most about. The iPhone recomputes its assessment of the white balance.

- **When you're in macro mode.** If the foreground object is very close to the lens—4 to 8 inches away—the iPhone automatically goes into *macro* (super closeup) mode. In this mode, you can do something really cool: You can *defocus the background.* The background goes soft, slightly blurry, just like the professional photos you see in magazines. Just make sure you tap the foreground object.

The Flash

The iPhone 4 has what, in the cellphone industry, is called a flash. It's actually just a very bright LED light on the back of the phone. You can make it turn on momentarily, providing a small boost of illumination when the lights are low. (That's a *small* boost—it won't do anything for subjects more than a few feet away.)

Ordinarily, the flash is set to Auto. It will turn on automatically when the scene is too dark, in the iPhone's opinion. But if you tap the (⚡ Auto) icon, two other options pop out: On (the flash will turn on no matter what the lighting conditions) and Off (the flash will not fire, no matter what).

Tip It took all of about 11 seconds before iPhone apps appeared that can control the flash even when you're not taking pictures. Free apps like Torch Flashlight and FlashLight 4g, for example, let you turn it on and leave it on, so you can see your key in the lock or read the tiny type in a program. Apps like Actual LED Flashlight and Strobe turn the flash into a blinking strobe light, at a rate you specify.

Zooming In

Here's an unexpected development in iOS 4: You now have a camera that can zoom in, bringing you "closer" to the subject.

There is, of course, some fine print. This is a digital zoom. It doesn't work like a real camera's zoom (which actually moves lenses to blow up the scene). Instead, it basically just blows up the image, making everything bigger, and degrading the picture quality in the process.

If you're still interested, all you have to do is tap the screen. A slider appears at one edge of the photo area; drag inside it, or tap inside it, toward the **+** button to zoom in on your subject (below, right). Sometimes, getting closer to the action is worth some image-quality sacrifice.

Taking the Shot

When the composition looks good, tap the ⊙ button. You hear the *snap!* sound of a picture successfully taken. (Mercifully, it's almost instantaneous in iOS 4—much faster than in previous software versions.)

You get to admire your work for only about half a second—and then the photo slurps itself into the ⊡ thumbnail icon at the lower-left corner of the screen.

That's Apple's subtle way of saying, "Tap here to see the picture you just took!" In the meantime, the camera's priority is getting ready to take another shot.

 Tip Technically, the iPhone doesn't record the image until the instant you take your finger *off* the screen. So for much greater stability (and therefore fewer blurrier shots), keep your finger pressed to the button while you compose the shot. Then take your finger off the button to snap the shot.

To look at other pictures you've taken, tap Camera Roll at the top of the screen. Camera Roll refers to pictures you've shot with the iPhone, as opposed to pictures from your computer. Here again, you see the table of contents showing your iPhone shots.

Note For details on copying your iPhone photography and videos back to your Mac or PC, see page 330.

Self-Portraits (the Front Camera)

Until the iPhone 4 came along, self-portraits were tricky. The chrome Apple logo on the back is not a self-portrait mirror, unless all you care about is how your nostril looks.

Everything's different on the iPhone 4. It has a second camera, right there on the front, above the screen. The point, of course, is that you can now use the screen itself as a viewfinder to help you frame yourself, experiment with your expression, and check your teeth.

To activate the front camera, open the Camera app, and then tap the ⟲ icon. Suddenly, you see yourself on the screen. Frame the shot, and then tap the ⟳ button to take the photo.

Now, don't get your expectations too high. The front camera is not the back camera. It's much lower resolution (640 × 480 pixels—not even enough resolution for a small print). There's no flash. Even the zoom slider is missing.

But when your goal is a well-framed self-portrait that you'll use on the screen—in an email or on a Web page, for example, where high resolution isn't very important—having the front-camera option is better than not having it.

Capturing the Screen

Let's say you want to write a book about the iPhone. (Hey, it could happen.) How on earth are you supposed to illustrate that book? How can you take pictures of what's on the screen?

For the first year of the iPhone's existence, that challenge was nearly insurmountable. People set up cameras on tripods to photograph the screen, or wrote hacky little programs that snapped the screen image directly to a JPEG file. Within Apple's walls, when illustrating iPhone manuals and marketing materials, they used a sneaky button press that neatly captured the screen image and added it directly to the Camera Roll of pictures already on the iPhone. But that function was never offered to the public—at least not until the iPhone 2.0 software came along.

Today, it's available to everyone. The trick is very simple: Start by getting the screen just the way you want it, even if that means holding your finger down on an onscreen button or a keyboard key. Now hold down the Home button, and while it's down, press the Sleep/Wake switch at the top of the phone. (Yes, you may need to invite some friends over to help you execute this multiple-finger move.)

But that's all there is to it. The screen flashes white. Now, if you go to the Photos program and open up the Camera Roll, you'll see a crisp, colorful pixel image, in PNG format, of whatever was on the screen. (Its resolution matches the screen: 480 × 320 pixels, or 960 × 480 on the iPhone 4.

At this point, you can send it by email (to illustrate a request for help, for example, or to send a screen from Maps to a friend who's driving your way); sync it with your computer (to add it to your Mac or Windows photo collection); or designate it as the iPhone's wallpaper (to confuse the heck out of its owner).

Recording Video

It's one of the biggest perks of the iPhone 3GS and iPhone 4: You can record video as well as still photos. And not just crummy, jerky, microscopic cellphone video, either—it's smooth (30 frames per second), sharp, colorful video that does surprisingly well in low light.

Using video is almost exactly like taking stills. Pop into the Camera mode. Then tap the ◉/◼◀ switch so that the ◼◀ is selected. You can hold the iPhone either vertically or horizontally; it doesn't care if your video is tall and thin or wide and squat.

Tap to compute focus, exposure, and white balance, as described on the previous pages. Then tap the Start/Stop button in the middle ((●))—and you're rolling! As you film, the button blinks red and a time counter ticks away in the corner.

You can't zoom in or out (except by walking). But look at the bright side: There's no easier-to-use camcorder on earth. You can hold the phone in either portrait or landscape orientation. And man, what a lot of capacity! Each individual shot can be one hour long—and on the 32-gigabyte iPhone, you can record *17 hours* of video.

Which ought to be just about long enough to capture the entire elementary-school talent show.

When you're finished recording, tap the (●) button again. The iPhone stops recording and plays a couple of notes; it's ready to record another shot.

iPhone 4 Goodies

The video features of the iPhone 4 have taken a giant leap forward. Actually, four leaps forward:

- **Hi-def video.** The iPhone 4's backside camera captures high-definition video (1280 × 720 pixels) instead of the standard-def footage of older iPhones (640 × 480). It looks absolutely fantastic. It's probably the best-looking video a cellphone can take.

- **Front-side camera.** For the first time, you can film yourself and see what you're doing. Just tap the icon before you film to make the iPhone use its front-mounted camera, so that the screen shows you. Be aware that videos you capture this way aren't hi-def—they're the standard 640 × 480-pixel quality of iPhones gone by.

- **Tap to focus.** You can change focus while you're filming, which is great when you're panning from a nearby object to a distant one. It's not automatic, as it is on regular camcorders. Still, you can tap somewhere in your "viewfinder" to specify a new focus point. The iPhone recalculates the focus, white balance, and exposure at that point, just as it does when you're taking stills (see page 156).

- **Video light.** You know the LED "flash" on the back of the phone? You can now use it as a video light, supplying some illumination to subjects within about five feet or so. Just tap the (⚡ Auto) icon, and then tap On. The light remains on until you tap to turn it off (or you exit the Camera app).

Editing Video

To review what you just shot, tap the 🔲 thumbnail icon at the lower-left corner of the screen (or lower-right if you're holding the iPhone horizontally). This opens up the video playback screen. Tap the big ▶ button to play back the video you just shot.

What's really cool, though, is that you can *edit* this video right on the phone. You can trim off the dead air at the beginning and the end.

To do that, tap the screen to make the scroll bar appear at the top. Then drag the vertical trim marks inward. Adjust them, hitting ▶ to see the effect as you go, until you've isolated the good stuff—and then tap Trim.

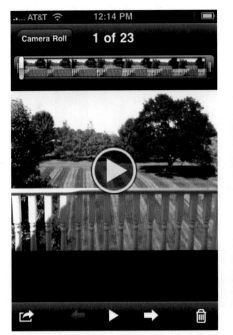

Finally, tap either Trim Original (meaning "shorten the original clip permanently") or Save as New Clip (meaning "leave the original untouched, and spin out the shortened version as a separate video").

iMovie for iPhone

Now, depending on your creative sophistication, you might be scoffing at the heading for the previous section. "Editing video? You call trimming the ends editing?"

It's true—there's more to editing than just snipping dead air from the ends of a clip. That's why Apple made iMovie for iPhone. This little $5 app lets you trim and rearrange video clips, add music and credits, drop in photos with zooming and crossfades, and then post the whole thing directly to YouTube.

Sure, the whole concept sounds a little ridiculous; video editing on a phone? You might as well introduce Microsoft Excel for Toaster Ovens.

But you watch. The way life goes, some iPhone production will win at Cannes next year.

If the idea appeals to you, you can buy the app from the App Store—and you can get instructions for using it in the free downloadable PDF appendix to this chapter, "iMovie for iPhone." It's available on this book's "Missing CD" at *www.missingmanuals.com*.

Uploading Your Video to YouTube (or MMS, Email...)

Now, here's something not every cellphone can do: Film a movie, edit out the boring parts, and then upload it to YouTube—right from the phone!

Call up the video, if it's not already on the screen before you. Tap the 📤 button. You get four choices: Email Video, MMS, Send to MobileMe (these are described earlier in this chapter)—or Send to YouTube.

If you tap that one, the iPhone asks for your YouTube account name and password. Next it wants a title, description, and *tags* (searchable keywords like "funny" or "babies"). Finally, tap Publish.

After the upload is complete, you're offered the chance to see the video as it now appears on YouTube, or to Tell a Friend (that is, email the YouTube link to a pal). Both are excellent ways to admire your masterful cinematography.

> **Tip** Although the iPhone 4 films in high-def, it doesn't transmit high-definition video to YouTube (the files are too big, too slow, too AT&T bandwidth-hogging). But a free app called PixelPipe HD handily works around that limitation. It can also upload to Facebook, Picasa, Flickr, and any of 100 other sites.

Geotagging

Mention to a geek that a gadget has both GPS and a camera, and there's only one possible reaction: "Does it do *geotagging*?"

Geotagging means "embedding your latitude and longitude information into a photo or video when you take it." After all, every digital picture you've ever taken comes with its time and date embedded in its file; why not its location?

The good news is that the iPhone can geotag every photo and movie you take. How you use this information, however, is a bit trickier. The iPhone doesn't geotag unless all the following conditions are true:

- **The location feature on your phone is turned on.** On the Home screen, tap Settings→General. Make sure Location Services is turned On, and make sure Camera is turned On.

- **The phone knows where it is.** If you're indoors, the GPS chip in the iPhone probably can't get a fix on the satellites overhead. And if you're not near cellular towers or WiFi base stations, then even the pseudo-GPS may not be able to triangulate your location.

- **You've given permission.** The first time you use the iPhone's camera, a peculiar message appears (shown on page 155). It's asking, "Do you want to geotag your pictures?" If you tap OK, then the iPhone's geographical coordinates will be embedded in each photo you take.

iPhoto (Get Info)   Preview (Inspector window)

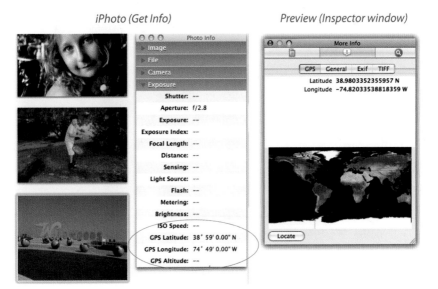

OK, so suppose all of this is true, and the geotagging feature is working. How will you know? Well, thanks to the Places feature described on page 140, you can put geotagging to work right on the phone. You can tap a pushpin on a map and see all the photos you took in that spot.

You can also transfer the photos to your computer, where your likelihood of being able to see the geotag information depends on what photo-viewing software you're using. For example:

- When you've selected a photo in iPhoto (on the Mac), you can press ⌘-I to view the Photo Info panel. At the very bottom, you'll see the GPS coordinates, expressed as latitude and longitude.

- If you export a photo and open it in Preview (on the Mac), then you can choose Tools→Inspector to open the Inspector panel. Its center tab offers a world map that pinpoints the photo's location.

- If you click Locate (on the Preview panel shown on the previous page, you pop into Google Maps online, where you get to see an aerial photo of the spot where you snapped the picture.

- Once you've posted your geotagged photos on Flickr.com (the world's largest photo-sharing site), people can use the Explore menu to search for them by location, or even see them clustered on a world map.

- If you import your photos into Picasa (for Windows), then you can choose Tools→Geotag→View in Google Earth to see a picture's location on the map (if the free Google Earth program is installed on your computer, that is).

  Or choose Tools→Geotag→Export to Google Earth File to create a .kmz file, which you can send to a friend. When opened, this file opens Google Earth (if it's on your friend's computer) and displays a miniature of the picture in the right place on the map.

Better Geotagging

iPhone geotagging is wicked cool, but, as the ads say, "There's an app for that" that can make the whole process easier. The App Store is full of little programs that make the iPhone's camera better.

For example, *SmugShot* correctly geotags your photos and sends that data (along with the photo) directly to SmugMug.com (membership required), which can show you the photos' locations using Google Maps online.

Better yet: *AirMe* correctly tags your photos and auto-uploads your shots to Flickr or AirMe.com. And it's free.

Get it? Get it!

7 All About Apps

Shortly before the iPhone went on sale in 2007, Apple CEO Steve Jobs announced that programmers wouldn't be able to write new programs for it. This was not a popular announcement. "It's a *computer,* for the love of Mike," groused the world's amateur and professional programmers. "It's got memory, a screen, a processor, WiFi…It runs a variant of Mac OS X! Jeez Louise, why can't we write new programs for the thing?!"

Apple said it was only trying to preserve the stability of the phone and of the AT&T network. It needed time to redesign the iPhone operating system, to create a digital sandbox where all those loose-cannon non-Apple programs could run without interfering with the iPhone's "real" functions.

During that year of preparation, new programs appeared on the iPhone, all right—but in forms that most ordinary iPhone fans didn't bother with. There were the semi-lame "Web apps," which were little more than iPhone-shaped Web pages; and there were hacks.

That's right, hacks. You can't sell 6 million of any electronic goody in one year and escape the notice of the hacking community. It didn't take long for these programmers to "jailbreak" the iPhone, using special software tools to open it up (metaphorically speaking) and shoehorn their own programs onto it.

The trouble with jailbreaking the iPhone, though, is that it's not foolproof. Everything may work for a while, but a subsequent Apple software update could actually "brick" your phone (render it inoperable, requiring a complete replacement)—and, in some cases, did. Some hacks required technical skill and a lot of patience, too.

Finally, though, Apple threw open its doors to independent programmers by the tens of thousands, and in July 2008, it offered a simple way for you to get the new iPhone programs they wrote: the iPhone App Store.

Welcome to App Heaven

"App" is short for *application,* meaning software program, and the App Store is a single, centralized catalog of every authorized iPhone add-on program in the world.

Nothing like the App Store had ever been attempted before. Oh, sure, there were thousands of programs for the Mac, Windows, Palm organizers, Treos, BlackBerries, and Windows Mobile phones—but there was never a *single* source of software for those platforms.

In the iPhone's case, there's only one place where you can get new programs (at least without hacking your phone): the App Store.

You hear people talking about downsides to this approach: Apple's stifling the competition, Apple's taking a 30 percent cut of every program sold, Apple's maintaining veto power over programs it doesn't like (or that may compete with its products and services).

But there are some enormous benefits to this setup, too. First, the whole universe of software programs is all in one place. Second, Apple checks out every program to make sure it's decent and runs decently. Third, the store is beautifully integrated with the iPhone itself, making it fast, simple, and idiotproof to download and install new software morsels.

There's an incredible wealth of software in the App Store. These programs can turn the iPhone into an instant-message tool, a pocket Internet radio, an eBay auction tracker, a medical reference, a musical keyboard, a time and expense tracker, a home-automation remote control, a photo editor, an Etch-a-Sketch, a recipe box, a tip calculator, a currency converter, an ebook reader, a restaurant finder, a friend finder, a teleprompter, a parenting handbook, and so on. The best of them exploit the iPhone's orientation sensor, WiFi, Bluetooth, GPS, and other features.

Above all, the iPhone is a dazzling handheld game machine. There are arcade games, classic video games, casino and card games, multiplayer games, puzzles, strategy games, and on and on. Some of them feature smooth 3-D graphics and tilt control; in one driving simulator, you turn the iPhone itself like a steering wheel, and your 3-D car on the screen banks accordingly. Watch out, Game.Boy.

It's so much stuff—200,000 apps in 2 years, 5 billion downloads—that the challenge is now just finding your way through it. Thank goodness for those Most Popular lists...

Two Ways to the App Store

You can get to the App Store in two ways: from the phone itself, or from your computer's copy of the iTunes software.

Using iTunes offers a much easier browsing and shopping experience, of course, because you've got a mouse, a keyboard, and that big screen. But downloading straight to the iPhone, without ever involving the computer, is also wicked cool—and it's your only option when you're out and about.

Shopping from the Phone

To check out the App Store from your iPhone, tap the App Store icon. You arrive at the colorful, scrolling wonder of the store itself.

Across the bottom, you see the now-familiar iPhone lineup of buttons that control your view of the store:

- **Featured.** Here are the 30 programs Apple is recommending this week. (If you tap the Genius button, you're shown a list of apps you might enjoy, based on the apps you've already downloaded.)

- **Categories.** This list shows the entire catalog, organized by category: Books, Business, Education, Entertainment, Finance, Games, and so on. Tap a category to see what's in it.

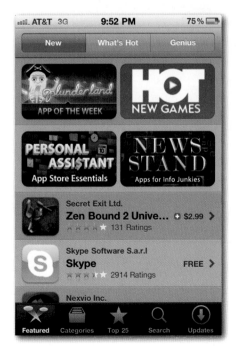

- **Top 25.** Tap this button to reveal a list of the 25 most popular programs at the moment, ranked by how many people have downloaded them. You can also tap the Top Free button at the top of the screen to see the most popular *free* programs. There are lots of them, and they're one of the great joys of the App Store. And Top Grossing shows which apps have made the most money, even if it's not a lot of copies.

- **Search.** Scrolling through those massive lists is a fun way to stumble onto cool things. But as the number of iPhone programs grows into the thousands, viewing by list begins to get awfully unwieldy.

  Fortunately, you can also *search* the catalog, which is a very efficient way to go if you know what you're looking for (either the name of a program, the kind of program, or the software company that made it). Tap in the Search box to make the keyboard appear. As you type, the list shrinks so that it's showing you only the matches. You might type *tetris,* or *piano,* or *Disney,* or whatever.

- **Updates.** Unlike its buddies, this button isn't intended to help you navigate the catalog. Instead, it lets you know when one of the programs you've *already* installed is available in a newer version. Details in a moment.

Once you're looking at the scrolling list of programs—no matter which button was your starting point—the next steps are the same. Each listing shows you the program's name, its icon, and its price. About a third of the App Store's programs are free; the rest are usually under $10, although a few, intended for professionals (pilots, for example), can cost a lot more.

Best of all, this listing shows each program's star rating, which may be the most important statistic of all. You can think of it as a letter grade, given to this program by everyone who's tried it out so far and expressed as an average. (In small type, you can even see how *many* people's opinions are included in this score. You can also see the average rating for *this version* of the program; these apps are constantly being revised and updated.)

Why is it so important? Because not all the App Store's goodies are equally good. Remember, these programs come from a huge variety of people—teenagers in Hungary, professional firms in Silicon Valley, college kids goofing around on weekends—and just because they made it into the store doesn't mean they're worth the money (or even the time to download).

Sometimes, a program has a low score because it's just not designed well or it doesn't do what it's advertised to do. And sometimes, of course, it's a little buggy.

The App Details Screen

When you tap a program's name, you wind up at a screen that contains even more detail. There's a description, a horizontally scrolling set of screenshots, details about the author, the date posted, the version number, and so on. You can also tap the Reviews link to dig beyond the average star rating into the *actual* written reviews from people who've already tried the thing.

If you decide something is worth getting, scroll back to the top of the page and tap its price button. That button changes to say Install, and it does just what it says. Once you tap Install, you've committed to downloading the program. There are only things that may stand in your way:

- **A request for your iTunes account info.** You can't use the App Store without an Apple account—even if you're just downloading free stuff. If you've ever bought anything from the iTunes Store, signed up for a .Mac or MobileMe account, or bought anything from Apple online, then you already have an iTunes account (an Apple ID).

    The iPhone asks you to enter your iTunes account name and password the first time you access the App Store, and every so often thereafter, just to make sure some marauding child in your household can't run up your bill without your knowledge.

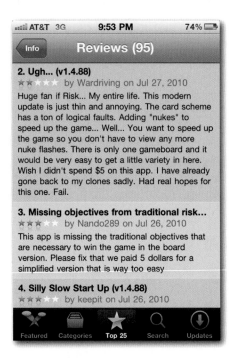

■■■ AT&T 3G   9:53 PM   74% ▭

Reviews (95)

2. Ugh... (v1.4.88)
★★★★★ by Wardriving on Jul 27, 2010
Huge fan if Risk... My entire life. This modern update is just thin and annoying. The card scheme has a ton of logical faults. Adding "nukes" to speed up the game... Well... You want to speed up the game so you don't have to view any more nuke flashes. There is only one gameboard and it would be very easy to get a little variety in here. Wish I didn't spend $5 on this app. I have already gone back to my clones sadly. Had real hopes for this one. Fail.

3. Missing objectives from traditional risk...
★★★★★ by Nando289 on Jul 26, 2010
This app is missing the traditional objectives that are necessary to win the game in the board version. Please fix that we paid 5 dollars for a simplified version that is way too easy

4. Silly Slow Start Up (v1.4.88)
★★★★★ by keepit on Jul 26, 2010

Featured   Categories   **Top 25**   Search   Updates

- **A file size over 20 megabytes.** Most iPhone apps are pretty small—small enough to download directly to the phone, even over a cellular connection. If a program is bigger than 20 MB, though, you can't download it over the cellular airwaves, a policy no doubt intended to soothe nerves at AT&T, whose network would be choked with 100 million iPhoners downloading huge files.

  Instead, over-20-meg files are available only when you're on a WiFi connection. Of course, you can also download them to your computer and sync them from there, as described later in this chapter.

Once you begin downloading a file, the iPhone automatically switches back to the Home screen, where you can see the new icon appear; a tiny progress bar inches across it to indicate the download's progress.

> You don't have to sit there and stare at the progress bar. You can go on working on the iPhone. In fact, you can even go back to the App Store and start downloading something else simultaneously.

Two Welcome Notes about Backups

Especially when you've paid good money for your iPhone apps, you might worry about what would happen if your phone gets lost or stolen, or if someone (maybe you) accidentally deleted one of your precious downloads.

You don't actually have to worry, for two reasons.

First, the next time you sync your iPhone with iTunes, iTunes asks if you want the newly purchased apps backed up onto your computer. If you click Transfer, then the programs eventually show up on the Applications tab in iTunes.

Second, here's a handy little fact about the App Store: It remembers your phone and what you've already bought. You can redownload a purchased program at any time without having to pay for it again.

 If some program doesn't download properly on the iPhone, don't sweat it. Go into iTunes and choose Store→Check for Purchases. And if a program does download to the phone but doesn't transfer to iTunes, then choose File→Transfer Purchases from "iPhone". These two commands straighten things out, clear up the accounting, and make all well with your two copies of each program (iPhone + computer).

Shopping in iTunes

You can also download new programs to your computer, using iTunes, and then sync them over to the phone. By all means use this method whenever you can. It's much more efficient to use a mouse, a keyboard, and a full screen.

In iTunes, click Store (in the Source list). In the iTunes Store box, click App Store.

Now the screen fills with starting points for your quest. There are Top 10 lists (meaning most popular), a Categories list, What's New and What's Hot listings, and so on. Start clicking away to browse the store.

Or use the Search box at top right. Be aware, though, that whatever you type here winds up searching the *entire* iTunes Store, complete with pop songs, TV shows, movies, and so on. The results are grouped by category, but you can click Apps (in the Filter box at left) to hide everything except actual apps. Or click Power Search, where you can limit the search to iPhone apps, to free ones, to iPhone-only programs (as opposed to ones that also work on the iPod Touch or iPad), and so on.

From here, the experience is the same as it is on the phone. Drill down to the Details page for a program, read its description and reviews, look at its photos, and so on. Click Buy App to download and, at the next sync, install it.

 Tip The little numbers next to the app names in the iTunes listings (like "4+") are age recommendations. Now you know.

Organizing Your Apps

As you add new apps to your iPhone, it sprouts new Home screens as necessary to accommodate them all, up to a grand total of 11 screens. That's 180 icons—and yet you can actually go all the way up to 2,160 apps, thanks to the miracle of *folders.*

 Tip Just because there are only 2,160 spots for icons on your Home screens doesn't mean you can't *install* more than that. You can! You can keep going until the iPhone is out of memory. Only 2,160 icons show up—but you can still find and open the others by using Spotlight (page 46). (Once you're over about 200, that's probably how you'll want to find them anyway.)

Until the iOS 4 software came along, this multiple-Home-page business was getting a little unwieldy. People were spending way too much time hunting through their decks of Home screens trying to find the one app they wanted.

Nowadays, the situation has improved. First, the Spotlight search feature can pluck the program you want out of your haystack, as described on page 46.

Second, you can now organize your apps into folders, which greatly alleviates the agony of TMHSS (Too Many Home-Screens Syndrome).

The bottom line: It's well worth taking a moment to arrange the icons on your Home screens into logical categories, tidy folders, or at least a sensible sequence.

You can do that either on the phone itself or in iTunes on your computer. (That's a far quicker and easier method, but of course it works only when your phone is actually connected to the Mac or PC.)

Rearranging/Deleting Apps using iTunes

To fiddle with the layout of your Home screens with the least amount of hassle, connect the iPhone to your computer using the white charging cradle. Open iTunes (Version 9 or later).

Click your iPhone's icon in the left-side list, and then click the Apps tab at the top of the screen. You see the display on the next page.

From here, it's all mouse power:

- Turn on Sync Apps, if necessary, and then turn on the checkboxes of the apps you want on your phone. In other words, you can store hundreds of apps in iTunes, but load only some of them onto your iPhone.

- Click one of the Home-page thumbnails in the scrolling far-right list to indicate which screen you want to edit. Then drag the app icons to rearrange them on that page.

- It's totally fine to drag an app onto a different page thumbnail. You can organize your icons on these Home pages by category, frequency of use, color, or whatever tickles your fancy. (The empty gray thumbnail at the bottom of the thumbnails list means, "Drag an app here to install an additional Home-page screen.")

Tip You can select several app icons simultaneously by ⌘-clicking them; that way, you can move a bunch of them at once.

- You can drag the page thumbnails up or down to rearrange *them*, too.

- To delete an app from the iPhone, point to its icon and click the ✖ that appears. (You can't delete the original iPhone apps like Safari and Mail.)

- Create a folder by dragging one app's icon on top of another (see page 180 for more on folders).

When your design spurt is complete, click Apply in the lower-right corner of the screen.

Rearranging/Deleting Apps Right on the Phone

If you're out and about, it may not be practicable to connect to iTunes. Fortunately, you can also redesign your Home screens right on the iPhone.

To enter this Home-screen editing mode, hold your finger down on any icon until, after about a second, the icons begin to—what's the correct term?—*wiggle.* (That's got to be a first in user-interface history.)

 Tip You can even move an icon onto the Dock. Just make room for it by first dragging an *existing* Dock icon to another spot on the screen.

At this point, you can rearrange your icons by dragging them around the glass into new spots; the other icons scoot aside to make room.

You can drag a single icon across multiple Home pages without having to lift your finger on each page and start a new drag. Just drag the icon against the right or left margin of the screen to "turn the page."

To create an additional Home screen, drag a wiggling icon to the right edge of the screen; keep your finger down. The first Home screen slides off to the left, leaving you on a new, blank one, where you can deposit the icon. You can create up to 11 Home screens in this way.

You may have noticed that, while your icons are wiggling, most of them also sprout little ⊗'s. That's how you *delete* a program you don't need anymore: Tap that ⊗. You'll be asked if you're sure; if so, it says bye-bye.

(You can't delete one of Apple's preinstalled apps, so no ⊗ appears on those icons.)

When everything looks good, press the Home button to stop the wiggling.

 You can also eliminate an app *temporarily*. In iTunes, while your iPhone is connected, click the iPhone's icon, and then click the Apps tab. Turn on Sync Applications, and then turn off the checkboxes of the apps you don't want on the phone. After the next sync, those apps will be gone from your iPhone—but a safety copy is still in iTunes. You can always turn that checkbox on (and then sync) to restore it to your iPhone.

Restoring the Home Screen

If you ever need to undo all the damage you've done, tap Settings→General→ Reset→Reset Home Screen Layout. That function preserves any new programs you've installed, but it consolidates them. If you'd put 10 programs on each of four Home screens, you wind up with only two screens, each packed with 20 icons. Any leftover blank pages are eliminated. (This function also places all of your downloaded apps in alphabetical order.)

Folders

Folders. Such a simple concept. So useful on your Mac or PC. But so, so missing during the first three years of the iPhone era.

Now, in iOS 4, they're here. Folders let you organize your apps, de-emphasize the ones you don't use often, and restore order to that horribly flat, multipage display of icons.

Setting Up Folders in iTunes

As usual, it's fastest and easiest to set up your folders within iTunes, on your Mac or PC, where you have a mouse and a big screen to help you. Connect your iPhone to your computer, open iTunes, click the iPhone's icon in the list at left, and click the Apps tab at the top. You see something like the illustration on page 178.

To create a folder, drag one app's icon on top of another. The software puts both of them into a single new folder. If they're the same kind of app, iOS 4 even tries to figure out what category they both belong to—and names the new folder accordingly ("Music," "Photos," "Kid Games," or whatever). As on the iPhone, this new name is only a proposal; an editing window also appears so that you can type a custom name you prefer.

Once you've got a folder, you can open it just by double-clicking. A special black panel sprouts from the folder icon, revealing its contents; the rest of the screen goes dim. Now you can edit the folder's name, drag the icons around inside it, or drag an app right out of the black strip to remove it from the folder.

If you remove all the apps from a folder, the folder disappears.

Setting Up Folders on the iPhone

iTunes is efficient for working with folders, but let's face it: You're not always seated at your computer. (If you were, you wouldn't have bought a pocket computer.)

To create and edit folders right on the phone, you must always begin by entering Home-screen editing mode. That is, hold your finger down on any icon until all the icons begin to wiggle.

At this point, to create a folder, drag one app's icon on top of another. Just like in iTunes, the software puts both of them into a new folder and gives it a proposed name, as shown on the next page.

Note When Steve Jobs unveiled iOS 4, he pointed out that you can fit up to 12 apps in each folder. And you can have 16 folders on each of your 11 Home screens. And you can have four more folders on the Dock that's always at the bottom of the home screen. So let's see: 12 apps × 16 folders × 11 home screens + (4 Dock folders × 12 apps) = 2,160 apps. That's 2,160 apps on an iPhone! Right?

Not quite. Once you've got 15 folder icons on the last page, the 16th icon would have to be a single app icon, and there'd be no way to create a final folder!

Did Apple lie to us? Not exactly. You can't set up 2,160 apps on the iPhone. But remember that you can also organize your Home screens in iTunes. There, you can drag apps around with the mouse—including dragging them from your list of apps in iTunes, freeing you from the "drop an app on an app" limitation. So yes, you can create 11 home screens full of folders, and therefore 2,160 apps, in iTunes.

(Actually, 2,160 is not the limit even then. That's only how many *icons* show up on the Home screen—but you can keep downloading and downloading, hundreds or thousands more. Even if the higher-numbered apps don't fit on your screen, you can still find and open them using the Spotlight search feature.

Drag one app onto another...   *...and a new folder is born.*

Drop more apps onto the folder to put them inside. Tap the folder to access its contents.

Once you've created a folder or two, they're easy to rename, move, delete, and so on. (Again, you can do all of this only in Home-screen editing mode.) Like this:

- **Take an app out of a folder** by dragging its icon anywhere else on the Home screen. The other icons scoot aside to make room, just as they do when you move them from one Home screen to another.

- **Move a folder around** by dragging around, as you would any other icon (page 179).

 Tip You can drag a folder icon onto the Dock, too, just as you would any app (page 179). Now you've got a popup subfolder full of your favorite apps—on the Dock, which is present on every Home screen. That's a very handy feature; it multiplies the handiness of the Dock itself.

- **Rename a folder** by opening it (tapping it). At this point, the folder's name box is ready for editing.

- **Delete a folder** by removing all of its contents. The folder disappears automatically.

When you're finished manipulating your folders, press the Home button to exit Home-screen editing mode—and stop all the wiggling madness.

App Preferences

If you're wondering where you can change an iPhone app's settings, consider backing out to the Home screen and then tapping Settings. Believe it or not, Apple encourages programmers to add their programs' settings *here*, way down below the bottom of the iPhone's own Settings screen.

Some programmers ignore the advice and build the settings right into their apps, where they're a little easier to find. But if you don't see them there, now you know where else to look.

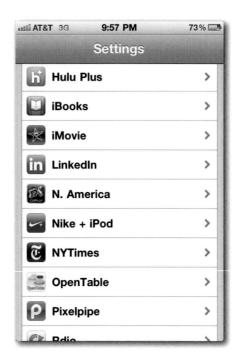

App Updates

When a circled number appears on the App Store's icon (on the Home screen), or when one appears on the Updates icon within the App Store program, that's Apple's way of letting you know that a program you already own has been updated. The beauty of a single-source catalog like the App Store is that Apple knows which programs you've bought—and notifies you automatically when new, improved versions are released.

When you tap Updates, you're shown a list of the programs with waiting updates. And when you tap a program's name, a details screen tells you precisely what the changes are—new features, perhaps, or some bug fixes.

You can download the update, or all the updates, with a single tap...no charge.

 You can also download your updates from iTunes. Click Applications in the Source list (under the Library heading); the lower edge of the window lets you know if there are updated versions of your programs waiting and offers buttons that let you download the updates individually or all at once.

How to Find Good Apps

If the Recommended, What's Hot, and Top 25 lists aren't getting you inspired, there are all kinds of Web sites dedicated to reviewing and recommending iPhone apps. There's *appcraver.com*, for example, and *iphoneappreviews.net*, *whatsoniphone.com*, and on and on.

But if you've never dug into iPhone apps before, you should at the very least try out some of the superstars, the big dogs that almost everybody has.

Here are a few—a very few, a drop in the bucket at the tip of the iceberg— meant only to suggest the infinite variety that's available from the App Store:

- **Drawing programs.** Etch-a-Sketch is just what it says. Shake the iPhone to erase your drawing. Or try any of thousands of full-color drawing apps.

- **Instant messaging.** Thanks to AIM (AOL Instant Messaging), or Yahoo Messenger, or apps that connect to multiple networks at once (like IM+ or Beejive IM), you can conduct instant-message chats right from the iPhone. Most are free.

- **Unlimited free calls.** Skype is another free program. Whenever you're in a WiFi hot spot, you can call 400 million other Skypers around the world, and talk as long as you like, for free. Or call regular telephone numbers for about 2 cents a minute, worldwide.

- **Radio.** AOL Radio is a free program that delivers more than 200 Internet radio stations, organized by musical genre. Or listen to live radio shows. All at no charge. Or go for Pandora or Last.fm instead. Not only do they play free Internet radio, but you can also hit Thumbs Up and Thumbs Down buttons to rate the songs you're hearing. Over time, they send you more and more of the kinds of songs you like.

- **Play the iPhone.** Ocarina is a magical app that turns the iPhone into a musical instrument. The screen displays four colored circles—the "holes" that you cover with your fingers, as on a flute. Then you blow into the microphone at the bottom of the iPhone, and presto: the haunting, expressive sound of a wind instrument. You can even *listen in* to other Ocarina players around the world as they play!

- **Twitter, Facebook…** If you're on Twitter, then you need Twitter, Twitterific, or one of the other Twitter apps for the iPhone. The Facebook app is also excellent: Update your status, exchange messages, post photos, and so on, right from the phone.

- **2-D physics.** In the amazing Crayon Physics app, you draw things with your finger—and they come to life, responding to real-life gravity and physics. It's enchanting, and an addictive puzzle game. Or try Rolando, an insanely popular puzzle-physics game.

- **Remote.** This amazing free program from Apple turns the iPhone into a WiFi, whole-house *remote control* for your Mac or PC's music playback.

 Tip Remote can also control an Apple TV. In fact, it's a great match for the Apple TV, because whenever you're supposed to enter text on the TV, the keyboard pops up on the iPhone's screen automatically. (It's a lot easier to type on the iPhone than to pluck out letters from a grid on the TV screen.)

Multitasking

Yes, it's true: In iOS 4, you don't have to exit one program before opening the next. The iPhone is, more or less, a multitasking phone now. (On the iPhone 3GS and iPhone 4, anyway. Earlier models are considered too slow.)

The big benefit here is speed. You can duck out of what you're doing, check some other app, and return to where you left off—without having to wait for your apps to close and then reopen (which often takes several seconds), and without having to reconstruct how you had things when you left.

But in iOS 4, switching out of a program doesn't actually close it. Instead, it's just suspended—frozen in the middle of whatever it was doing—and therefore not using up any battery power or slowing down your little iComputer.

That, of course, is not real multitasking. Just freezing a background program isn't the same as letting it run.

That, however, is just how Apple wants it. If you left a bunch of apps running in the background all the time, they'd run down your battery in no time (see also: Android phones).

There are some exceptions, however: special cases when Apple permits actual multitasking to take place, where programs are allowed to keep processing away, even in the background. These happy, authorized exceptions:

- **Internet audio.** At long last, you can keep listening to an Internet music service like Pandora or Last.fm, or listen to the game on an Internet radio station, while you tap out some email, surf the Web, or whatever. Just start the radio app playing, and then switch into a different program.

- **GPS apps.** GPS programs are allowed to keep going in the background, too. For navigation apps, that means they'll continue tracking your position, and even speaking the turn-by-turn directions, while you work in other programs. (But not while you're driving, of course…right?)

  Nice touch: If you're listening to music in one app while your GPS app continues to direct you, the iPhone automatically lowers the music volume each time the GPS program speaks an instruction.

  Social-networking apps like Foursquare, which also rely on GPS, can work in the background, too. That is, your friends can track your location even when Foursquare isn't the frontmost app.

- **Internet phone apps.** Apps that let you make calls over WiFi networks, thereby avoiding using up any of your monthly cellular minutes, are one of the greatest joys of iPhonedom. But these programs, like Skype and Line2, always had one huge downside: You couldn't *receive* calls unless the phone app was open and running. Kind of a bummer, really.

  But now, thanks to multitasking, they can answer incoming calls (and make your iPhone ring) even when they're in the background—even when the phone is asleep. And once you've answered, you can switch to another app without losing the call—great when you want to consult your calendar, get Google Maps driving instructions, or look up someone's phone number, without having to hang up.

- **Notifications.** Background apps may not be allowed to run in all their glory. They are, however, allowed to send notices to you from the background. They can send you little alert messages, which pop up on the screen much like text messages do. You might get news headlines, requests to play online games, reminders, and other notices, without having to open the relevant program.

The Task Switcher

If you hadn't read about it, you might not even realize that your iPhone can do this multitasking thing. The key to the whole feature is the *task switcher,* the row of icons that appears at the bottom of the screen when you double-press the Home button.

The task switcher is introduced on page 18, but here are the basics:

- **It slides to the left (older apps).** When you double-press the Home button, whatever's on the screen gracefully slides upward to reveal the first segment of the task switcher: the icons of the four apps you've used most recently. This is awesome; it's amazing how often those are what you want when you need to duck out of what you're doing. You can tap one to open it, without having to return to the Home screen or hunt through *multiple* Home screens.

But if you swipe your finger to the left, you pull into view the next four most recent apps you had open. Swipe again for the *next* four. And so on, and so on, until you're 10 or 12 swipes deep, and you've just wasted a lot of time. (If you have to look that far, you might as well have just used Spotlight!)

Rotation lock   Playback   Current
                   controls   music app

When you tap an icon on the task switcher, you open that app. A cool, carousellish animation makes it look like the incoming app is a card flipping out from behind the outgoing one.

- **It slides to the right (Widget bar).** If you double-press the Home button and then swipe to the *right,* you reveal five handy buttons, as shown on the previous page. The first one is Rotation Lock (page 17). The next three are playback controls for your iPod music; the last is the iPod app's icon.

  The thought here is that these are functions you need often, so they've been installed on the task switcher, where they're always a couple of clicks away.

- **You can remove the icons.** If the task switcher contains the icon of an app you just used but don't intend to use again for a long time, it doesn't have to stay there, taking up valuable space away from more worthy icons. You can delete icons from the lineup, in other words.

  To do that, open the task switcher. Hold down your finger on any one of the apps there until they all start to wiggle (sound familiar?) At this point, a little ⊖ icon appears in the corner of each icon; tap that button to delete the icon. The ones to its right slide in to take its place.

  (The app will return to the lineup the next time you open it from the Home screen; it's not really gone.)

 This isn't a task *manager,* like the one you use to exit programs on Android or Windows Mobile phones. You never have to worry about open apps using up memory, for example; remember, they're frozen when not in use. Instead, this business about removing an icon is strictly a visual convenience, to be used when you want to bring two icons on the task switcher closer together.

Troubleshooting Apps

Let's face it: Little freebie apps created by amateur programmers aren't always as stable and well-designed as, say, Apple's programs. Plenty of them are glitchy around the edges.

If a program is acting up—opening it returns you immediately to the Home screen, for example, or even restarts the iPhone—follow these steps, in sequence:

- **Open the program again.** Sometimes, second time's the charm. ·

- **Restart the iPhone.** That is, hold down the Sleep switch on the top until the slide to power off note appears. Slide your finger to turn off the iPhone, and then turn it back on again. In many cases, that little micro-nap is all the iPhone needs to get its memory straight again.

- **Reinstall the annoying program.** This one could take several steps. It involves deleting the program from the iPhone, as described on page 180, and then re-downloading it from the App Store. You'll get a message that says, "You have already purchased this item," which you already knew. Just tap OK.

- **Reset the iPhone.** If the iPhone is actually *frozen*—nonresponsive— then *reset* it instead. Follow the sequence described on page 412.

Finally, if you're feeling goodwill toward your fellow iPhone-lovers, consider reporting the problem so other people might be spared the headache you've just endured.

To do that, open the App Store on your iPhone. Navigate back to the program as though you were going to download it again. But on its info screen, scroll down and then tap Report a Problem.

Here, you can specify what kind of problem you're having (technical or cultural) and type in the specifics.

When you tap Report and then tap OK in the confirmation box, your bug report gets sent along—not to Apple, but to the author of the program, who may or may not be moved to do something about it.

8 Maps, Apps, & iBooks

Your Home screen comes already loaded with the icons of about 20 programs. These are the essentials, the starting points; eventually, of course, you'll fill that Home screen, and many overflow screens, with additional programs you install yourself.

The starter programs include major gateways to the Internet (Safari), critical communications tools (Phone, Messages, Mail, Contacts), visual records of your life (Photos, Camera), Apple shopping centers (iTunes, App Store), and a well-stocked entertainment center (iPod).

Most of those programs get chapters of their own. This chapter covers the smaller programs: Calendar, YouTube, Stocks, Maps, Weather, Voice Memos, Notes, Clock, Calculator, and Compass.

Calendar

What kind of digital companion would the iPhone be if it didn't have a calendar program? In fact, not only does it have a calendar—but it even has one that syncs with your computer.

If you maintain your life's schedule on a Mac (in iCal or Entourage) or a PC (in Outlook), then you already have your calendar on your iPhone. Make a change in one place, and it changes in the other, every time you sync over the USB cable.

Better yet, if you have a MobileMe account or work for a company with an Exchange server (Chapters 13 and 14), then your calendar can be synchronized with your computer *automatically,* wirelessly, over the air.

Or you can use Calendar all by itself.

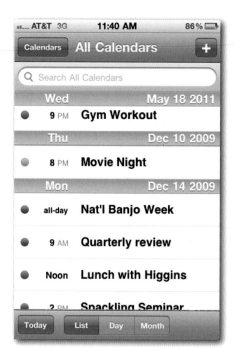

Working with Views

By clicking one of the view buttons at the bottom of the screen, you can switch among these views:

- **List view** offers you a tidy chronological list of everything you've got going on, from today forward. Flick or drag your finger to scroll through it.

 Tip List view also houses the Spotlight box, which can search your whole calendar. Type a few letters of the appointment's name, and then tap the result in the list to open it; tap Show in Calendar to jump to that event in Day view.

- **Day** shows a single day's events, broken down by time slot. Tap the ◄ and ► buttons to move backward or forward a day at a time.

Tip *Hold down* one of the ◀ and ▶ buttons to zoom through the dates quickly. You can skip into a date next month in just a few seconds.

- **Month** shows the entire month, as shown on the previous page. Dots on the date squares show you when you're busy. Tap a date square to read, in the bottom part of the screen, what you've got going on that day. (You can flick or drag that list to scroll it, although this list isn't what you'd call roomy.)

In all three views, you can tap Today (bottom left) to return to today's date.

Making an Appointment

The basic calendar is easy to figure out. After all, with the exception of one unfortunate Gregorian incident, we've been using calendars successfully for centuries.

Even so, recording an event on this calendar is quite a bit more flexible than entering one on, say, one of those "Hunks of the Midwest Police Stations" paper calendars.

Start by tapping the ✚ button (top-right corner of the screen). The Add Event screen pops up, filled with tappable lines of information. Tap one (like Title/

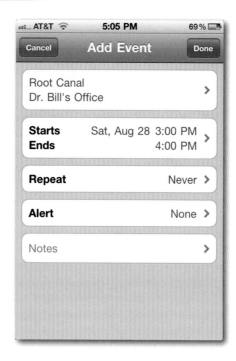

Location, Starts/Ends, or Repeat) to open a configuration screen for that element.

For example:

- **Title/Location.** Name your appointment here. For example, you might type *Fly to Phoenix.*

  The second line, called Location, makes a lot of sense. If you think about it, almost everyone needs to record *where* a meeting is to take place. You might type a reminder for yourself like *My place,* a specific address like *212 East 23rd,* a contact phone number, or a flight number.

  Use the keyboard as usual. When you're finished, tap Save.

- **Starts/Ends.** On this screen, tap Starts, and then indicate the starting time for this appointment, using the four spinning dials at the bottom of the screen. The first sets the date; the second, the hour; the third, the minute; the fourth, AM or PM. If only real alarm clocks were so much fun!

  Then tap Ends, and repeat the process to schedule the ending time. (The iPhone helpfully presets the Ends time to one hour later.)

Appointment, with times

All-day event

An All-day event, of course, has no specific time of day: a holiday, a birthday, a book deadline. When you turn this option on, the Starts and Ends times disappear. The event appears at the top of the list for that day.

 Tip Calendar can handle multiday appointments, too, like trips away. Turn on All-day—and then use the Starts and Ends controls to specify beginning and ending *dates*. On the iPhone, you'll see it as a list item that repeats on every day's square. Back on your computer, you'll see it as a banner stretching across the Month view.

Tap Save when you're done.

- **Repeat.** The screen here contains common options for recurring events: every day, every week, and so on. It starts out saying None.

  Once you've tapped a selection, you return to the Edit screen. Now you can tap the End Repeat button to specify when this event should *stop* repeating. If you leave the setting at Repeat Forever, you're stuck seeing this event repeating on your calendar until the end of time (a good choice for recording, say, your anniversary, especially if your spouse might be consulting the same calendar).

  In other situations, you may prefer to spin the three dials (month, day, year) to specify an ending date, which is useful for car and mortgage payments.

- **Alert.** This screen tells Calendar how to notify you when a certain appointment is about to begin. Calendar can send any of four kinds of flags to get your attention. Tap how much notice you want: 5, 15, or 30 minutes before the big moment; an hour or two before; a day or two before; or on the day of the event.

When you tap Save and return to the main Add Event screen, you see that a new line, called Second Alert, has sprouted up beneath the first Alert line. This line lets you schedule a *second* warning for your appointment, which can occur either before or after the first one. Think of it as a backup alarm for events of extra urgency. Tap Save.

Once you've scheduled these alerts, you'll see a message appear on the screen at the appointed time(s). (Even if the phone was asleep, it appears briefly.) You'll also hear a chirpy alarm sound.

 Note The iPhone doesn't play the sound if you turned off Calendar Alerts in Settings→Sounds. It also doesn't play if you silenced the phone with the silencer switch on the side.

- **Calendar.** Tap here to specify which color-coded *calendar* (category, like Home, Kids, or Work) this appointment belongs to. Turn the page for details on the calendar concept.

- **Notes.** Here's your chance to customize your calendar event. You can type any text you want in the notes area—driving directions, contact phone numbers, a call history, or whatever. Tap Save when you're finished.

When you've completed filling in all these blanks, tap Done. Your newly scheduled event now shows up on the calendar.

Editing, Rescheduling, and Deleting Events

To examine the details of an appointment in the calendar, tap it once. The Event screen appears, filled with the details you previously established.

To edit any of these characteristics, tap Edit. You return to what looks like a clone of the New Event screen shown on page 196.

Here, you can change the name, time, alarm, repeat schedule, or any other detail of the event, just the way you set them up to begin with. (Except the calendar category. For some reason, you can't change that once you've set it.)

This time, there's a big red Delete Event button at the bottom. That's the only way to erase an appointment from your calendar.

 Tip The Calendar program doesn't have a to-do list, as you may have noticed. It may someday, as Apple adds new software features via free updates.

In the meantime, you can always fire up Safari and head over to *www.tadalist.com*, a free, iPhone-friendly, online To Do–list program.

The Calendar (Category) Concept

A *calendar,* in Apple's somewhat confusing terminology, is a color-coded sub-set—a *category*—into which you can place various appointments. They can be anything you like. One person might have calendars called Home, Work, and TV Reminders. Another might have Me, Spouse 'n' Me, and The Kidz. A small business could have categories called Deductible Travel, R&D, and R&R.

You can't create calendar categories, or change their colors, on the iPhone—only in your desktop calendar program. Or, if you're a MobileMe member, you can also set up your categories at *www.me.com*; all your categories and color codings show up on the iPhone automatically.

What you *can* do, in iOS 4 for the first time, is choose which subset of catego-ries you want to see. Just tap Calendars at the top of any Calendar view. You arrive at the big color-coded list of your categories.

This screen exists partly as a reference, a cheat sheet to help you remem-ber what color goes with which category, and partly as a tappable subset-chooser. That is, if you tap the Work category, you return to the calendar view you were just viewing, but now all categories are hidden except the one you tapped.

Tip You can set up real-time, wireless connections to calendars published on the Web in the CalDAV format—notably your Yahoo or Google calendar. Just tap your way to Settings→Mail, Contacts, Calendars→Add Account→Other→Add CalDAV Account. For Server, type (for example) *www.google.com*; fill in your account info.

Now you have a two-way synced calendar between your iPhone and (in this case) your Google calendar. To read about other ways of syncing the iPhone with online calendars, including read-only .ics files (like sports-team schedules), download the PDF appendix called "Syncing Calendar with .ics Files" from this book's "Missing CD" page at *www.missingmanuals.com*.

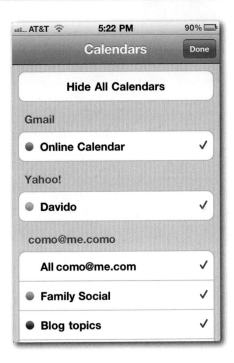

YouTube

YouTube, of course, is the stratospherically popular video-sharing Web site where people post short videos of every description: funny clips from TV, homemade blooper reels, goofy short films, musical performances, bite-sized serial dramas, and so on. YouTube's fans watch 200 million little videos a day.

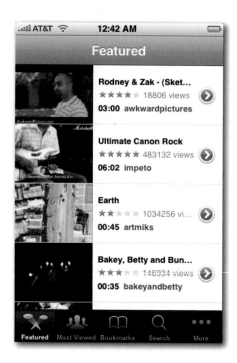

Of course, there's a Web browser on the iPhone. So why does it need a special YouTube *program?* (Especially when YouTube now offers a specialized Web site, *m.youtube.com,* that many iPhoners actually prefer to the app?)

Long story: When the iPhone debuted, YouTube movies were in a format called Flash, which the iPhone didn't (and still doesn't) recognize. (Apple says Flash video is a buggy battery-drainer.)

So Apple persuaded YouTube to re-encode all of its millions of videos into H.264, a *much* higher-quality format? Amazingly enough, YouTube agreed—and you are the lucky benefactor. (Here's what a Flash video and an H.264 video look like, so you can see the difference.)

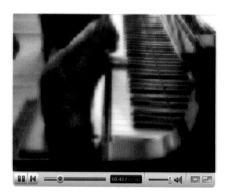

Finding a Video to Play

The YouTube program is basically a collection of lists. Tap one of the icons at the bottom of the screen, for example, to find videos in any of these ways:

- **Featured.** A scrolling, flickable list of videos handpicked by YouTube's editors. You get to see the name, length, star rating, and popularity (viewership) of each one.

- **Most Viewed.** A popularity contest. Tap the buttons at the top to look over the most-viewed videos Today, This Week, or All (meaning "of all time"). Scroll to the bottom of the list and tap Load 25 More to see the next chunk of the list.

- **Favorites.** A list of videos you've flagged as your own personal faves, as described in a moment.

- **Search.** Makes the iPhone keyboard appear so you can type a search phrase. YouTube produces a list of videos whose titles, descriptions, keywords, or creator names match what you typed.

If you tap More, you get some additional options:

- **Most Recent.** These are the very latest videos posted on YouTube.

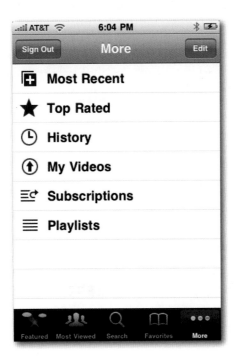

- **Top Rated.** Whenever people watch a video on YouTube, they have the option of giving it a star rating. (You can rate videos right from the iPhone, too.) This list rounds up the highest-rated videos. Beware—you may be disappointed in the taste of the masses.

- **History.** This is a list of videos you've viewed recently on the iPhone—and a Clear button that nukes the list, so people won't know what you've been watching.

- **My Videos, Subscriptions, Playlists.** These options appear only if you have a YouTube account (which is free at *www.youtube.com*) and have logged into it on your iPhone. My Videos are, of course, the videos you've posted on YouTube. Subscriptions are videos you've signed up to receive in installments (many YouTubers produce a new video every week, for example). And Playlists are handpicked sets of videos you've grouped together yourself. Details follow.

> **Tip** Once you've tapped More to see the additional options, you also get an Edit button. It opens a Configure screen that works exactly like the one described on page 119. That is, you can now rearrange the four icons at the bottom of the YouTube app's screen, or you can replace those icons with the ones that are usually hidden (like Most Recent or Top Rated) just by dragging them into place.

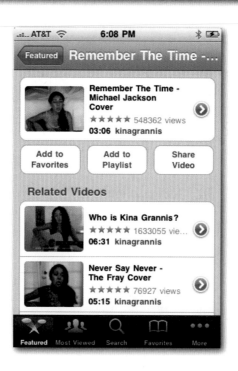

Each list offers a  button at the right side. Tap it to open the Details screen for that video, featuring a description, date, category, tags (keywords), uploader name, play length, number of views, links to related videos, and so on.

Also on this screen are Add to Favorites, which adds this video to your own personal list of favorites (tap Favorites at the bottom of the screen to see it); Add to Playlist, which opens a Playlist screen where you can add, edit, and delete these self-playing sequences of videos; and Share Video, which creates an outgoing message containing a link to that video.

Address it and send it along to anyone you think would be interested, thus fulfilling your duty as a cog in the great viral YouTube machine.

Playing YouTube Videos

To play a video, tap its row in any of the lists. Turn the iPhone 90 degrees counterclockwise—at least if you want to see the video full-screen. The video begins playing automatically; you don't have to tap the ▶ button. (In iOS 4, you *can* turn the iPhone upright once the video starts, but that makes it play all shrunken in the screen, with huge, black, empty areas above and below.)

Here, you'll discover a basic truth about the YouTube app on the iPhone: Videos look *great* if you're connected to the Internet through a WiFi hot spot or the 3G network. They look *not* so great if you're connected over AT&T's cellular EDGE network. When you're on EDGE, you get a completely different version of the video—smaller, coarser, and grainier. In fact, you may not be able to get videos to play at all over EDGE.

When you first start playing a video, you get the usual iPhone playback controls (▶❙ ❙◀◀ ❙❙) the volume slider, and the progress scrubber at the top. Here again, you can double-tap the screen to magnify the video slightly, just enough to eliminate the black bars on the sides of the screen (or tap the ⬕ button at the top-right corner to do the same).

The controls fade away after a moment so they don't block your view. You can make them appear and disappear with a single tap on the video.

There are two icons on these controls, however, that *don't* also appear when you're playing iPod videos. First is the ⌓ button, which adds the video you're watching to your Favorites list so you won't have to hunt for it later.

Second is the ✉ button, which pauses the video and sends you to the Mail app, where a link to the video is pasted into an outgoing message for you.

The Done button at the top-left corner takes you out of the video you're watching and back to the list of YouTube videos.

Stocks

This one's for you, big-time day trader. The Stocks app tracks the rise and fall of the stocks in your portfolio. It connects to the Internet to download the very latest stock prices.

(All right, maybe not the *very* latest. The price info may be delayed as much as 20 minutes, which is typical of free stock-info services.)

When you first fire it up, Stocks shows you a handful of sample high-tech stocks—or, rather, their abbreviations. (They stand for the Dow Jones Industrial Index, the NASDAQ Index, the S&P 500 Index, Apple, Google, and Yahoo. AT&T, one of the starter listings on the original iPhone, has been dumped.)

Next to each, you see its current share price, and next to *that*, you see how much that price has gone up or down today. As a handy visual gauge to how elated or depressed you should be, this final digit appears on a *green* background if it's gone up, or a *red* one if it's gone down.

Tap a stock name to view its stock-price graph at the bottom of the screen. You can even adjust the time scale of this graph by tapping the little interval buttons along the top edge: 1d means "one day" (today); 1w means "one week"; 1m, 3m, and 6m refer to numbers of months; and 1y and 2y refer to years.

Finally, to get more detailed information about a stock, tap its name and then tap the ⓨ! button in the lower-left corner. The iPhone fires up its Web browser and takes you to the Yahoo Finance page for that particular stock, showing the company's Web site, more detailed stock information, and even recent news articles that may have affected the stock's price.

Landscape View

If you turn the iPhone sideways, you get a much bigger, more detailed, widescreen graph of the stock in question. (Flick horizontally to view the previous or next stock.)

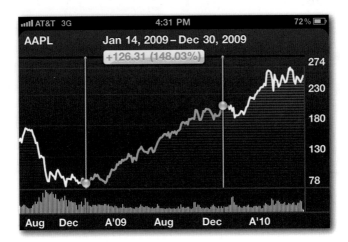

Better yet, you can pinch with two fingers or two thumbs to isolate a certain time period; pop-up bubbles show you how much of a bath you took (or how much of a windfall you received) during the interval you highlighted. Cool!

Customizing Your Portfolio

It's fairly unlikely that *your* stock portfolio contains just Apple, Google, and Yahoo. Fortunately, you can customize the list of stocks to reflect the companies you *do* own (or you want to track).

To edit the list, tap the ❶ button in the lower-right corner. You arrive at the editing screen, where the following choices await:

- **Delete a stock** by tapping the ⊖ button and then the Delete confirmation button.

- **Rearrange the list** by dragging the grip strips on the right side.

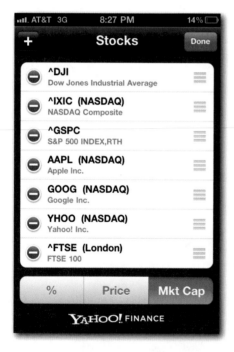

- **Add a stock** by tapping the ✚ button in the top-left corner; the Add Stock screen and the keyboard appear.

  The idea here is that you're not expected to know every company's stock-symbol abbreviation. So type in the company's *name,* and then tap

Search. The iPhone shows you, just above the keyboard, a scrolling list of companies with matching names. Tap the one you want to track. You return to the stocks-list editing screen.

- **Choose %, Price, or Numbers.** You can specify how you want to see the changes in stock prices in the far-right column: as *percentages* ("+ 0.65%"), *numbers* ("+2.23") or as *market capitalization* ("120.3B," meaning $120 billion total corporate value). Tap the corresponding button at the bottom of this screen.

When you're finished setting up your stock list, tap Done.

Maps

Google Maps on the Web is awesome already. It lets you type in any address or point of interest in the U.S. or many other countries—and see it plotted on a map. You have a choice of a street-map diagram or an actual aerial photo, taken by satellite. Google Maps is an incredible resource for planning a drive, scoping out a new city before you travel there, investigating the proximity of a new house to schools and stores, seeing how far a hotel is from the beach, or just generally blowing your mind with a new view of the world.

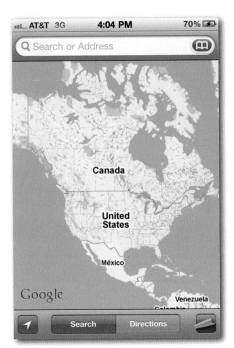

And now you've got Google Maps on the iPhone, with even more features—like turn-by-turn driving directions, a live national Yellow Pages business directory, GPS that pinpoints your current location, and real-time traffic-jam alerts, represented by color coding on the roads shown on the map.

Browsing the Maps

The very first time you open Maps, you see a miniature U.S. map. Double-tap to zoom in, over and over again, until you're seeing actual city blocks. You can also pinch or spread two fingers to magnify or shrink the view. Drag or flick to scroll around the map.

To zoom *out* again, use the rare *two-finger tap.* So—zoom in with *two* taps using one finger; zoom out with *one* tap using two fingers.

At any time, you can tap the curling-page button in the corner of the screen (◢) to open a secret panel of options. Here you can tap your choice of amazing map views: Map (street-map illustration), Satellite (stunning aerial photos), or Hybrid (photos superimposed with street names).

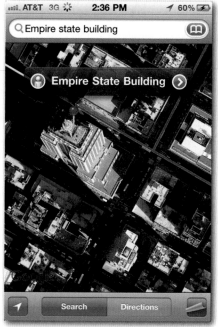

There's no guarantee that the Satellite view provides a very *recent* photo—different parts of the Google Maps database use photography taken at different times—but it's still very cool.

 Note You'll know when you've zoomed in to the resolution limits of Google's satellite imagery; it will just stop zooming. Do some two-finger taps to back out again.

Location, Location, Location

If any phone can tell you where you are, it's the iPhone. It has not one, not two, but *three* ways to determine your location.

- **GPS.** First, the iPhone contains a traditional GPS chip, of the sort that's found in automotive navigation units from Garmin, TomTom, and other companies.

  Don't expect it to work as well as those car units, though. This is a cellphone, for goodness' sake—not some much bigger, single-purpose, dedicated-GPS car unit.

  Still, Apple's designers used every trick in the book to maximize the iPhone's sensitivity, including using the tiny metal ring around the camera lens as part of the GPS antenna. If the iPhone has a good view of the sky, and isn't confounded by skyscrapers or the metal of your car, then it can do a decent job of consulting the 24 satellites that make up the Global Positioning System and determining its own location.

  But what if it can't see the sky? Or what if you have an original iPhone, which has no GPS chip? Fortunately, all iPhones have two other fallback location features.

- **Skyhook's Wi-Fi Positioning System.** Metropolitan areas today are blanketed by overlapping WiFi signals. At a typical Manhattan intersection, you might be in range of 20 base stations. Each one broadcasts its own name and unique network address (its *MAC address*—nothing to do with Mac computers) once every second. Although you'd need to be within 150 feet or so to actually get onto the Internet, a laptop or phone can detect this beacon signal from up to 1,500 feet away.

  A company called Skyhook had a huge idea: Suppose you could correlate all those beacon signals with their physical locations. Why, you'd be able to simulate GPS—without the GPS!

So since 2003, 500 full-time Skyhook employees have been driving every road, lane, and highway in major cities around the world, measuring all those WiFi signals, noting their network addresses and locations. (Neither these vans nor the iPhone ever has to *connect* to these base stations. They're just reading the one-way beacon signals.)

So far, Skyhook's database knows about 50 million hot spots—and the precise longitude and latitude of each. The company licenses this information to companies, like Apple, who want to build location services into their gadgets.

If the iPhone can't get a fix on GPS, then it sniffs around for WiFi base stations. If it finds any, it transmits their IDs back to Skyhook (via cellular network), which looks up those network addresses—and sends coordinates back to the iPhone.

That accuracy is good only to within 100 feet at best, and of course the Skyhook system fails completely once you're out of populated areas. On the other hand, it works indoors, which GPS definitely doesn't.

- **Google's cellular triangulation system.** Finally, as a last resort, any iPhone can turn to a system of location-guessing based on your proximity to the cellphone towers around you. Software provided from Google works a lot like Skyhook's software but relies upon its knowledge of cellular towers' locations rather than WiFi base stations. The accuracy isn't as good as Skyhook or GPS—you're lucky if it puts you within a block or two of your actual location—but it's something.

 Tip The iPhone's location circuits eat into battery power. To shut them down when you're not using them, use the Settings switch described on page 375.

Finding Yourself

All right—now that you know how the iPhone gets its location information, here's how you can use it. It does *not* give you GPS-like navigation instructions, with a voice saying, "Turn left on Elm Street"—at least not unless you get an app that does that from the App Store. (Most require a monthly fee, but not all; try MapQuest 4 Mobile, for example.)

What it can do, though, is show you where you are. Tap the Locate button (➤) at the bottom of the Maps screen. The button turns blue, indicating that the iPhone is consulting its various references—GPS, WiFi network, cellular network—to try to figure out where you are.

What you see now depends on what kind of luck the phone is having (read the illustration below from right to left):

- **Good: The Location circle pulsates.** The first thing that usually happens when you tap the ↗ button is that a big, crosshairs-like circle appears on the map. That's the iPhone's first guess, a quick stab based on triangulation of the local cell towers. As long as it's bouncing inward and outward, it's saying: "I think you're around here. But hold on—let me see if I can be a little more specific."

 Note Actually, the *first* thing that may happen is you may be asked: "'Maps would like to use your current location." (A similar query appears the first time you use *any* program that uses the iPhone's location info.) It's just a little heads-up for the privacy-conscious. Unless you're paranoid, tap OK.

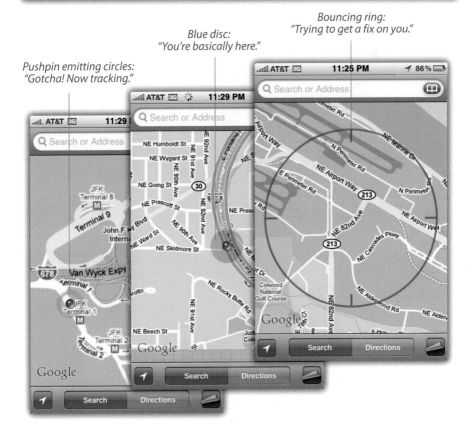

Pushpin emitting circles: "Gotcha! Now tracking."

Blue disc: "You're basically here."

Bouncing ring: "Trying to get a fix on you."

- **Better: The circle sits still.** The blue circle stops pulsing when it's exhausted all the iPhone's location technologies. It's saying: "You're in here somewhere, mate, but I'm afraid this is the best I can do."

- **Best: The blue pushpin appears—and moves with you.** If you're outdoors (so that the GPS can work), or indoors in a big city (so that the WiFi location circuit works), the iPhone may drop a blue pushpin onto the map. That's it saying, "OK, pal, I've got you. You're *here.*"

The iPhone is now tracking you, moving along the map *with* you as you drive, ride, or walk. (The smoothness of the animation depends on the iPhone's success at getting a good location signal.)

The iPhone keeps tracking you until you push the ✈ button again.

Sometimes a blue, see-through disc appears around the pushpin, indicating the iPhone's degree of uncertainty. Still, in times of navigational confusion, that guidance can be extremely useful. It's not just seeing where you are on a map—it's seeing which way you're *going* on the map.

 Tip Once you've found something on the map—your current position, say, or something you've searched for—you can drop a pin there for future reference. Tap the ▤ button; when the page curls up, tap Drop Pin. A blue pushpin appears on the map.

You can drag the pin to move it, or tap ◉ to add it to your Bookmarks (described in a moment), or use it as a starting point for directions. And if you tap Directions, the iPhone lists "Dropped Pin" as your starting point—usually a good guess.

Orienting the Map

It's great to see a blue pin on the map, and all—but how do you know which way you're facing? Legions of iPhone fans have developed a peculiar ritual known as the iPhone Circle, in which they run the perimeter of an imaginary 50-yard circle, holding out the iPhone before them, in an attempt to figure out which way is up on the map.

If you have an iPhone 3GS or iPhone 4, you don't have to bother. Thanks to the built-in magnetometer (compass), the map can orient itself for you.

Just tap the ➹ button twice. The map spins so that the direction you're facing is upward. A "flashlight beam" emanates from your blue dot; its width indicates the iPhone's degree of confidence. (The narrower the beam, the surer it is.)

Searching the Maps

You're not always interested in finding out where you are; often enough, you know that much perfectly well. Instead, you want to see where something *else* is. That's where the Search button comes in.

Tap it to summon the Search box and the iPhone keyboard. (If there's already something in the Search box, tap the ⊗ button to clear it out.)

Here's what Maps can find for you:

- **An address.** You can skip the periods (and usually the commas, too). And you can use abbreviations. Typing *710 w end ave ny ny* will find 710 West End Avenue, New York, New York. (In this and any of the other examples, you can type a Zip code instead of a city and a state.)

- **An intersection.** Type *57th and lexington, ny ny*. Maps will find the spot where East 57th Street crosses Lexington Avenue in New York City.

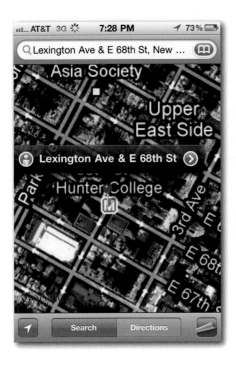

- **A city.** Type *chicago il* to see a map of the city. You can zoom in from there.

- **A Zip code.** Type *10024* to see that region.

- **A point of interest.** Type *washington monument* or *niagara falls*.

When Maps finds a specific address, an animated, red-topped pushpin comes flying down onto its precise spot on the map. A translucent bubble identifies the location by name.

 Tip Tap the bubble to hide it. Tap the map pin to bring the bubble back. Tap the ⊘ to bookmark the spot, to get directions, or to add it to Contacts.

Finding Friends and Businesses

Maps is also plugged into your Contacts list, which makes it especially easy to find a friend's house (or just to see how ritzy his neighborhood is).

Instead of typing an address into the empty Search bar, tap the 🕮 button at the right end of it. You arrive at the Bookmarks/Recents/Contacts screen, containing three lists that can save you a lot of typing.

Two of them are described in the next section. But if you tap Contacts, you see your master address book (Chapter 3). Tap the name of someone you want to find. In a flash, Maps drops a red, animated pushpin onto the map to identify that address.

 Tip If you're handy with the iPhone keyboard, then you can save a few taps. Type part of a person's name into the Search bar. As you go, the iPhone displays a list of matching names. Tap the one you want to find on the map.

That pushpin business also comes into play when you use Maps as a glorified national Yellow Pages. If you type, for example, *pharmacy 60609*, those red pushpins show you all the drugstores in that Chicago Zip code. It's a great way to find a gas station, a cash machine, or a hospital in a pinch. Tap a pushpin to see the name of the corresponding business.

As usual, you can tap the ⊘ button in the map pin's label bubble to open a details screen. If you've searched for a friend, then you see the corresponding Contacts card. If you've searched for a business, then you get a screen containing its phone number, address, Web site, and so on. Remember that you can tap a Web address to open it, or tap a phone number to dial it. ("Hello, what time do you close today?")

 Tip If the cluster of map pins makes it hard to see what you're doing, then tap *List*. You see a neat text list of the same businesses. Tap one to see it alone on the map, or tap ⊙ to see its details card.

In both cases, you get two useful buttons, labeled Directions To Here and Directions From Here. Turn the page for details.

You also get buttons like Add to Bookmarks and Create New Contact, which save this address for instant recall (read on).

Bookmarks and Recents

Let's face it: The iPhone's tiny keyboard can be a little fussy. One nice thing about Maps is the way it tries to eliminate typing at every step.

If you tap the ⌘ button at the right end of the Search bar, for example, you get the Bookmarks/Recents/Contacts screen—three lists that spare you from having to type stuff.

- **Bookmarks** are addresses you've flagged for later use by tapping Add to Bookmarks, an option that appears whenever you tap the ⊙ in a push-pin's label. For sure, you should bookmark your home and workplace. They'll make it much easier to request driving directions.

- **Recents** are searches you've conducted. You'd be surprised at how often you want to call up the same spot again later—and now you can, just by tapping its name in this list. You can also tap Clear to empty the list (if, for example, you intend to elope and don't want your parents to find out).

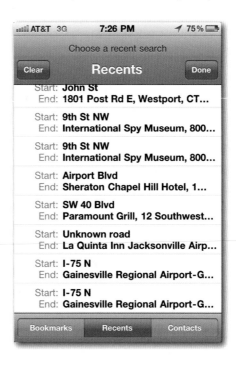

- **Contacts** is your iPhone address book. One tap maps out where someone lives.

Directions

If you tap Directions, the Search bar turns into *two* Search bars: one labeled Start and the other, End. Plug in two addresses—if you've used the Location function, the Start address already says "Current Location"—and let Google Maps guide you from the first to the second.

The iPhone *does* give you turn-by-turn directions—but only as written instructions on the screen, not as a spoken voice. Also, you have to *ask* for each successive instruction; this app doesn't display them automatically based on your current position. It's not a Garmin, in other words.

Still, for a phone, it's not bad.

Begin by filling in the Start and End boxes. You can use any of the address shortcuts on pages 215-216, or you can tap 📖 to specify a bookmark, a recent search, or a name in Contacts. (Or, after performing any search that produces a pushpin, you can tap the ⊙ button in its label bubble and then tap Directions To Here or Direction From Here on the details screen.)

Then tap Route. In just a moment, Maps displays an overview of the route you're about to drive. At the top of the screen, you see the total distance and the amount of time it'll take (if you stay within the speed limit). Amazingly, you also see buttons for 🚌 (public transportation) and 🚶 (walking) directions. These usually take you longer, and public transport isn't always available, but it's amazing that they're even an option.

Tap Start to see the first driving instruction. The map also zooms in to the actual road you'll be traveling, which looks like it's been drawn in with purple highlighter. It's just like having a printout from MapQuest—the directions at the top of the screen say, for example, "Head east on Canterbury Ln toward Blackbird Ave – go .5 mi." Unlike MapQuest, though, you see only one instruction at a time (the current step)—and you don't have to clutch and peer at a crumpled piece of paper while you're driving.

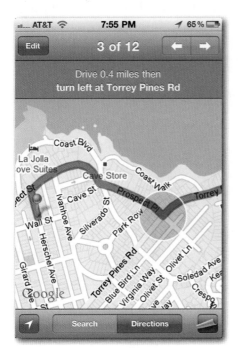
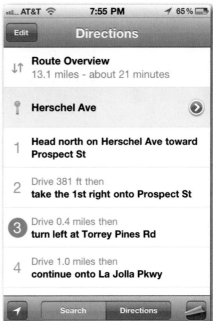

Tap the ← or → buttons to see the previous or next driving instruction. At any time, you can also tap ⤴ and then List to see the master list of turns. Tap an instruction to see a closeup of that turn on the map.

To adjust one of the addresses, tap the current driving instruction; the Search boxes reappear. And to exit the driving mode, tap the ⏸ button again.

 Tip If you tap the ⟳ button, you swap the Start and End points. That's a great way to find your way back after your trip.

Traffic

How's this for a cool feature? Free, real-time traffic reporting—the same information you'd have to pay Sirius XM Satellite Radio $10 a month for. Just tap ⤴ (lower-right corner), and then tap Show Traffic. Now the stretches of road change color to indicate how bad the traffic is.

- **Green** means the traffic is moving at least at 50 miles an hour.

- **Yellow** indicate speeds from 25 to 50 mph.

- **Red** means the road is like a parking lot. The traffic is moving under 25 mph. Time to start up the iPod mode and entertain yourself.

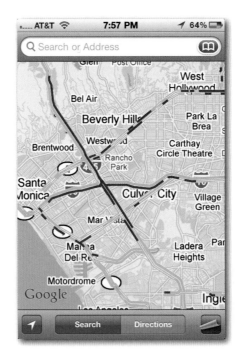

If you don't see any color-coding, it's because Google doesn't have any information for those roads. Usually, the color-coding appears only on highways, and only in metropolitan areas.

Street View

OK, if your brain isn't already boggled by the iPhone, this'll do it.

Most people think of Google Maps as an overhead view, like any other map. But these days, there's more to it than that. And it's all lurking in the little 🅰 icon. Look for him on the red pushpin label after any search. He's likely to appear whenever you search for a street address in a suburb or city (or when you search for the city itself).

When you tap this guy, you open up Street View. It's a 360-degree photographic view of the entire area at street level. You can actually perform a virtual walk-through of an entire city this way! The illustration below tells you all you need to know.

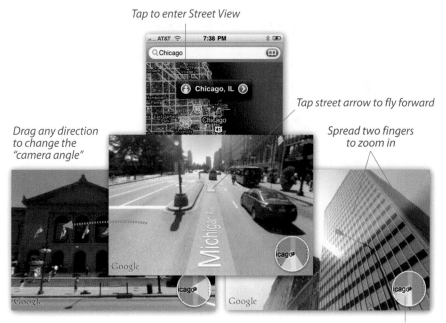

Tap to enter Street View

Tap street arrow to fly forward

Drag any direction to change the "camera angle"

Spread two fingers to zoom in

Tap to return to Map View

What a great way to check out a neighborhood before you visit, shop—or move—there.

Weather

This little widget shows a handy current-conditions display for your city (or any other city) and, at your option, even offers a six-day forecast.

Before you get started, the most important step is to tap the ❶ button at the lower-right corner. The widget flips around.

On the back panel, shown below on the right, you can delete the sample city (Cupertino, California, which is Apple's headquarters) by tapping ⊖ and then Delete. And you can add your own city, or cities of interest, by tapping ✚. The Add Location screen and keyboard appear so you can type your city and state or Zip code. You can rearrange the sequence of cities by dragging the grip strips up or down.

 Tip This Weather widget is world-friendly. You can type the name of any reasonably sized city on earth to find out its weather. Remember to check before you travel.

When you tap Search, you're shown a list of matching cities; tap the one whose weather you want to track. When you return to the configuration screen, you can also specify whether you prefer degrees Celsius or degrees Fahrenheit. Tap Done.

Now the front of the widget (facing page, left) displays the name of your town, today's predicted high and low, the current temperature, a six-day forecast, and a graphic representation of the sky conditions (sunny, cloudy, rainy, and so on).

There's nothing to tap here except the icon at lower left. It fires up the Safari browser, which loads itself with Yahoo's information page about that city. Depending on the city, you might see a City Guide, city news, city photos, and more.

If you've added more than one city to the list, by the way, just flick your finger right or left to shuffle through the Weather screens for the different cities on your list. The tiny bullets beneath the display correspond to the number of Weather cities you've set up—and the white bold one indicates where you are in the sequence.

Voice Memos

This audio app is ideal for recording lectures, musical performances, notes to self, and cute child utterances. The best part: When you sync your iPhone, all of your voice recordings get copied back to the Mac or PC automatically. You'll find them in iTunes, in a folder called Voice Memos.

> **Tip** On a new iPhone, the Voice Memos app comes in a folder called Utilities on the first Home screen.

Start by doing a "testing, testing" check, and make sure the VU meter's needle is moving. (If it's not, maybe the iPhone thinks you're recording from the wrong source—a Bluetooth headset, for example.)

Tap the red Record button to start recording. You can pause at any time by pressing the same button—which now bears a pause symbol (**II**). Stop recording by tapping the Stop button (**■**) on the right.

You can also switch out of the app to do other work. A red banner across the top of the screen reminds you that you're still recording. (You can make *very* long recordings with this thing. Let it run all day, if you like. Even your most long-winded friends can be immortalized.)

To review your recordings, tap what used to be the Stop button, which now looks like a list (☰). This opens the recordings list. Tap one to hear it; tap Delete to get rid of it; tap Share to send it by email or MMS. (If the recording is too long for email or MMS, you're offered the chance to edit it, as described next.)

Editing Your Recording

You might not guess that such a tiny, self-effacing app might actually offer some basic editing functions, but it does. Tap the ⊙ button to the right of any recording to open its Info screen.

Here, you can give yourself some clue what it is by choosing a label (Podcast, Interview, and so on, shown on the facing page at left). Or tap Custom and type in any name you prefer.

If you tap Trim Memo, you get the display shown below at right. Drag the endpoints of the scroll bar inward to cut the dead air off the beginning and end, playing the sound as necessary to guide you (▶). Tap Trim Voice Memo.

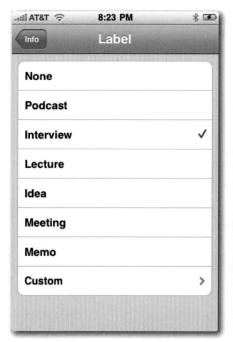
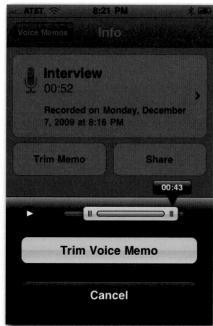

Notes

The Notes app is the iPhone's answer to a word processor. It's simple in the extreme—there's no formatting, for example; let's hope you love that Marker Felt font. Still, it's nice to be able to jot down lists, reminders, and brainstorms. (You can email them to yourself when you're finished—or sync them right to your Mac or PC's email program.)

Tip You can't change the font in Notes. But you can change the font *size*. See page 381.

The first time you open Notes, you see what looks like a yellow, lined legal pad. Tap on the lines to make the keyboard appear so you can begin typing.

Tip Turn the iPhone! This is one of the blessed apps where you can get a much larger, widescreen keyboard by rotating the phone 90 degrees counterclockwise.

When you're finished with a note for now, tap Done. The keyboard goes away, and a ✚ button appears at the top right. It opens a new note.

Whenever you put away the keyboard by tapping Done, a handy row of icons appears at the bottom of your Notes page. The rundown:

- ⬅ ➡. These buttons let you skip to the previous or next page without requiring a detour to the master Notes list.

- ✉. Tap to send your note by email to someone. The iPhone creates a new outgoing message, pastes the first line of the note into the Subject line, and then pastes the note's text into the body. All you have to do is address the note, edit the body if necessary, and hit Send. Afterward, the iPhone politely returns you to the note you were editing.

- 🗑. Tap to delete the current note. After you confirm your decision, the Trash's lid opens, the note folds itself up and flies in, and then the lid closes up again. Cute—real cute.

As you create more pages, the Notes button (top left) becomes more useful. It's your table of contents for the Notes pad. It displays the first lines of your notes (most recent at the top), along with the time or date you last edited it. (The ✚ button appears here, too.) To open a note, tap its name.

There's a Search box hiding here, too. Drag down on the Notes list to bring the Spotlight box into view. Tap it to open the keyboard. You can now search all your notes instantly—not just their titles, but also the text inside them.

Syncing Notes

The iPhone can synchronize your collection of notes with all kinds of other notes sources, so the same notes are waiting for you everywhere you look.

For example, most email programs let you create notes. To that end, you can set up iTunes to sync your iPhone notes with Mail (Apple's email program for the Mac) or with Microsoft Outlook 2003, 2007, or 2010 on a PC. Page 281 has the details.

Your notes can also sync wirelessly with the Notes modules on MobileMe, Google, Yahoo, AOL, or another IMAP email account. To set this up, open Settings→Mail, Contacts, Calendars. Tap the account you want (MobileMe, Gmail, Yahoo, AOL, or whatever); finally, turn the Notes switch On.

That should do it. Now your notes are synced, both ways, with Mail or Outlook when you connect the iPhone to your computer with the cable. With a MobileMe account, notes are synced nearly instantly, wirelessly, both directions.

One catch: Notes you create at *gmail.com, aol.com,* or *yahoo.com* don't wind up on the phone. Those accounts sync wirelessly in one direction only: *from* the iPhone to the Web site, where the notes arrive in a Notes folder. (There's no problem , however, if you get your AOL or Gmail mail in an email *program* like Outlook or Gmail. Then it's two-way syncing as usual.)

Clock

It's not just a clock—it's more like a time factory. Hiding behind this single icon on the Home screen are four programs: a world clock, an alarm clock, a stopwatch, and a countdown timer.

 Tip On a new iPhone, the Clock comes stored in a folder called Utilities on the first Home screen.

World Clock

When you tap World Clock on the Clock screen, you start out with only one clock, showing the current time in Apple's own Cupertino, California.

The neat part is that you can open up *several* of these clocks, and set each one up to show the time in a different city. The result looks like the row of clocks in a hotel lobby, making you look Swiss and precise.

By checking these clocks, you'll know what time it is in some remote city, so you don't wind up waking somebody up at what turns out to be 3 a.m.

To specify which city's time appears on the clock, tap the **+** button at the upper-right corner. The keyboard pops up so you can type the name of a major city. As you type, a scrolling list of matching city names appears above the keyboard; tap the one whose time you want to track.

As soon as you tap a city name, you return to the World Clock display. The color of the clock indicates whether it's daytime (white) or night (black). Note, too, that you can scroll the list of clocks. You're not limited to four, although only four fit on the screen at once.

> **Note** Only the world's major cities are in the iPhone's database. If you're trying to track the time in Squirrel Cheeks, New Mexico, consider adding a major city in the same time zone instead—like Albuquerque.

To edit the list of clocks, tap Edit. Delete a city clock by tapping and then Delete, or drag clocks up or down using the ≡ as a handle. Then tap Done.

Alarm

If you travel much, this feature could turn out to be one of your iPhone's most useful functions. It's reliable, it's programmable, and it even wakes *the phone* first, if necessary, to wake *you*.

To set an alarm, tap Alarm at the bottom of the Clock program's screen. Tap the ✚ button at the upper-right corner to open the Add Alarm screen.

You have several options here:

- **Repeat.** Tap to specify what days this alarm rings. You can specify, for example, Mondays, Wednesdays, and Fridays by tapping those three buttons. (Tap a day-of-the-week button again to turn off its checkmark.) Tap Back when you're done.

- **Sound.** Here's where you specify what sound you want to ring when the time comes. You can choose from any of the iPhone's 25 ringtone sounds, or any you've added yourself. Tap Back.

 Tip Alarm, Crickets, Digital, and Old Phone are the longest and highest sounds. They're the ones most likely to get your attention.

- **Snooze.** If this option is on, then at the appointed time, the alarm message on the screen offers you a Snooze button. Tap it for 10 more minutes of sleep, at which point the iPhone tries again to get your attention.

- **Label.** Tap to give this alarm a description, like "Get dressed for wedding." That message appears on the screen when the alarm goes off.

- **Time dials.** Spin these three vertical wheels—hour, minute, AM/PM—to specify the time you want the alarm to go off.

When you finally tap Save, you return to the Alarm screen, which lists your new alarm. Just tap the On/Off switch to cancel an alarm. It stays in the list, though, so you can quickly reactivate it another day, without having to redo the whole thing. You can tap the ✚ button to set another alarm, if you like.

Note, too, that the ● icon appears in the status bar at the top of the iPhone screen. That's your indicator that the alarm is set.

To delete or edit an alarm, tap Edit. Tap ⊖ and then Delete to get rid of an alarm completely, or tap the alarm's name to return to the setup screen, where you can make changes to the time, name, sound, and so on.

So what happens when the alarm goes off? The iPhone wakes itself up, if it was asleep. A message appears on the screen, identifying the alarm and the time.

And, of course, the sound rings. This alarm is one of the only iPhone sounds that you'll hear *even if the silencer switch is turned on.* Apple figures that if you've gone to the trouble of setting an alarm, you probably *really* want to know about it, even if you forget to turn the ringer back on.

In that case, the screen says, slide to stop alarm.

To cut the ringing short, tap OK or Snooze, or press the Sleep switch, or tap a volume button. After the alarm plays (or you cut it short), its On/Off switch goes to Off (on the Alarm screen).

 Tip With some planning, you can also give yourself a silent, *vibrating* alarm. It can be a subtle cue that it's time to wrap up your speech, conclude a meeting, or end a date so you can get home to watch *Lost*.

You have to set this up right, though. If you just turn on the iPhone's silencer switch, then the alarm will ring *and* vibrate. If you choose None as the alarm sound, it won't ring *or* vibrate.

Here's the trick, then: *Do* choose an alarm sound. And *don't* turn off your ringer. Instead, use the volume keys to crank the iPhone's volume all the way to zero. Now the phone vibrates at the appointed time—but it won't make a sound.

Stopwatch

You've never met a more beautiful stopwatch than this one. Tap Start to begin timing something: a runner, a train, a long-winded person who's arguing with you.

While the digits are flying by, you can tap Lap as often as you like. Each time, the list at bottom identifies how much time elapsed since the *last* time you tapped Lap. It's a way for you to compare, for example, how much time a runner is spending on each lap around a track.

(The tiny digits at the *very* top measure the *current* lap.)

You can do other things on the iPhone while the stopwatch is counting, by the way. In fact, the timer keeps ticking away even when the iPhone is asleep! As a result, you can time long-term events, like how long it takes an ice sculpture to melt, the time it takes for a bean seed to sprout, or the length of a Michael Bay movie.

Tap Stop to freeze the counter; tap Start to resume the timing. If you tap Reset, you reset the counter to zero and erase all the lap times.

Timer

The fourth Clock mini-app is a countdown timer. You input a starting time, and it counts down to zero.

Countdown timers are everywhere in life. They measure the time of periods in sports and games, of cooking times in the kitchen, of stunts on *Survivor*. But on the iPhone, the timer has an especially handy function: It can turn off the music or video after a specified amount of time. In short, it's a Sleep timer that plays you to sleep, then shuts off to save power.

To set the timer, open the Clock app and then tap Timer. Spin the two dials to specify the number of hours and minutes you want to count down.

Then tap the When Timer Ends control to set up what happens when the timer reaches 0:00. Most of the options here are ringtone sounds, so you'll have an audible cue that the time's up. The top one, though, Sleep iPod, is the aforementioned sleep timer. It stops audio and video playback at the appointed time, so that you (and the iPhone) can go to sleep. Tap Set.

Finally, tap Start. Big clock digits count down toward zero. While it's in progress, you can do other things on the iPhone, change the When Timer Ends settings, or just hit Cancel to forget the whole thing.

Calculator

The iPhone wouldn't be much of a computer without a calculator, now would it? And here it is, your everyday memory calculator—with a secret twist.

 Tip On a new iPhone, the Calculator sits in a folder called Utilities on the first Home screen.

In its basic four-function mode, you can tap out equations (like *15.4 × 300 =*) to see the answer at the top. (You can *paste* things you've copied into here, too; just hold your finger down until the Paste button appears.)

 Tip When you tap one of the operators (like ×, +, −, or ÷) it sprouts a white outline to help you remember which operation is in progress. Let's see an ordinary calculator do *that!*

The Memory function works like a short-term storage area that retains numbers temporarily, making it easier to work on complicated problems. When you tap m+, whatever number is on the screen gets added to the number already in the memory; the mr/mc button glows with a white ring to let you know you've stored something there. Press m- to *subtract* the currently displayed number from the number in memory.

And what *is* the number in memory? Press mr/mc to display it—to use it in a subsequent calculation, for example. Finally, tap mr/mc twice to clear the memory and do away with the white ring.

Now the twist: If you rotate the iPhone 90 degrees in either direction, the Calculator morphs into a full-blown HP *scientific* calculator, complete with trigonometry, logarithmic functions, exponents, roots beyond the square root, and so on. Go wild, ye engineers and physicists!

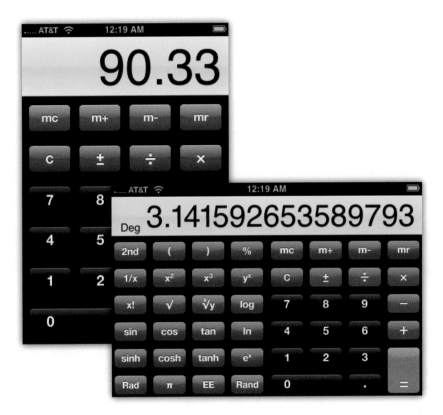

Compass

Yeah, yeah: WiFi, camera, Bluetooth, music, touchscreen, tile sensor—all phones have that stuff these days. But the iPhone still has something the also-rans lack: A compass.

There's an actual magnetometer in the iPhone 3GS and iPhone 4—a magnetic-field sensor. When you open the Compass app, you get exactly what you'd expect: a classic Boy Scout wilderness compass that always points north.

Except it does a few things the Boy Scout compasses never did. Like displaying a digital readout of your heading (shown below, right) or displaying your precise geographical coordinates at the bottom, or offering a choice of *true* north (the "top" point of the Earth's rotational axis) or *magnetic* north (the spot traditional compasses point to, which is about 11 degrees away from true north). (Tap the ❶ to specify which north you prefer.)

The very first time you use the Compass (or anytime you're standing near something big and metal—or magnetic, like stereo speakers), you get the little message shown on the facing page at left. It's telling you to move away from the big metal thing, and to de-confuse the Compass by moving it through 3-D space in a big figure 8. (Yes, you look like a deranged person, but it's good exercise.)

Once the Compass is working, hold it roughly parallel to the ground, and then read it like…a compass.

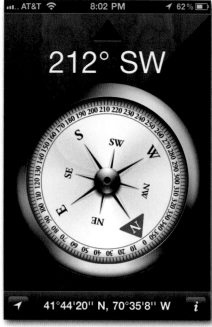

For many people, the real power of the Compass isn't even on display here. It's when you're using the Maps program. (You can jump directly from Compass to Maps by tapping the ➤ button in the lower-left corner.)

The Compass powers the map-orientation feature—the one that shows you not just where you are on the map, but which way you're facing (page 221). That's a rather critical detail when you're lost in a city, trying to find a new address, or emerging from the subway with no idea which way to walk.

But there's more magic yet. People who write iPhone programs can tap into the Compass's information, too, and use it in clever new ways. There's an "augmented reality" app called New York Nearest Subway, for example. By using the Compass, GPS, and tilt-sensor information, it knows exactly where you are, which way you're facing, and how you're holding the phone—and so it superimposes, in real time, arrows that show you where to find the nearest New York subway stop, and which line it's on. Freaky.

iBooks

iBooks is Apple's ebook reading program. It's a free download from the App Store, and it turns the iPhone into a sort of pocket-sized Kindle. With iBooks, you can carry around dozens or hundreds of books in your pocket, which, in the pre-ebook days, would have drawn some funny looks in public.

Most people think of iBooks as a reader for books that Apple sells on its iTunes bookstore—bestsellers and current fiction, for example—and it does that very well. But you can also load it up with your own PDF documents, as well as millions of free, older, out-of-copyright books.

 Tip iBooks is very cool and all. But in the interest of fairness, it's worth noting that Amazon's free Kindle app, and Barnes & Noble's free B&N eReader app, are much the same thing—but offer much bigger book libraries at lower prices than Apple's.

Buying Books

To shop the iBooks bookstore, open the iBooks app. Tap Store in the upper-right corner. Here's the literary equivalent of the App Store, complete with the icons across the bottom. Tap Featured to see what Apple's plugging this week; Browse to see the most popular books in each category (tap Categories at top left to specify which category); Charts to see this week's bestsellers, including what's on the New York Times Best Seller list; Search to search by name; and Purchases to see what you've bought.

Tip Once you've bought a book from Apple, you can download it again on other iPhones, iPod Touches, iPads, and (someday, when Apple releases the necessary reader software), Macs and PCs. Buy once, read many.

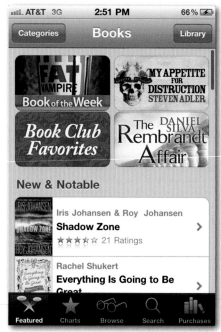

Once you find a book that looks good, you can either tap Get Sample to download a free chapter, read ratings and reviews, or tap the price itself to buy the book and download it straight to the phone.

PDFs and ePub Files

Apple's bookstore isn't the only way to get books. You can also load up your ebook reader from your computer, feeding it with PDF documents and ePub files.

Note ePub is the normal iBooks format. It's a very popular standard for ebook readers, Apple's and otherwise. The only difference between ePub documents you create and the ones Apple sells is that Apple's are copy-protected.

As usual, iTunes is the most convenient loading dock for files bound for your iPhone. Open the program on your Mac or PC. Click Books in the Library list at the left side. Here you'll see all the books, PDF documents, and ePub files that you've slated for transfer.

To add to this set, just drag files off of your desktop and directly into this window, as shown here.

And where are you supposed to get all these files? Well, PDF documents are everywhere—people send them as attachments, and you can turn any document into a PDF file. (For example, on the Mac, in any program, choose File→Print; in the resulting dialog box, click PDF→Save as PDF.)

 Tip If you get a PDF document as an email attachment, adding it to iBooks is even easier. Tap the attachment to open it; now tap Open in iBooks in the corner of the page. (The iPhone may not be able to open really huge PDFs, though.)

But free ebooks in ePub format are everywhere, too. There are 33,000 free downloadable books at *gutenberg.org*, for example, and over a million at *books.google.com*—oldies, but classic oldies, with lots of Mark Twain, Agatha Christie, Herman Melville, H.G. Wells, and so on.

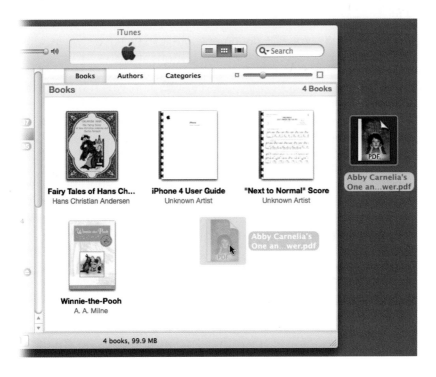

Once you've got some books loaded up in iTunes, you specify which ones you want synced to the phone by connecting the iPhone, clicking its icon in the list at left, clicking the Books tab at top, and turning on the checkboxes of the books you want to transfer. (Details are on page 329.)

Your Library

Once you've supplied your iBooks app with some reading material, the fun begins. When you open the app, you see a handsome wooden bookshelf, with your own personal library represented as little book covers. Mostly what you'll do here is tap a book to open it. But there are all kinds of other activities waiting for you:

- You can reorganize your bookshelf. Hold down your finger on a book until it swells with pride, then drag it into a new spot.

- If you've loaded some PDF documents, you can switch between Books and PDFs bookshelves by tapping the buttons at top.

- If you drag your finger down, you reveal a ☰ icon, which switches the book-cover view to a much more boring (but more compact) list view. (Buttons at the bottom let you sort the list by author, title, category, and so on.) And there's a Search box, too, which lets you search your books' titles—helpful if you have an enormous library.

- Tap Edit if you want to rearrange the book thumbnails (just drag them around without having to hold your finger down) or delete a book (tap the ⊗ icon in the thumbnail corner). Of course, deleting a book from the phone doesn't delete your safety copy in iTunes.

Reading

But come on—you're a reader, not a librarian. Here's how you read an ebook.

Open the book or PDF by tapping the book cover. Now the book opens, ready for you to read. Looks great, doesn't it? (If you're returning to a book you've been reading, iBooks remembers your place.)

 Tip Turn the phone 90 degrees for a wider column of text. The whole page image rotates with you.

In general, reading is simple: Just read. Turn the page by tapping the edge of the page—or swiping your finger across the page. (If you swipe slowly, you can actually see the "paper" bending over—in fact, you can see through to the "ink" on the other side of the page! Amaze your friends.) You can tap or swipe the left edge (to go back a page) or the right edge (forward).

 Tip This, incidentally, is the Rotation Lock's big moment. When you want to read lying down, you can prevent the text from rotating 90 degrees using the Rotation Lock (page 17).

But if you tap a page, a row of additional controls appear:

- Library takes you back to the bookshelf view.

- ≔ opens the Table of Contents. The chapter or page names are "live"— you can tap one to jump there.

- ☼ opens a screen-brightness slider (next page, left). That's a nice touch, because the brightness of the screen makes a big difference in the comfort of your reading—and going all the way to Settings to make the change is a real pain. (The brightness you set here doesn't affect the brightness level of all the other apps—only iBooks.)

- ₐA lets you change the type size. That's a huge feature for people with tired or over-40 eyes. And it's something paper books definitely can't do.

  The same pop-out panel offers a Fonts button, where you can choose from five different typefaces for your book, as well as a Sepia On/Off button, which lets you specify whether the page itself is white or off-white.

- Q opens the Search box (next page, right). It lets you search for text within the book you're reading, which can be extremely useful. As a bonus, there are also Search Google and Search Wikipedia buttons, so that you can hop online to learn more about something you've just read.

- **Page dots.** At the bottom of the screen, the row of horizontal dots represent the pages of your book. Tap or drag the slider to jump around in the book. (If you've magnified the font size, of course, your book suddenly consumes more pages.)

 Tip An iBook can include pictures and even videos. Double-tap a picture in a book to zoom in on it.

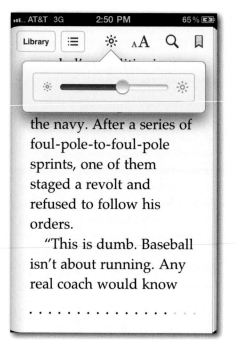

When you're reading a PDF document, by the way, you can do something you can't do when reading regular books: zoom in and out using the usual two-finger pinch-and-spread gestures. Very handy indeed.

 Note On the other hand, here are some features that don't work in PDF files (only ebooks): font and type-size changes; page-turn page-curling animations; Sepia background on/off; Dictionary; Highlights; and Notes.

Notes, Bookmarks, Highlighting, Dictionary

Here are some more stunts that you'd have trouble pulling off in a printed book. If you hold your finger down on a word, you get this effect:

- **Dictionary.** Opens up a graceful, elegant page from iBooks' built-in dictionary. You know—in the unlikely event that you encounter a word you don't know.

- **Highlight.** Adds yellow transparent highlighting to the word you tapped. For best results, don't tap the Highlight button until you've first grabbed the blue dot handles and dragged them to enclose the entire passage you want highlighted.

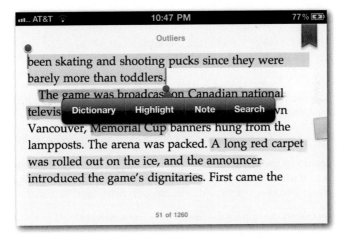

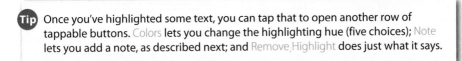

Tip Once you've highlighted some text, you can tap that to open another row of tappable buttons. Colors lets you change the highlighting hue (five choices); Note lets you add a note, as described next; and Remove Highlight does just what it says.

- **Note.** This feature creates highlighting on the selected passage *and* opens an empty yellow sticky note, complete with keyboard, so you can type in your own annotations. When you tap Done, your note collapses down to a tiny yellow post-it peeking out from the right edge of the margin. Tap it to reopen it.

To delete a note, tap the highlighted text. Tap Remove Note.

- **Search** opens the same Search box that you'd get by tapping the Q icon—except this time, the highlighted word is already filled in, saving you a bit of typing.

- adds a bookmark to the current page. This isn't like a physical book-mark, where there's only one in the whole book; you can use it to flag as many pages, for as many reasons, as you like.

There are a couple of cool things going on with your bookmarks, notes, and highlighting, by the way. Once you've added them to your book, they're mag-ically and wirelessly synced to any other copies of that book—on other gad-gets, like the iPad or iPod Touch (or other iPhones). Very handy indeed.

Furthermore, if you tap the ≡ button to open the Table of Contents, you'll see a Bookmarks tab. It presents a tidy list of all your bookmarked pages, notes, and highlighted passages. As usual, tap a page to jump there.

Tip iBooks can actually read to you! Just turn on VoiceOver (see page 109, which also explains some of the other changes in your lifestyle that are required when VoiceOver is turned on).

Then open a book. Tap the first line (to get the highlighting off the buttons at top).

Now swipe down the page with two fingers to make the iPhone start reading the book to you, out loud, with a synthesized voice. It even turns the pages automatically and keeps going until you tap with two fingers to stop it.

Yes, this is exactly the feature that debuted in the Amazon Kindle and was then removed when publishers screamed bloody murder—but somehow, so far, Apple has gotten away with it.

9

Getting Online

The iPhone's concept as an all-screen machine is a curse and a blessing. You may curse it when you're trying to type text, wishing you had real keys. But when you're online—oh, baby. That's when the Web comes to life, looming larger and clearer than on any other cellphone. That's when you see real email, full-blown YouTube videos, hyperclear Google maps, and all kinds of Internet goodness, larger than life.

Well, at least larger than on most other cellphones.

A Tale of Three Networks

The iPhone can get onto the Internet using any of three methods—three kinds of wireless networks. Which kind you're on makes a huge difference to your iPhone experience; there's nothing worse than having to wait until the next ice age for some Web page to arrive when you need the information *now*. Here they are, listed from slowest to fastest.

- **AT&T's EDGE cellular network.** Your iPhone can connect to the data over the same airwaves that carry your voice, thanks to AT&T's EDGE cellular data network. The good part is that it's almost everywhere; your iPhone can get online almost anywhere you can make a phone call.

 The bad news is that EDGE is slow. *Dog* slow—sometimes dial-up slow. Finding a faster way was Apple's #1 priority when it designed its second iPhone.

 You can't be on a phone call while you're online using EDGE, either.

- **AT&T's 3G cellular network.** For the last several years, cellphone companies have quietly been building high-speed cellular data networks—so-called *3G* networks. (3G stands for "third generation." The ancient analog cellphones were the first generation; EDGE-type networks were the second.) Geeks refer to AT&T's 3G network standard by its official name: HSDPA, for High-Speed Download Packet Access.

 Baby, when you're on 3G, the iPhone is awesome. Web pages that take 2 minutes to appear using EDGE show up in about 20 seconds when you're on 3G. Email downloads much faster, especially when there are attachments involved. Voice calls sound better, too, even when the signal strength is very low, since the iPhone's 3G radio can communicate with multiple towers at once.

 Oh, and you can talk on the phone and use the Internet simultaneously, which can be very handy indeed.

 3G is not all sunshine and bunnies, however; it has two huge downsides.

 First: coverage. In an attempt to serve the most people with the least effort, cell companies always bring 3G service to the big cities first. AT&T's 3G coverage is available in about 350 U.S. cities, which is a good start. But that still leaves most of the country, including 10 entire states, without any 3G coverage at all. Whenever you're outside of the blue chicken pox on the AT&T coverage map, your iPhone falls back to the old EDGE speeds.

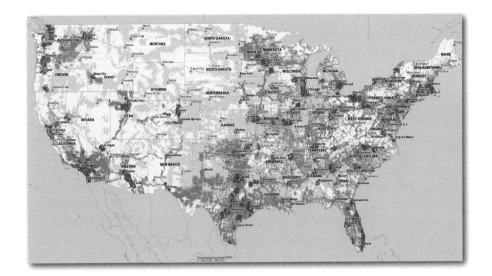

The second big problem with 3G is that, to receive its signal, a phone's circuitry uses a lot of power. That's why the iPhone gets *twice* the talk time (on the iPhone 4, 14 hours instead of 7) when you turn off 3G.

- **WiFi hot spots.** WiFi, known to geeks as 802.11 and to Apple fans as AirPort, is the fastest of all. It's wireless networking, the same technology that laptops get online at high speed in any WiFi *hot spot*.

Hot spots are everywhere these days: in homes, offices, coffee shops (notably Starbucks), hotels, airports, and thousands of other places. Unfortunately, a hot spot is a bubble about 300 feet across; once you wander out of it, you're off the Internet. So WiFi is for people who are sitting still.

> **Tip** At *www.jiwire.com*, you can type an address or a city and find out exactly where to find the closest WiFi hot spots. Or, quicker yet: Open Maps on your iPhone and type in, for example, *wifi austin tx* or *wifi 06902*. Pushpins on the map show you the closest WiFi hot spots.

When you're in a WiFi hot spot, your iPhone has a *very* fast connection to the Internet, as though it's connected to a cable modem or DSL. And when you're online this way, you can make phone calls and surf the Internet simultaneously. And why not? Your iPhone's WiFi and cellular antennas are independent.

So those are the three networks, from slowest to fastest; the iPhone looks for them from fastest to slowest. (You'll always know which kind of network you're on, thanks to the status icons on the status bar: 🛜, 🄴, or 🅱🄶.)

And how much faster is one than the next? Well, network speeds are measured in kilobits per second (which isn't the same as the more familiar kilo-*bytes* per second; divide by 8 to get those).

The EDGE network is supposed to deliver data from 70 to 200 kbps, depending on your distance from the cell towers. 3G gets 300 to 700 kbps. And a WiFi hot spot can spit out 650 to 2,100 kbps. You'll never get speeds near the high ends—but even so, you can see that there's quite a difference.

The bottom line: 3G and WiFi are *awesome,* and EDGE is…well, not so much.

 Tip The iPhone 3GS and iPhone 4 are technically capable of getting onto even faster cellular networks—something called 7.2 Mbps HSDPA, if you're scoring at home— once AT&T installs them. Check back here in 2013.

Sequence of Connections

The iPhone isn't online all the time. To save battery power, it opens the connection only on demand: when you check email, request a Web page, and so on. At that point, the iPhone tries to get online following this sequence:

- First, it sniffs around for a WiFi network that you've used before. If it finds one, it connects quietly and automatically. You're not asked for permission, a password, or anything else.

- If the iPhone can't find a previous hot spot, but it detects a *new* hot spot, a message appears. It displays the new hot spots' names, as shown at left on the facing page; tap the one you want. (If you see a 🔒 icon, then that hot spot been protected by a password, which you'll have to enter.)

- If the iPhone can't find any WiFi hot spots to join, or if you don't join any, it connects to the cellular network: 3G if it's available, and EDGE if not.

Silencing the "Want to Join?" Messages

Sometimes, you might be bombarded by those "Do you want to join?" messages at a time when you have no need to be online. You might want the iPhone to stop bugging you—to *stop* offering WiFi hot spots. In that situation, from the Home screen, tap Settings→Wi-Fi, and then turn off Ask to Join Networks. When this option is off, the iPhone never interrupts your work by bounding in, wagging, and dropping the name of a new network at your feet. In this case, to get onto a new network, you have to visit the aforementioned Settings screen and select it, as described next.

The List of Hot Spots

At some street corners in big cities, WiFi signals bleeding out of apartment buildings sometimes give you a choice of 20 or 30 hot spots to join. But whenever the iPhone invites you to join a hot spot, it suggests only a couple of them: the ones with the strongest signal and, if possible, no password requirement.

But you might sometimes want to see the complete list of available hot spots—maybe because the iPhone-suggested hot spot is flaky. To see the full list, from the Home screen, tap Settings→Wi-Fi. Tap the one you want to join, as shown below at right.

Commercial Hot Spots

Tapping the name of the hot spot you want to join is generally all you have to do—if it's a home WiFi network. Unfortunately, joining a *commercial* WiFi hot spot—one that requires a credit-card number (in a hotel room or airport, for example)—requires more than just connecting to it. You also have to *sign into* it, exactly as you'd do if you were using a laptop.

To do that, return to the Home screen and open Safari. You'll see the "Enter your payment information" screen, either immediately or as soon as you try to open a Web page of your choice.

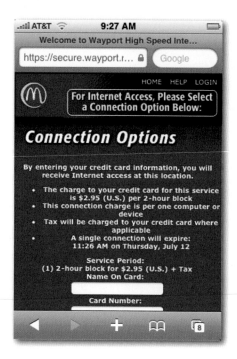

Supply your credit-card information or (if you have a membership to this WiFi chain, like Boingo or T-Mobile) your name and password. Tap Submit or Proceed, try *not* to contemplate the cost, and enjoy your surfing.

 Tip Mercifully, the iPhone memorizes your password. The next time you use this hot spot, you won't have to enter it again.

How to Turn Off 3G

"How to Turn Off 3G?" Is this author mad? Everyone's paying AT&T a lot more money for the privilege of getting 3G. Why on earth would you want to turn it off?

Because 3G is a power hog; it *cuts your iPhone' battery life in half.* Therefore, be grateful that the iPhone even *has* an on/off switch for its 3G radio; that's a luxury most 3G phone owners don't have.

You might consider turning off 3G when, for example, you're not in a 3G area anyway, or you're not using the Internet. You could turn it off when you have a long work day ahead of you, and you can't risk running out of juice halfway through the day. Or maybe you're getting the "20% battery left" warning, and you're many hours away from a chance to recharge.

Turning off 3G forces the iPhone to use the older, less congested AT&T network, which sometimes means you can complete a call in a crowded place where a 3G attempt would fail.

In those situations, from the Home screen, tap Settings→General→Network; where it says Enable 3G, tap to turn it Off. Now, if you want to get online, your phone will use only WiFi and the slow EDGE network.

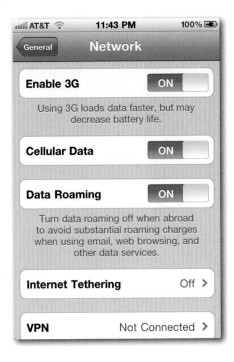

Airplane Mode and WiFi Off Mode

To save even more battery power, you can turn off all three of the iPhone's network connections in one fell swoop. You can also turn off WiFi alone.

- **To turn all radios off.** In Airplane mode (tap Settings, turn on Airplane Mode), you turn off *both* the WiFi *and* the cellular circuitry. Now you can't make calls or get onto the Internet. You're saving power, however, and also complying with flight regulations that ban cellphones in flight.

- **To turn WiFi on or off.** From the Home screen, tap Settings→Wi-Fi. Tap the On/Off switch to shut this radio down (or turn it back on).

 Tip Once you've turned on Airplane mode, you can actually tap Wi-Fi and turn that feature back *on* again. Why on earth? Because some airlines offer WiFi on selected flights. You'll need a way to turn WiFi *on*, but your cellular circuitry *off*.

In Airplane mode, anything that requires voice or Internet access—text messages, Web, email, and so on—triggers a message. "Turn off Airplane mode or use WiFi to access data." Tap either OK (to back out of your decision) or Settings (to turn off Airplane mode and get online).

You can, however, enjoy all the other iPhone features: iPod, camera, clock, calculator, and so on. You can also work with stuff you've *already* downloaded to the phone, like email and voicemail messages.

Tethering

Tethering means using your iPhone as a glorified Internet antenna, so that your laptop can get online. (The laptop connects to the phone either with a USB cable or over wireless Bluetooth.) AT&T charges $20 a month extra for this feature, and offers it only if you've signed up for the 2-gigabytes-of-Internet-data-a-month plan.

To sign up, choose Settings→General→Network. Then tap Set Up Internet Tethering. (The purpose of this button is to make sure that you've signed up for AT&T's tethering plan, which you can do either over the phone or at *www.att.com/mywireless*.) Once you've signed up for tethering, getting your laptop online is simple.

Tethering via Cable

If you can connect your laptop to your iPhone using the white charging cable, you should. Tethering eats up a lot of the phone's battery power, so keeping it plugged into the laptop means you won't wind up with a dead phone when you're finished surfing.

Once you've plugged the iPhone into the laptop, choose Settings→ General→Network. Tap Internet Tethering and turn Internet Tethering on.

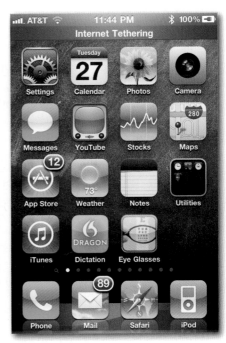

That should be all there is to it. A blue "Internet Tethering" banner at the top of the iPhone's screen gently pulses to remind you of the big favor it's doing you. Wait about 10 seconds and then try using your laptop's Web browser.

If you don't seem to be online, open System Preferences→Network (on the Mac) or the Network and Sharing Center (Windows). Make sure that the new iPhone USB connection gets first priority (there are more troubleshooting details at *http://support.apple.com/kb/ts2756*).

Tethering via Bluetooth

Tethering by wireless Bluetooth connection is even cooler, because you can leave the iPhone in your pocket or purse. You'll surf away on your laptop, baffling every Internet-less soul around you.

Before you can pull off this stunt, you have to *pair* your laptop with the phone. It's an easy, one-time procedure, but the steps differ depending on your laptop brand. It always starts, though, with you turning on Bluetooth on the iPhone. (Tap Settings→General→Bluetooth→On.)

Now go to your computer. For example:

- **Mac OS X.** Open System Preferences→Bluetooth. Click the + button in the lower-left corner; when your iPhone's name shows up in the list, click it and then click Continue. After a moment, a huge six-digit number appears on both the Mac screen and the iPhone screen; on the phone, tap Pair, and on the Mac, click Continue, and then Quit.

 Tip You can make life for yourself a lot easier later if, before you click Quit, you turn on "Show Bluetooth status in the menu bar." You'll see why in a moment.

- **Windows 7.** Open the Start menu; type *Bluetooth.* Click Add a Bluetooth device. When your iPhone's name shows up in the list, click it and then click Next. After a moment, a huge six-digit number appears on both the PC screen and the iPhone screen; on the phone, tap Pair, and on the PC, tap Close.

On the phone, choose Settings→ General→Network. Tap Internet Tethering and turn Internet Tethering on.

Now, the pairing business was a one-time operation, but you still have to connect to the phone manually each time you want to go online.

- On the Mac, click the ✳ icon in the menu bar (which appears there because you wisely followed the preceding Tip). Choose iPhone 4→Connect to Network. (The menu lists whatever your actual iPhone's name is, which might not be "iPhone 4.")

- In Windows, click the ✳ icon on the system tray and connect to the iPhone.

After about 10 seconds, you're online (and using up iPhone battery power like there's no tomorrow). Conveniently enough, you can still use all functions of the iPhone, including making calls and even surfing the Web, while it's channeling your laptop's Internet connection.

10 The Web

T he Web on the iPhone looks like the Web on your computer, and that's one of Apple's greatest accomplishments. You see the real deal—the actual fonts, graphics, and layouts—not the stripped-down, bare-bones mini-Web on cellphones of years gone by.

Treo

iPhone

The iPhone's Web browser is Safari, a lite version of the same one that comes with every Macintosh and is also available for Windows. It's fast (at least in a WiFi hot spot), simple to use, and very pretty indeed.

Safari Tour

You get on the Web by tapping Safari on the Home screen (below, left); the very first time you do this, a blank browser window appears (below, right). As noted in the previous chapter, the Web on the iPhone can be either fast (when you're in a WiFi hot spot), medium (in a 3G coverage area) or excruciating (on the EDGE cellular network). Even so, some Web is usually better than no Web at all.

Tip You don't have to wait for a Web page to load entirely. You can zoom in, scroll, and begin reading the text even when only part of the page has appeared.

Safari has most of the features of a desktop Web browser: bookmarks, autocomplete (for Web addresses), scrolling shortcuts, cookies, a pop-up ad blocker, password memorization, and so on. (It's missing niceties like streaming music, Java, Flash, and other plug-ins.)

Here's a quick tour of the main screen elements, starting from the upper left:

- **(Google).** Tap this word (which you can change to say Bing or Yahoo) to open the search bar and the keyboard; see page 269.

- **Address bar.** This empty white box is where you enter the *URL* (Web address) for a page you want to visit. (URL is short for the even-less-self-explanatory *Uniform Resource Locator*.) See page 258.

- **✕, ↻ (Stop, Reload).** Tap ✕ to interrupt the downloading of a Web page you've just requested (if you've made a mistake, for instance, or if it's taking too long).

  Once a page has finished loading, the ✕ button turns into a ↻ button. Click this circular arrow if a page doesn't look or work quite right, or if you want to see the updated version of a Web page (such as a breaking-news site) that changes constantly. Safari redownloads the Web page and reinterprets its text and graphics.

- **◀, ▶ (Back, Forward).** Tap the ◀ button to revisit the page you were just on.

  Once you've tapped ◀, you can then tap the ▶ button to return to the page you were on *before* you tapped the ◀ button.

- **✚ (Share/Bookmark).** When you're on an especially useful page, tap this button. It offers three choices: Add Bookmark (page 261), Add to Home Screen (page 264), or Mail Link to this Page (page 260).

- **⊞ (Bookmarks).** This button brings up your list of saved bookmarks (page 261).

- **⬚, ⬚ (Page Juggler).** Safari can keep multiple Web pages open, just like any other browser. Page 255 has the details.

Zooming and Scrolling

These two gestures—zooming in on Web pages and then scrolling around them—have probably sold more people on the iPhone than any other demonstration. It all happens with a fluid animation, and a responsiveness to your finger taps, that's positively addicting. Some people spend all day just zooming in and out of Web pages on the iPhone, simply because they can.

When you first open a Web page, you get to see the *entire thing*. Unlike most cellphones, the iPhone crams the entire Web site onto its 3½-inch screen, so you can get the lay of the land.

At this point, of course, you're looking at .004-point type, which is too small to read unless you're a microbe. So the next step is to magnify the *part* of the page you want to read.

The iPhone offers three ways to do that:

- **Rotate the iPhone.** Turn the device 90 degrees in either direction. The iPhone rotates and magnifies the image to fill the wider view.

- **Do the two-finger spread.** Put two fingers on the glass and drag them apart. The Web page stretches before your very eyes, growing larger. Then you can pinch to shrink the page back down again. (Most people do several spreads or several pinches in a row to achieve the degree of zoom they want.)

- **Double-tap.** Safari is intelligent enough to recognize different *chunks* of a Web page. One article might represent a chunk. A photograph might qualify as a chunk. When you double-tap a chunk, Safari magnifies *just that chunk* to fill the whole screen. It's smart and useful.

  Double-tap again to zoom back out.

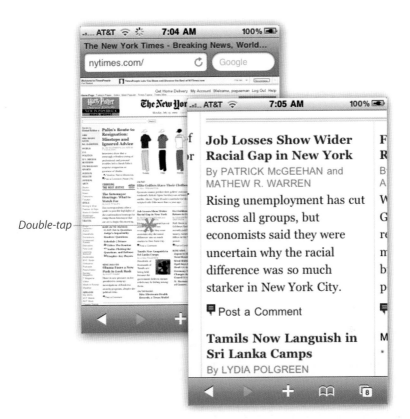

Double-tap

Once you've zoomed out to the proper degree, you can then scroll around the page by dragging or flicking with a finger. You don't have to worry about "clicking a link" by accident; if your finger's in motion, Safari ignores the tapping action, even if you happen to land on a link.

It's awesome.

 Tip Once you've double-tapped to zoom in on a page, you can use these little-known tricks: Double-tap anywhere on the *upper* half of the screen to scroll up, or the *lower* half to scroll down. The closer you are to the top or bottom of the screen, the more you scroll.

By the way, you'll occasionally encounter a *frame* (a column of text) on a page—an area that scrolls independently of the main page. If you have a MobileMe account (Chapter 13), for example, the Messages list is a frame. The iPhone has a secret, undocumented method for scrolling one of these frames without scrolling the whole page: the *two-finger drag.* Try it out.

The Address Bar

As on a computer, this Web browser offers four tools for navigating the Web: the address bar, bookmarks, the History list, and good old link-tapping. These pages cover each of these methods in turn.

The address bar is the strip at the top of the screen where you type in a Web page's address. And it so happens that *four* of the iPhone's greatest tips and shortcuts all have to do with this important navigational tool:

- **Insta-scroll to the top.** You can jump directly to the address bar, no matter how far down a page you've scrolled, just by tapping the very top edge of the screen (on the status bar). That "tap the top" trick is timely, too, when a Web site is designed to *hide* the address bar.

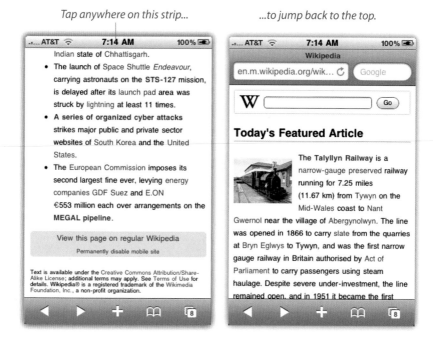

Tap anywhere on this strip...   ...to jump back to the top.

- **Don't delete.** There *is* a ⊗ button at the right end of the address bar whose purpose is to erase the entire current address so you can type another one. (Tap inside the address bar to make it, and the keyboard, appear.) But the ⊗ button is for suckers.

Instead, whenever the address bar is open for typing, *just type*. Forget that there's already a URL there—just start typing. The iPhone is smart enough to figure out that you want to *replace* that Web address with a new one.

- **Don't type *http://www or .com*.** Safari is also smart enough to know that most Web addresses use that format—so you can leave all that stuff out, and it will supply them automatically. Instead of *http://www.cnn.com*, for example, you can just type *cnn* and hit Go.

- **Don't type *.net, .org,* or *.edu,* either.** Safari's secret pop-up menu of canned URL choices can save you four keyboard taps apiece. To see it, hold your finger down on the .com button. Then tap the common suffix you want.

Otherwise, this address bar works just like the one in any other Web browser. Tap inside it to make the keyboard appear. (If the address bar is hidden, then tap the top edge of the iPhone screen.)

The Safari Keyboard

In Safari, the keyboard works just as described in Chapter 2, with a couple of exceptions.

First, there are no spaces allowed in Internet addresses; therefore, in the spot usually reserved for the space bar, this keyboard has three keys for things that *do* appear often in Web addresses: period, slash, and ".com." These nifty special keys make typing Web addresses a lot faster.

Second, tap the blue Go key when you're finished typing the address. That's your Enter key. (Or tap Cancel to hide the keyboard *without* "pressing Enter.")

As you type, a handy list of suggestions appears beneath the address bar (facing page, left). These are all Web addresses that Safari already knows about, because they're either in your Bookmarks list or in your History list (meaning you've visited them recently).

If you recognize the address you're trying to type, then by all means tap it instead of typing out the rest of the URL. The time you save could be your own.

Tip You can copy and paste Web addresses right in the address bar (just hold your finger down in it). You can also send the URL of an open Web page to a friend by email. Just tap the **+** button at the bottom of the screen. In the pop-up button box (shown on the next page), tap Mail Link to this Page. The iPhone's email program opens, and a new outgoing message appears. The Subject line and body are already filled in; you just address the message and send it. (Return to Safari by pressing Home and then tapping Safari.)

By the way, remember that you can *rotate* the keyboard into landscape orientation, as shown here. This is a big deal; when it's stretched out the wide way, you get much bigger, broader keys, and typing is much easier and faster. (In iOS 4, you can even rotate the iPhone *after* you tap the address bar or text box; the keyboard rotates even after it's on the screen.)

Bookmarks

Safari comes prestocked with bookmarks (Favorites)—that is, tags that identify Web sites you might want to visit again without having to remember and type their URLs. Amazingly, all these canned bookmarks are interesting and useful to *you* in particular! How did it know?

Easy—it copied your existing desktop computer's browser bookmarks from Internet Explorer (Windows) or Safari (Macintosh) when you synced the iPhone (Chapter 12). Sneaky, eh?

To see them, tap 📖 at the bottom of the screen. You see the master list of bookmarks (below, right). Some may be "loose," and many more are probably organized into folders, or even folders *within* folders.

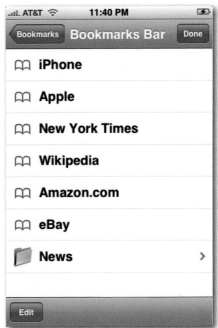

Tapping a folder shows you what's inside, and tapping a bookmark begins opening the corresponding Web site.

Creating New Bookmarks

You can add new bookmarks right on the phone. Any work you do here is copied *back* to your computer the next time you sync the two machines.

When you find a Web page you might like to visit again, tap the **+** button (bottom of the screen) and then tap Add Bookmark (below, left). The Add Bookmark screen appears. You have two tasks here:

- **Type a better name.** In the top box, you can type a shorter or clearer name for the page than the one it comes with. Instead of "Bass, Trout, & Tackle—the Web's Premier Resource for the Avid Outdoorsman," you can just call it "Fish site."

  The box below this one identifies the underlying URL, which is totally independent from what you've *named* your bookmark. You can't edit this one.

- **Specify where to file this bookmark.** If you tap Bookmarks >, you open Safari's hierarchical list of bookmark folders, which organize your book-marked sites. Tap the folder where you want to file the new bookmark so you'll know where to find it later.

 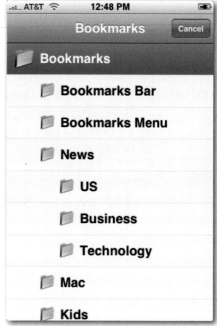

Tip Here's a site worth bookmarking: *http://google.com/gwt/n*. It gives you a bare-bones, superfast version of the Web, provided by Google for the benefit of people on slow connections (like EDGE). You can opt to hide graphics for even more speed. Yeah, the iPhone's browser is glorious and all—but sometimes you'd rather have fast than pretty.

Editing Bookmarks and Folders

It's easy enough to massage your Bookmarks list within Safari—to delete favorites that aren't so favorite anymore, make new folders, rearrange the list, rename a folder or a bookmark, and so on.

The techniques are the same for editing bookmark *folders* and editing the bookmarks themselves—after the first step. To edit the folder list, start by opening the Bookmarks list (tap the button), and then tap Edit.

To edit the bookmarks themselves, tap , tap a folder, and ***then*** tap Edit. Now you can get organized:

- **Delete something.** Tap the button next to a folder or bookmark, and then tap Delete to confirm.

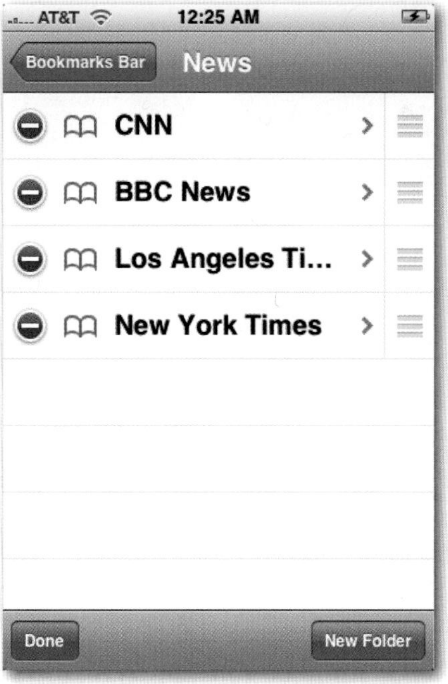

- **Rearrange the list.** Drag the grip strip (☰) up or down in the list to move the folders or bookmarks up or down. (You can't move or delete the top three folders—History, Bookmarks Bar, and Bookmarks Menu.)

- **Edit a name and location.** Tap a folder or bookmark name. If you tap a folder, then you arrive at the Edit Folder screen; you can edit the folder's name and which folder it's inside of. If you tap a bookmark, Edit Bookmark lets you edit the name and the URL it points to.

  Tap the Back button (upper-left corner) when you're finished.

- **Create a folder.** Tap New Folder in the lower-right corner of the Edit Folders screen. You're offered the chance to type a name for it and to specify where you want to file it (that is, in which *other* folder).

Tap Done when you're finished.

Web Clips

If there's a certain Web site you visit all the time, like every day, even the four taps necessary to open it in the usual way (Home, Safari, Bookmarks, your site's name) can seem like overwhelming amounts of red tape. That's why Apple made it simple to add the icon of a certain Web page right on your Home screen.

Start by opening the page in question. Tap the **+** button at the bottom of the screen. In the button list, tap Add to Home Screen. Now you're offered the chance to edit the icon's name; finally, tap Add.

When you return to your Home screen, you'll see the new icon. You can move it around, drag it to a different Home screen, and so on, exactly as described on page 177.

Or, to delete it, touch its icon until all the Home icons begin to wiggle. Tap the Web clip's badge (facing page, right) to remove its icon.

> **Tip** You can turn *part* of a Web page into one of these Web clips, too. You might want quick access to *The New York Times'* "most emailed" list, or the bestselling children's books on Amazon, or the most-viewed video on YouTube, or the box scores for a certain sports league.
>
> All you have to do is zoom and scroll the page in Safari *before* you tap the **+** button, isolating the section you want. Later, when you open the Web clip, you'll see exactly the part of the Web page you wanted.

The History List

Behind the scenes, Safari keeps track of the Web sites you've visited in the last week or so, neatly organized into subfolders like Earlier Today and Yesterday. It's a great feature when you can't recall the address for a Web site you visited recently—or when you remember it had a long, complicated address and you get the psychiatric condition known as iPhone Keyboard Dread.

To see the list of recent sites, tap the 📖 button, and then tap the History folder, whose icon bears a little clock to make sure you know it's special. Once the History list appears, just tap a bookmark (or a folder name and *then* a bookmark) to revisit that Web page.

Erasing the History List

Some people find it creepy that Safari maintains a complete list of every Web site they've seen recently, right there in plain view of any family member or coworker who wanders by. They'd just as soon their wife/husband/boss/parent/kid not know what Web sites they've been visiting.

You can't delete just one particularly incriminating History listing. You can, however, delete the *entire* History menu, thus erasing all your tracks. To do that, tap Clear; confirm by tapping Clear History.

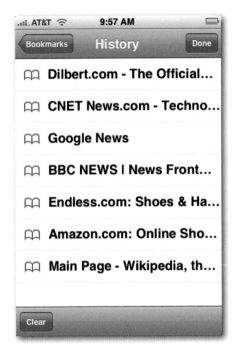
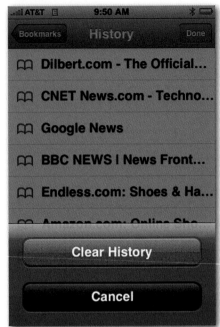

You've just rewritten History.

Tapping Links

You'd be surprised at the number of iPhone newbies who stare dumbly at the screen, awestruck at the beauty of full-blown Web pages—but utterly baffled as to how to click links.

The answer: Tap with your finger.

Here's the fourth and final method of navigating the Web: tapping links on the screen, much the way you'd click them if you had a mouse. As you know from desktop-computer browsing, not all links are blue and underlined. Sometimes, in fact, they're graphics.

The only difference is that on the iPhone, not all links take you to other Web pages. If you tap an email address, it opens up the iPhone's Mail program (Chapter 11) and creates a preaddressed outgoing message. If you tap a phone number you find online, the iPhone calls it for you. There's even such a thing as a *map* link, which opens the Google Maps program (page 209).

Each of these links, in other words, takes you out of Safari. If you want to return to your Web browsing, then you have return to the Home screen and tap Safari. The page you had open is still there, waiting.

Saving Graphics

In the original iPhone software, if you found a picture online that you wished you could keep forever, you had only one option: Stare at it until you'd memorized it.

Now, however, life is much easier. Just keep your finger pressed on the image, very still, for about a second. You'll see a sliding button sheet appear, offering a Save Image button. (If the graphic is also a tappable link, then an Open Link button is also on this sheet.)

If you tap Save Image, the iPhone thoughtfully deposits a copy of the image in your Camera Roll (page 159) so it will be copied back to your Mac or PC at the next sync opportunity. If you tap Copy, you nab that graphic, and can now paste it into another program. (There's another way to snag a graphic, too: Copy it. Use the technique described on page 215.)

AutoFill

On the real Safari—on the Mac or PC—a feature called AutoFill saves you an awful lot of typing. It fills out your name and address automatically when you're ordering something online. It stores your passwords so you don't have to re-enter them every time you visit passworded sites.

On the iPhone, where you're typing on glass, the convenience of AutoFill goes to a whole new level.

 Tip Here's the obligatory speech about security. You know: If your iPhone is stolen, then the bad guy could see your bank account if the password's been stored, and so on. You've been warned.

To turn on AutoFill, visit Settings→Safari→AutoFill. Two features await (shown on the facing page at left):

- **Use Contact Info.** Turn this on. Then tap My Info. From the address book, find your own listing. You've just told Safari *which* name, address, city, state, Zip code, and phone number belong to you.

    From now on, whenever you're asked to input your address, phone number, and so on, you'll see an AutoFill button at the top of the keyboard. Tap it to make Safari auto-enter all those details, saving you no end of typing. (It works on *most* sites.) If there are extra blanks that AutoFill doesn't fill, then you can tap the Previous and Next buttons to move your cursor from one to the next instead of tapping and scrolling manually.

- **Names & Passwords.** If you turn this on, then Safari will offer to memorize each name and password you enter on a Web site. You can tap Yes (good idea for your PTA or library account), Never for this Website (good idea for your bank), or Not Now (you'll be asked again next time).

Searching the Web

You might have noticed that whenever the address bar appears, so does a search bar just to the right of it. (It bears the name of your chosen search service—Google, for example.)

That's an awfully handy shortcut. It means you can perform a search without having to leave whatever page you're already on. Just tap into that box, type your search phrase, and then tap the big blue Search button in the corner.

You can tell the iPhone to use Yahoo's search or Microsoft's Bing instead of Google, if you like. From the Home screen, tap Settings→Safari→Search Engine, as shown on the next page.

Tip There are all kinds of cool things you can type here—special terms that tell Google, "I want *information,* not Web-page matches."

You can type a movie name and Zip code or city/state (*Titanic Returns 10024*) to get a list of today's showtimes in theaters near you. Get the forecast by typing *weather chicago* or *weather 60609*. Stock quotes: Type the symbol (*AMZN*). Dictionary definitions: *define schadenfreude*. Unit conversions: *liters in 5 gallons*. Currency conversions: *25 usd in euros*. Then tap Search to get instant results.

Audio and Video on the Web

In general, streaming audio and video on the iPhone is a bust. The iPhone doesn't recognize the Real, Windows Media, or Flash file formats. This means the iPhone can't play the huge majority of online video and audio recordings. That's a crushing disappointment to news and sports junkies.

But the iPhone isn't *utterly* clueless about streaming online goodies. It can play some QuickTime movies, like movie trailers, as long as they've been encoded (prepared) in certain formats (like H.264).

It can also play MP3 audio files right off the Web. That can be extremely handy for people who like to know what's going on in the world, because many European news agencies offer streaming MP3 versions of their news broadcasts. Here are a few worth bookmarking:

- **BBC News.** You can find 5-minute news bulletins at *www.bbc.co.uk/ worldservice/programmes/newssummary.shtml.* (Here's a shortcut: *http:// bit.ly/2xhEKF.*)

- **Deutsche Welle.** English-language news, sports, arts, and talk from Germany. *www.dw-world.de/dw/0,2142,4703,00.html*. (Shortcut: *http://bit. ly/HHwog.*)

- **Radio France.** English-language broadcasts from France. *www.rfi.fr/ langues/statiques/rfi_anglais.asp*. (Shortcut: *http://bit.ly/10ol5A.*)

- **Voice of America.** The official external radio broadcast of the U.S. government. *www.voanews.com/english/.*

Actually, any old MP3 files play fine right in Safari. If you've already played through your 4 or 8 gigabytes of music from your computer, then you can always do a Web search for *free mp3 music.*

Manipulating Multiple Pages

Like any self-respecting browser, Safari can keep multiple pages open at once, making it easy for you to switch among them. You can think of it as a miniature version of tabbed browsing, a feature of browsers like Safari Senior, Firefox, and the latest Internet Explorer. Tabbed browsing keeps a bunch of Web pages open simultaneously—in a single, neat window.

The beauty of this arrangement is that you can start reading one Web page while the others load into their own tabs in the background.

On the iPhone, it works like this:

- **To open a new window,** tap the button in the lower right. The Web page shrinks into a mini version. Tap New Page to open a new, untitled Web-browser tab; now you can enter an address, use a bookmark, or whatever.

> **Note** Alternatively, hold your finger down on a link instead of tapping it. You get a choice of three commands, one of which is Open in New Page. (The others are Open and Copy, meaning copy the Web address.)
>
> Sometimes, Safari sprouts a new window *automatically* when you click a link. That's because the link you tapped is programmed to open a new window. To return to the original window, read on.

- **To switch back to the first window,** tap again. Now there are two dots (• •) beneath the miniature page, indicating that *two* windows are open. (The boldest, whitest dot indicates where you are in the horizontal row of windows.) Bring the first window's miniature onto the screen by flicking horizontally with your finger. Tap it to open it full-screen.

    You can open a third window, and a fourth, and so on, and jump among them, using these two techniques. The icon sprouts a number to let you know how many windows are open; for example, it might say ⬚.

- **To close a window,** tap . Flick over to the miniature window you want to close, and then tap the ❌ button at its top-left corner.

> **Note** Safari requires at least one window to be open. If you close the very last window, Safari gives you a blank, empty window to take its place.

RSS: The Missing Manual

In the beginning, the Internet was an informational Garden of Eden. There were no banner ads, pop-ups, flashy animations, or spam messages. Back then, people thought the Internet was the greatest idea ever.

Those days, alas, are long gone. Web browsing now entails a constant battle against intrusive advertising and annoying animations. And with the proliferation of Web sites of every kind—from news sites to personal weblogs (*blogs*)—just reading your favorite sites can become a full-time job.

Enter RSS, a technology that lets you subscribe to *feeds*—summary blurbs provided by thousands of sources around the world, from Reuters to Apple to your nerdy next-door neighbor. The result: You spare yourself the tediousness of checking for updates manually, plus you get to read short summaries of new articles without ads or blinking animations. And if you want to read a full article, you just tap its headline.

 Note RSS stands for either Rich Site Summary or Really Simple Syndication. Each abbreviation explains one aspect of RSS—either its summarizing talent or its simplicity.

Safari, as it turns out, doubles as a handy RSS reader. Whenever you tap an "RSS Feed" link on a Web page, or whenever you type the address of an RSS feed into the address bar (it often begins with *feed://*), Safari automatically displays a handy table-of-contents view that lists all the news blurbs on that page.

Scan through the summaries. When you see an article that looks intriguing, tap its headline. You go to the full Web page to read the full-blown article.

 Tip It's worth bookmarking your favorite RSS feeds. One great one for tech fans is *feed://www.digg.com/rss/index.xml*, a constantly updated list of the coolest and most interesting tech and pop-culture stories of the day. Most news publications offer news feeds, too. (Your humble author's own daily *New York Times* blog has a feed that's *http://pogue.blogs.nytimes.com/?feed=rss2*.)

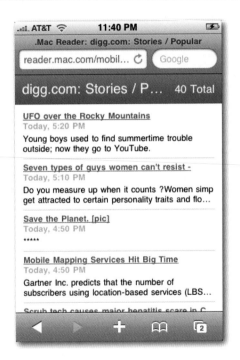

Web Security

Safari on the iPhone isn't meant to be a full-blown Web browser like the one on your desktop computer, but it comes surprisingly close—especially when it comes to privacy and security. Cookies, pop-up blockers, parental controls…they're all here, for your paranoid pleasure.

Pop-up Blocker

The world's smarmiest advertisers have begun inundating us with pop-up and pop-under ads—nasty little windows that appear in front of the browser window, or, worse, behind it, waiting to jump out the moment you close your window. Fortunately, Safari comes set to block those pop-ups so you don't see them. It's a war out there—but at least you now have some ammunition.

The thing is, though, pop-ups are sometimes legitimate (and not ads)—notices of new banking features, seating charts on ticket-sales sites, warnings that the instructions for using a site have changed, and so on. Safari can't tell these from ads—and it stifles them, too. So if a site you trust says, "Please turn off pop-up blockers and reload this page," then you know you're probably missing out on a *useful* pop-up message.

In those situations, you can turn off the pop-up blocker. From the Home screen, tap Settings→Safari. Where it says Block Pop-ups, tap the On/Off switch.

Cookies

Cookies are something like Web page preference files. Certain Web sites—particularly commercial ones like Amazon.com—deposit them on your hard drive like little bookmarks so they'll remember you the next time you visit. Ever notice how Amazon.com greets you "Welcome, Chris" (or whatever your name is)? It's reading its own cookie, left behind on your hard drive (or in this case, on your iPhone).

Most cookies are perfectly innocuous—and, in fact, are extremely useful, because they help Web sites remember your tastes. Cookies also spare you the effort of having to type in your name, address, and so on, every time you visit these Web sites.

But fear is widespread, and the media fan the flames with tales of sinister cookies that track your movement on the Web. If you're worried about invasions of privacy, Safari is ready to protect you.

From the Home screen, tap Settings→Safari→Accept Cookies. The options here are like a paranoia gauge. If you click Never, you create an acrylic shield around your iPhone. No cookies can come in, and no cookie information can go out. You'll probably find the Web a very inconvenient place; you'll have to re-enter your information upon every visit, and some Web sites may not work properly at all. The Always option means, "Oh, what the heck—just gimme all of them."

A good compromise is From Visited, which accepts cookies from sites you *want* to visit, but blocks cookies deposited on your phone by sites you're not actually visiting—cookies an especially evil banner ad gives you, for example.

This screen also offers a Clear Cookies button (deletes all the cookies you've accumulated so far), as well as Clear History (page 391) and Clear Cache.

The *cache* is a patch of the iPhone's storage area where pieces of Web pages you visit—graphics, for example—are retained. The idea is that the next time you visit the same page, the iPhone won't have to download those bits again. It already has them on board, so the page appears much faster.

If you worry that your cache eats up space, poses a security risk, or is confusing some page (and preventing the most recent version of the page from appearing), then tap this button to erase it and start over.

Parental Controls

If your child (or employee) is old enough to have an iPhone but not old enough for the seedier side of the Web, then don't miss the Restrictions feature in Settings. The iPhone makes no attempt to separate the good Web sites from the bad—but it *can* remove the Safari icon from the iPhone altogether so that no Web browsing is possible at all. See page 378 for instructions.

Web Applications

For the first year of the iPhone, there was no App Store. No add-on programs, no way to make the iPhone do new, cool stuff (at least not without hacking it). Apple gave iPhone programmers only one bit of freedom: They could write iPhone-shaped *Web pages* tailored for the iPhone.

Some of these iPhone Web applications look like desktop widgets that do one thing really well—like showing you a Doppler radar map for local weather. Some are minipages that tap directly into sites like Flickr and Twitter. Some even let you tap into Web-based word processing sites if you need to create a document *right this very instant*.

Today, regular iPhone programs do everything those Web apps once did. Web apps were essentially a workaround, a placeholder solution until Apple could get its App Store going. So Web apps are fast fading away now that the App Store is in business.

If you're still interested, you can read about these antique iPhone artifacts in the free downloadable appendix to this chapter. It's available from this book's "Missing CD" page at *www.missingmanuals.com*.

11 Email

You ain't never seen email on a phone like this. It offers full format-ting, fonts, graphics, and choice of type size; file attachments like Word, Excel, PowerPoint, PDF, Pages, Numbers, and photos; and compatibility with Yahoo Mail, Gmail, AOL Mail, MobileMe mail, corporate Microsoft Exchange mail, and just about any standard email account. Dude, if you want a more satisfying portable email machine than this one, buy a laptop.

This chapter covers the basic email experience, which has been thoroughly overhauled in iOS 4. If you've gotten yourself hooked up with MobileMe or Exchange ActiveSync, though, you'll soon find out how wireless email syncing makes everything better. Or at least different. (See Chapters 13 and 14 for details.)

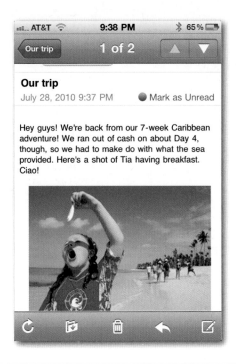

Setting Up Your Account

If you play your cards right, you won't *have* to set up your email account on the phone. The first time you set up the iPhone to sync with your computer (Chapter 12), you're offered the chance to *sync* your Mac's or PC's mail with the phone. That doesn't mean it copies actual messages—only the email settings, so the iPhone is ready to start downloading mail.

You're offered this option if your Mac's mail program is Mail or Entourage or if your PC's mail program is Outlook, Outlook Express, or Windows Mail.

But what if you don't use one of those email programs? No sweat. You can also plug the necessary settings right into the iPhone.

Free Email Accounts

If you have a free email account from Google, AOL, or Yahoo; a MobileMe account (Chapter 13); or a Microsoft Exchange account run by your employer (Chapter 14), then setup on the iPhone is easy.

From the Home screen, tap Settings→Mail, Contacts, Calendars→Add Account. Tap the colorful logo that corresponds to the kind of account you have (Google, Yahoo, or whatever).

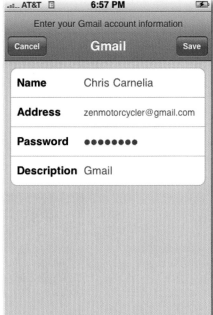

Now you land on the account-information screen. Tap into each of the four blanks and, when the keyboard appears, type your name, email address, account password, and a description (that one's optional). Tap Save.

Your email account is ready to go!

 Tip If you don't have one of these free accounts, they're worth having, if only as a backup to your regular account. They can help with spam filtering, too, since the iPhone doesn't offer any; see page 299. To sign up, go to Google.com, Yahoo.com, AOL.com, or Me.com.

POP3 and IMAP Accounts

Those freebie, Web-based accounts are super-easy to set up. But they're not the whole ball of wax. Millions of people have a more generic email account, perhaps supplied by their employers or Internet providers. They're generally one of two types:

- **POP accounts** are the oldest, most compatible, and most common type on the Internet. (POP stands for Post Office Protocol, but this won't be on the test.) But a POP account can make life miserable if you check your mail on more than one machine (say, a PC and an iPhone), as you'll discover shortly.

  A POP server transfers incoming mail to your computer (or iPhone) before you read it, which works fine as long as you're using *only that machine* to access your email.

- **IMAP accounts** (Internet Message Access Protocol) are newer and have more features than POP servers, and they're quickly catching up in popularity. IMAP servers keep all your mail online, rather than making you store it on your computer; as a result, you can access the same mail from any computer (or phone) . IMAP servers remember which messages you've read and sent, and they even keep track of how you've filed messages into mail folders. (Those free Yahoo email accounts are IMAP accounts, and so are Apple's MobileMe accounts and corporate Exchange accounts. Gmail accounts *can* be IMAP, too, which is awesome.)

  There's really only one downside to this approach: If you don't conscientiously delete mail after you've read it, your online mailbox eventually overflows. On IMAP accounts that don't come with a lot of storage, the system sooner or later starts bouncing new messages, annoying your friends.

The iPhone can communicate with both kinds of accounts, with varying degrees of completeness.

If you haven't opted to have your account-setup information transferred automatically to the iPhone from your Mac or PC, then you can set it up manually on the phone.

From the Home screen, tap Settings→Mail, Contacts, Calendars→Add Account. Tap Other, tap Add Mail Account, and then enter your name, email address, password, and an optional description. Tap Next.

Apple's software attempts to figure out which kind of account you have (POP or IMAP) by the email address. If it can't make that determination, then you arrive at a second screen, where you're asked for such juicy details as the Host Name for Incoming and Outgoing Mail servers. (This is also where you tap either IMAP or POP, to tell the iPhone what sort of account it's dealing with.)

If you don't know this stuff offhand, you'll have to ask your Internet provider, corporate tech-support person, or next-door teenager to help you.

When you're finished, tap Save.

 To *delete* an account, open Settings→Mail, Contacts, Calendars→[account name]. At the bottom of the screen, you'll find the Delete Account button.

The "Two-Mailbox Problem"

It's awesome that the iPhone can check the mail from a POP mail account, which is the sort provided by most Internet providers. This means, however, that now you've got *two* machines checking the same account—your main computer and your iPhone.

Now you've got the "two-mailbox problem." What if your computer downloads some of the mail and your iPhone downloads the rest? Will your mail stash be split awkwardly between two machines? How will you remember where to find a particular message?

Fortunately, the problem is halfway solved by a factory setting deep within the iPhone that says, in effect: "The iPhone may download mail, but it will leave a copy behind for your desktop computer to download later."

 If you must know, this setting is at Settings→Mail, Contacts, Calendars→[your account name]→Account Info→Advanced.

Unfortunately, that doesn't stop the opposite problem. It doesn't prevent the *computer* from downloading messages before your *iPhone* can get to them. When you're out and about, therefore, you may miss important messages.

Most people would rather not turn off the computer every time they leave the desk. Fortunately, there's a more automatic solution: Turn on the Leave messages on server option in your Mac or PC email program. Its location depends on which email program you use. For example:

- **Entourage.** Choose Tools→Accounts. Double-click the account name; click Options. Turn on Leave a copy of each message on the server.

- **Mail.** Choose Mail→Preferences→Accounts→[account name]→ Advanced. Turn off Remove copy from server after retrieving a message.

- **Outlook.** Choose Tools→E-mail Accounts→E-mail. Click View or Change E-Mail Accounts→Next→[your account name]→Change→More Settings→Advanced. Turn on Leave a copy of messages on the server.

- **Outlook Express.** Choose Tools→Accounts→[your account name]→ Properties→Advanced. Turn on Leave a copy of messages on the server.

With this arrangement, both machines download the same mail; messages aren't deleted until you delete them from the bigger computer.

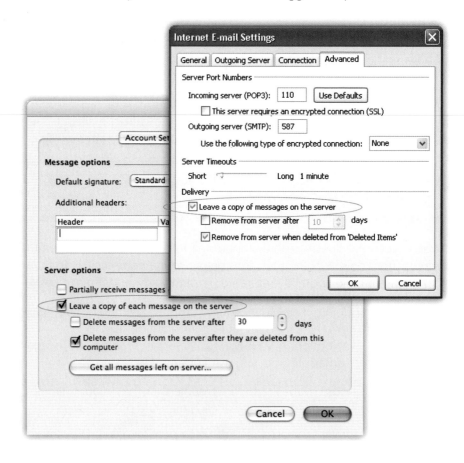

And consider getting (or forwarding your mail to) an IMAP account like MobileMe, Gmail, or Yahoo Mail, which avoids this whole mess. Then any changes you make on one machine are magically reflected on the other.

Downloading Mail

If you have "push" email (Yahoo, MobileMe, or Exchange), then your iPhone doesn't *check* for messages; new messages show up on your iPhone *as they arrive,* around the clock.

If you have any other kind of account, then the iPhone checks for new messages automatically on a schedule—every 15, 30, or 60 minutes. It also checks for new messages each time you open the Mail program, or whenever you tap the Check button (↻) within the Mail program.

You can adjust the frequency of these automatic checks or turn off the "push" feature (because it uses up your battery faster) in Settings; see page 382.

When new mail arrives, you'll know it by a glance at your Home screen, because the Mail icon sprouts a circled number that tells you how many new messages are waiting. You'll also hear the iPhone's little "You've got mail" sound, unless you've turned that off in Settings (page 372). To read your new mail, tap Mail.

The Unified Inbox

If you have more than one email address, then iOS 4 was written for you. For the first time, the iPhone offers a *unified Inbox*—an option that displays all the incoming messages from all your accounts in a single place. (If you don't see it—if Mail opened up to some other screen—keep tapping the upper-left button until you do.)

This Mailboxes page has two sections:

- **Inboxes.** To see all the incoming messages in one unified box, tap All Inboxes. You can, of course, also view the Inbox for any *individual* account in the top section shown here at left.

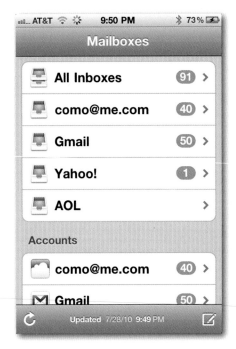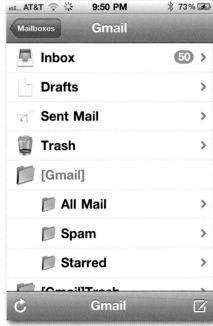

- **Accounts.** Farther down the Mailboxes screen, you see your accounts listed again. Tap one to view the traditional mail folders: Inbox, Drafts (written but not sent), Sent, Trash, and any folders you've created yourself (Family, Little League, Old Stuff, whatever), as shown above at right. If you have a Yahoo, MobileMe, Exchange, or another IMAP account, then these folders are automatically created on the iPhone to match what you've set up online.

 Note Not all kinds of email accounts permit the creation of your own filing folders, so you may not see anything but Inbox, Sent, and Trash.

The Message List—and Threading

If you tap an Inbox's name, you wind up face-to-face with the list of incoming messages. At first, you see only the subject lines of your messages, plus, in light-gray type, the first few lines of its contents; that way, you can scan through new messages and see if there's anything important. You can flick your finger to scroll this list, if it's long. Blue dots indicate messages you haven't yet opened. Tap a message to read it in all its formatted glory.

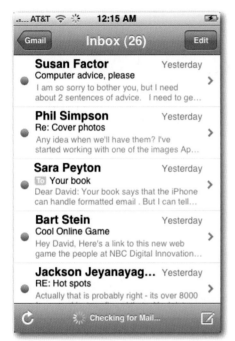

Here and there, you may spot another new iOS 4 feature: threaded messages. That's where several related messages—back-and-forths on the same subject—appear only once, in a single, consolidated Inbox entry. (You'll know one when you see one, because the number of volleys in this exchange appears at the right side of the message list, like this: ❸ ❯). The idea is to reduce Inbox clutter and help you remember what people were talking about.

To read a normal message in the message list, you just tap it. But when you tap a threaded message, you first open an intermediate screen that lists the messages in the thread. Tap one of those to read, at last, the message itself.

Of course, this also means that to return to the Inbox, you have more back-tracking to do (tap the upper-left button twice).

In general, threading is a nice feature, even if it accidentally clumps in a message that has nothing to do with the subject from time to time.

But if it bugs you, you can turn it off. Open Settings→Mail, Contacts, Calendars, scroll down, and turn off Organize By Thread.

What to Do with a Message

Once you've opened a message, you can respond to it, delete it, file it, and so on. Here's the drill.

Read It

The type size in email messages can be pretty small. Fortunately, you have some great iPhoney enlargement tricks at your disposal. For example:

- **Spread two fingers** to enlarge the entire email message.

- **Double-tap a narrow block of text** to make it fill the screen, if it doesn't already.

Drag or flick your finger to scroll through or around the message.

> **Tip** You can also, of course, just ask the iPhone to use a larger type size. From the Home screen, tap Settings→Mail, Contacts, Calendars→Minimum Font Size. You can choose the minimum type size you want from these options: Small, Medium, Large, Extra Large, or Giant. (What, no Humongous?)

It's nice to note that links are "live" in email messages. Tap a phone number to call it, a Web address to open it, a YouTube link to watch it, an email address to write to it, a time and date to add it to your calendar, and so on.

 Tip If you're using a Gmail account—a great idea—then any message you send, reply to, delete, or file into a folder is reflected on the Web at Gmail.com. Whether deleting a message really deletes it (after 30 days) or adds it to Gmail's "archived" stash depends on the tweaky settings described at *http://tinyurl.com/yokd27*.

Reply to It

To answer a message, tap the Reply/Forward icon (◀) at the bottom of the screen. You're asked if you want to Reply or Forward; tap Reply. If the message was originally addressed to multiple recipients, then you can send your reply to everyone simultaneously by hitting Reply All instead.

A new message window opens, already addressed. As a courtesy to your correspondents, Mail places the original message at the bottom of the window.

 Tip If you select some text (page 43) before you tap, then the iPhone pastes only that selected bit into the new, outgoing message. In other words, you're quoting back only a portion—just the way it works on a full-sized computer.

At this point, you can add or delete recipients, edit the Subject line or the original message, and so on. When you're finished, tap Send.

 Tip Use the Return key to create blank lines in the original message. (Use the Loupe— page 34—to position the insertion point at the proper spot.)

Using this method, you can splice your own comments into the paragraphs of the original message, replying point by point. The brackets by each line of the original message help your correspondent keep straight what's yours and what's hers.

Forward It

Instead of replying to the person who sent you a message, you may sometimes want to pass the note on to a third person.

To do so, tap the ◀ button at the bottom of the screen. This time, tap Forward.

 Tip If there's a file attached to the inbound message, the iPhone says, "Include attachments from original message?" and offers Include/Don't Include buttons. Rather thoughtful, actually—the phone can forward files it can't even open.

A new message opens, looking a lot like the one that appears when you reply. You may wish to precede the original message with a comment of your own, like, "Frank: I thought you'd be interested in this joke about your mom."

Finally, address and send it as you would any outgoing piece of mail.

Filing or Deleting One Message

As noted earlier, some mail accounts let you create filing folders to help manage your messages. Once you've opened a message that's worth keeping, you file it by tapping the 🗂 button at the bottom of the screen. Up pops the list of your folders (next page, left); tap the one you want.

It's a snap to delete a message you no longer want, too. If it's open on the screen before you, simply tap the 🗑 button at the bottom of the screen. Frankly, it's worth deleting tons of messages just for the pleasure of watching the animation as they funnel down into that tiny icon, whose lid pops open and shut accordingly (facing page, right).

 Tip If that one-touch Delete method makes you a little nervous, you can ask the iPhone to display a confirmation box before trashing the message forever. See page 385.

You can also delete a message from the message *list*—the Inbox, for example. Just swipe your finger across the message listing, in either direction. (It doesn't have to be an especially broad swipe.) The red Delete button appears; tap it to confirm, or tap anywhere else if you change your mind.

> **Tip** In a Gmail account, swiping like this produces a button that says Archive, not Delete. That's the Gmail way: It wants you to save everything. But you can change the button back so it says Delete. Tap Settings→Mail, Contacts, Calendars→[your Gmail account name]. Here, you can turn off Archive Messages. The button will now say Delete, and the messages you delete will really be deleted.

There's a long way to delete messages from the list, too, as described below. But for single messages, the finger-swipe method is *much* more fun.

Filing or Deleting Batches of Messages

You can also file or delete a bunch of messages at once. In the message list, tap Edit. A dot appears beside each message title. You can tap as many of these circles as you like, scrolling as necessary, adding a ● with each touch.

Finally, when you've selected all the messages in question, tap either Delete or Move. (The number in parentheses shows how many you've selected).

If you tap Move, you're shown the folder list so you can say where you want them moved. If you tap Delete, the messages disappear.

 Note When you delete a message, it goes into the Deleted folder. In other words, it works like the Macintosh Trash or the Windows Recycle Bin. You have a safety net.

Email doesn't have to stay in the Deleted folder forever, however. You can ask the iPhone to empty that folder every day, week, or month. From the Home screen, tap Settings→Mail, Contacts, Calendars. Tap your account name, then Account Info→Advanced→Remove. Now you can change the setting from "Never" to "After one day" (or week, or month).

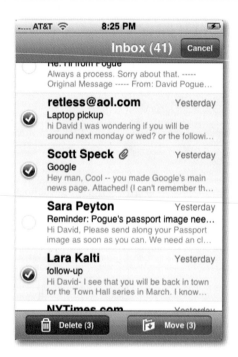

Add the Sender to Contacts

When you get a message from someone new who's worth adding to your iPhone's Contacts address book, tap the blue, oval-shaped email address (where it says "From:"). You're offered two buttons: Create New Contact and Add to Existing Contact. Use the second button to add an email address to an existing person's "card."

Open an Attachment

The Mail program downloads and displays the icons for *any* kind of attachment—but it can *open* only documents from Microsoft Office (Word, Excel, PowerPoint), Apple iWork (Pages, Keynote, Numbers), PDF, text, RTF, .vcf, graphics, and un-copy-protected audio and video files.

Just scroll down, tap the attachment's icon, wait a moment for downloading, and then marvel as the document opens up, full-screen. You can zoom in and zoom out, flick, rotate the phone 90 degrees, and scroll just as though it's a Web page or photo.

 Tip If you hold your finger down on the attachment's name, you get a list of ways to open it. "Quick Look" means the same non-editable preview as you'd get with a quick tap. But you might also see "Open in iBooks," for example, or the name of another app that can open it. Tap the one you want.

When you're finished admiring the attachment, tap Message (top-left corner) to return to the original email message.

Snagging a Graphic—Two Ways

One of the great joys of iPhone mail is its ability to display graphics that the sender embedded right in the message. And one of the great joys of iOS 4 is its flexibility in handling these graphics. Just hold your finger still on the picture. You're offered two choices:

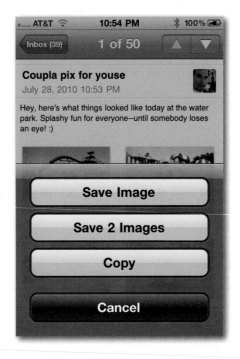

- **Save Image.** Tap this button to copy the photo into your Photos program, along with the pictures you've taken yourself. To see it later, tap Photos on the Home screen, and then tap Camera Roll.

- **Copy.** Here's another place where Copy and Paste pay off. After tapping Copy, you can paste the photo into another email message, into an outgoing picture (MMS) message, or anywhere fine graphics are pasted.

View the Details

When your computer's screen measures only 3½ inches diagonally, there's not a lot of extra space. So Apple designed Mail to conceal the details that you might need only occasionally. They reappear, naturally enough, when you tap Details in the upper-right corner of a message.

Now you get to see a few more details about the message. For instance:

- **Who it's to.** Well, duh—it's to *you*, right? °Yes, but it might have been sent to other people, too. When you open the Details, you see who else got this note—along with anyone who was Cc'ed (sent a copy).

When you tap the person's name in the blue oval, you open the corresponding info card in Contacts. It contains one-touch buttons for calling someone back (tap the phone number) or sending a text message (tap Text Message)—which can be very handy if the email message you just received is urgent.

- **Mark as Unread.** In the Inbox, any message you haven't yet read is marked by a blue dot (●). Once you've opened the message, the blue dot goes away.

  By tapping Mark as Unread, however, you make that blue dot *reappear*. It's a great way to flag a message for later, to call it to your own attention. The blue dot can mean not so much "unread" as "un–dealt with."

Details/Hide button

Hidden stuff

Tap Hide to collapse these details.

Move On

Once you've had a good look at a message and processed it to your satisfaction, you can move on to the next (or previous) message in the list by tapping the ▲ or ▼ button in the upper-right corner.

Or you can tap the button in the upper-left corner to return to the Inbox (or whatever mailbox you're in).

Searching

Praise be—there's a Search box in Mail. It's hiding *above* the top of every mail list, like your Inbox. To see it, scroll up, or just tap the status strip at the top of the screen.

Tap inside the Search box to make the keyboard appear. As you type, Mail hides all but the matching messages; tap one of the results to open it. (Note, however, that the iPhone doesn't search the *body* of your messages—it can search only the From, To, or Subject lines, or all three at once. Bummer.)

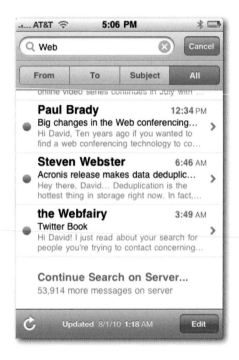

At the very bottom, you may see a link called Continue Search on Server. It doesn't appear for all email accounts, but it's there when you're in MobileMe, Gmail, and most other IMAP accounts. It's intended to let you continue your To/From/Subject line search on email that's not on your iPhone—that's still out there on the Internet, usually because it's so old that it's scrolled off your phone. If the message you seek hasn't appeared, Continue Search on Server is worth a try.

> **Tip** New in iOS 4: If, after typing a few letters, you tap Search, the keyboard goes away and an Edit button appears. Tapping it lets you select a whole bunch of the search results—and then delete or file them simultaneously.

Writing Messages

To compose a new piece of outgoing mail, open the Mail program, and then tap the ✒ icon in the lower-right corner. A blank new outgoing message appears, and the iPhone keyboard pops up.

> **Tip** Remember: You can turn the phone 90 degrees to get a much bigger widescreen keyboard for email. It's *much* easier to type this way.

Here's how you go about writing a message:

❶ **In the "To:" field, type the recipient's email address—or grab it from Contacts.** Often, you won't have to type much more than the first couple of letters of the name *or* email address. As you type, Mail automatically displays all matching names and addresses so you can tap one instead of typing. (It thoughtfully derives these suggestions by analyzing both your Contacts *and* which people you've recently exchanged email with.)

> **Tip** If you hold your finger down on the period (.) key, you get a pop-up palette of common email-address suffixes, like .com, .edu, .org, and so on.

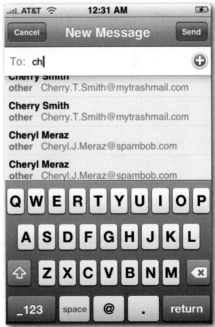

Alternatively, tap the button to open your Contacts list. Tap the name of the person you want. (Note, though, that the Contacts list shows you *all* names, even those that don't have email addresses.)

You can add as many addressees as you like; just repeat the procedure.

Incidentally, if you've set up your iPhone to connect to a corporate Exchange server (Chapter 14), then you can look up anybody in the entire company directory at this point. Page 358 has the instructions.

❷ **To send a copy to other recipients, enter the address(es) in the "Cc:" or "Bcc:" fields.** If you tap Cc/Bcc, From, the screen expands to reveal two new lines beneath the "To:" line: Cc: and Bcc:.

Cc stands for *carbon copy*. Getting an email message where your name is in the Cc line implies: "I sent you a copy because I thought you'd want to know about this correspondence, but I'm not expecting you to reply."

Bcc stands for *blind carbon copy*. It's a copy that goes to a third party secretly—the primary addressee never knows you sent it. For example, if you send your coworker a message that says, "Chris, it bothers me that you've been cheating the customers," you could Bcc your supervisor to clue her in without getting into trouble with Chris.

Each of these lines behaves exactly like the "To:" line. You fill each one up with email addresses in the same way.

❸ **Change the email account you're using, if you like.** If you have more than one email account set up on your iPhone, then you can tap Cc/Bcc, From to expand the form and then tap From: to open up a spinning list of your accounts (shown on the facing page). Tap the one you want to use for sending this message.

❹ **Type the topic of the message in the Subject field.** It's courteous to put some thought into the Subject line. (Use "Change in plans for next week," for instance, instead of "Yo.") And leaving it blank only annoys your recipient. On the other hand, don't put the *entire* message into the Subject line, either.

⑤ **Type your message in the message box.** All the usual iPhone keyboard tricks apply (Chapter 2). Don't forget that you can use Copy and Paste, too, within Mail or from other programs. Both text and graphics can appear in your message.

> **Note** You can't attach anything to an outgoing message—at least not directly. You can email a photo or a video from within the Photos program (page 150), though; you can *forward* a file attached to an incoming piece of mail; and you can *paste* a copied photo or video (or several) into an open email message. Close enough.

⑥ **Tap Send (to send the message) or Cancel (to back out of it).** If you tap Cancel, the iPhone asks if you want to save the message. If you tap Save Draft, then the message lands in your Drafts folder.

Later, you can open the Drafts folder, tap the aborted message, finish it up, and send it.

> **Tip** If you *hold down* the button for a moment, the iPhone automatically opens your most recently saved draft. Wicked cool!

Signatures

A *signature* is a bit of text that gets stamped at the bottom of your outgoing email messages. It can be your name, a postal address, or a pithy quote.

Unless you intervene, the iPhone stamps "Sent from my iPhone" at the bottom of every message. You may be just fine with that, or you may consider it the equivalent of gloating (or free advertising for Apple). In any case, you can change the signature if you want to.

From the Home screen, tap Settings→Mail, Contacts, Calendars→Signature. The Signature text window appears, complete with keyboard, so you can compose the signature you want.

Surviving Email Overload

If you don't get much mail, you probably aren't lying awake at night trying to think of ways to manage so much information overload on your tiny phone.

If you do get a lot of mail, here are some tips.

The Spam Problem

Mail is an awfully full-fledged email program for a *phone*. But compared with a desktop email program, it's really only half-fledged. You can't send file attachments, can't create mail rules—and can't screen out spam.

Spam, the junk mail that makes up more than 80 percent of email, is only getting worse. So how are you supposed to keep it off your iPhone?

The following solution will take 15 minutes to set up, but it will make you very happy in the long run.

Suppose your regular email address is *iphonecrazy@comcast.net*.

❶ **Sign up for a free Gmail account.** You do that at *www.gmail.com*.

The idea here is that you're going to have all your *iphonecrazy@comcast.net* messages sent on to this Gmail account, and you'll set up your iPhone to check the *Gmail* account instead of your regular account.

Why? Because Gmail has excellent spam filters. They'll clean up the mail mess before it reaches your iPhone.

Unfortunately, just *forwarding* your mail to the Gmail account won't do the trick. If you do that, then the return address on every message that reaches your iPhone will be *iphonecrazy@comcast.net*. When you tap Reply on the iPhone, your response won't be addressed to the original sender; it'll be addressed right back to you!

But the brainiacs at Google have anticipated this problem, too.

❷ **Sign in to Gmail. Click Settings→Accounts→"Add another mail account," and fill in the email settings for your main address. Turn on "Leave a copy of retrieved message on the server."** What you've just done is told Gmail to *fetch the mail* from your main address. The return addresses of your incoming messages remain intact!

As you complete the setup process in Gmail, you'll see a message that says: "You can now retrieve mail from this account. Would you also like to be able to send mail as *iphonecrazy@comcast.net*?"

If you click "Yes, I want to be able to send mail as [your real email address]," your iPhone should not only *receive* spam-filtered mail from your main account—but when you reply, your main email address also will be the return address, and not your Gmail address. In theory, at least.

This feature turns Gmail into a convenient, automatic, behind-the-scenes spam filter for your iPhone that leaves little trace of its involvement. (You can always change the outgoing account on a per-message basis; see page 296.) In the meantime, at least all mail sent to your main address (*iphonecrazy@ comcast.net*) will come to your iPhone prefiltered.

And as an added, *added* bonus, you can check your *iphonecrazy@comcast.net* email from any computer that has a Web browser—at Gmail.com.

> **Tip** Next time, keep your email address out of spammers' hands in the first place. Use one address for the public areas of the Internet, like chat rooms, online shopping, Web site and software registration, and newsgroup posting. Spammers use automated software robots that scour these pages, recording email addresses they find. Create a separate email account for person-to-person email—and *never* post that address on a Web page.

Settings

General   **Accounts**   Labels   Filters   Forwarding and POP   Web Clips

Send mail as:
(Use Gmail to send from your other email addresses)
Learn more

David Pogue <dpogue@gmail.com>   edit info
Reply-to address:
mail@davidpogue.com

Add another email address

Get mail from other accounts:
(download mail using POP3)

Add another mail account

How Many Messages

In Settings→Mail, Contacts, Calendars→Show (next page, left), you can specify how many messages you want to appear in the list before scrolling off the screen: 25, 50, 200, whatever.

It's only a false sense of being on top of things—you can always tap the Load 25 More Messages button to retrieve the next batch—but at least you'll never have a 2,000-message Inbox.

Condensing the Message List

As you may have noticed, the messages in your Inbox are listed with the Subject line in bold type *and* a couple of lines, in light-gray text, that preview the message itself.

You can control how many lines of the light-gray preview text show up here. From the Home screen, tap Settings→Mail, Contacts, Calendars→Preview. Choosing None means you fit a lot more message titles on each screen without scrolling; choosing 5 Lines shows you a lot of each message, but means you'll have to do more scrolling.

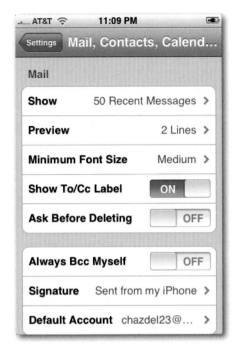 

Spotting Worthwhile Messages

The iPhone can display a little **To** or **Cc** logo on each message in your Inbox. At a glance, it helps you identify which messages are actually intended for *you*. Messages without those logos are probably spam, newsletters, mailing lists, or other messages that weren't specifically addressed to you.

To turn on these little badges, visit Settings→Mail, Contacts, Calendars and turn on Show To/CC Label. There's no downside to using this feature.

Managing Accounts

If you have more than one email account, you might want to deactivate one for a while—for example, to accommodate your travel schedule. You can also delete an account.

Visit Settings→Mail, Contacts, Calendars. In the list of accounts, tap the one you want. At the top of the screen, you see the On/Off switch, which makes an account dormant. And at the bottom, you see the Delete Account button.

Tip If you have several accounts, which one does the iPhone use when you send mail from other apps—like when you email a photo from Photos or a link from Safari?

It uses the *default* account, of course. You determine which one is the default account in Settings→Mail, Contacts, Calendars→Default Account.

12 Syncing with iTunes

Just in case you're one of the six people out there who've never heard of it, iTunes is Apple's multifunction, multimedia jukebox software. It's been loading music onto iPods since the turn of the twenty-first century. And without it, you won't get very far with your iPhone.

Most people use iTunes to manipulate their digital movies, photos, and music, from converting songs off a CD into iPhone-ready music files to buying songs, audiobooks, and movies online.

But as an iPhone owner, you need iTunes even more urgently, because it's how you get music, videos, email, addresses, appointments, ringtones, and other stuff *onto* the phone. It also backs up your iPhone automatically.

If you already have a copy of iTunes on your Mac or PC, then you may have encountered a warning that iTunes wants to update itself to version 9.2 (or later). With a click on the OK button, you can download and install that version. And you should; iOS 4 phones don't work with earlier versions.

If you've never had *any* version of iTunes, then fire up your Web browser and go to *www.apple.com/itunes/download*. Once the file lands on your computer, double-click the installer icon and follow the onscreen instructions to add iTunes to your life.

This chapter gives you a crash course in iTunes and tells you how to sync it with your iPhone.

The iTunes Window: What's Where

Here's a quick tour of the main iTunes window and what all its parts do.

The Source panel on the left side lists all the audio and video sources you can tap into at the moment. Clicking a name in the Source list makes the main song-list area change accordingly, like so:

- **Library.** Click this icon to see the contents of all your different collections. As you add movies, App Store downloads, music, podcasts, ringtones, and other stuff to iTunes, subheadings appear under the Library heading (like Music, TV Shows, Podcasts, Ringtones, and so on). Click one to see what audio, video, or software your computer has in that category.

- **Store.** Click the icons to shop for new stuff in the iTunes Store (music, movies, TV shows, free podcasts, ringtone snippets to customize your phone) or to see the list of things you've already bought.

- **Devices.** If there's a CD in the computer's drive, it shows up under this heading. Click it to see, and play, the songs on it. If there's an iPod or iPhone connected to the computer, then its icon shows up here, too, so you can see what's on it. If you have an Apple TV, it hangs out here, too.

- **Shared.** This list lets you browse the music libraries of *other* iTunes addicts on your network and play their music on your own computer. (Yes, it's legal.)

- **Playlists.** *Playlists* are lists of songs that you assemble yourself, mixing and matching music from different CDs and other sources as you see fit (page 309). Here's where you see them listed.

Here's the basic rule of using iTunes: Click one of these headings in the Source list to reveal what's *in* that source. The contents appear in the center part of the iTunes window.

The playback and volume controls, which work just as they do on the iPhone, are at the top-left corner of iTunes. At the upper-right corner is a Search box that lets you pluck one track out of a haystack. Next to it, you'll find handy buttons to change views within the window. (Cover Flow, which works just as it does on the iPhone, is the third button in this grouping.)

Five Ways to Get Music and Video

Once you have iTunes, the next step is to start filling it with music and video so you can get all that goodness onto your iPhone. iTunes gives you at least five options right off the bat.

Let iTunes Find Your Existing Songs

If you've had a computer for longer than a few days, you probably already have some songs in the popular MP3 format on your hard drive, perhaps from a file-sharing service or a free music Web site. If so, the first time you open iTunes, it offers to search your PC or Mac for music and add it to its library. Click Yes; iTunes goes hunting around your hard drive.

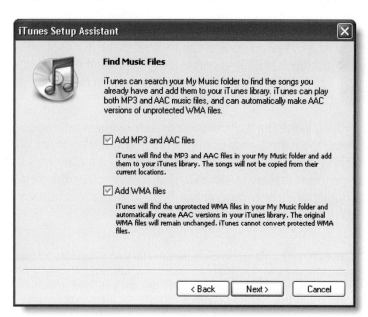

Visit the iTunes Store

Another way to feed your iPhone is to shop at the iTunes Store.

Click the iTunes Store icon in the list on the left side of the iTunes window. Once you land on the store's main page and set up your iTunes account, you can buy and download songs, audiobooks, and videos. This material goes straight into your iTunes library, just a sync away from the iPhone.

After years of conflict and controversy, the record companies have finally allowed Apple to start selling songs that aren't copy protected. Today, there's almost nothing left in the music department of iTunes that still has copy protection. (The little + symbol next to a song's price means "Not copy protected.")

Your iPhone, of course, can also get to the iTunes Store, wirelessly; just tap that alluring purple iTunes icon on the Home screen. Page 135 has the details. Any songs you buy on the phone get copied back to iTunes the next time you sync.

Not everything in the iTunes Store costs money, by the way. In addition to free iPhone apps, there are plenty of free audio and video podcasts, suitable for your iPhone, in the Podcasts area of the store. And there are tons of iPhone-compatible movie trailers to download at *www.apple.com/trailers/*. Hit that link on your iPhone's browser and watch the trailers stream down, perfectly formatted to the palm of your hand.

Import Music from a CD

iTunes can also convert tracks from audio CDs into iPhone-ready digital music files. Just start up iTunes, and then stick a CD into your computer's CD drive. The program asks you if you want to convert the songs to audio files for iTunes. (If it doesn't ask, click Import CD at the bottom of the window.)

Once you tell it to import the music, iTunes walks you through the process. If you're connected to the Internet, the program automatically downloads song titles and artist information from the CD and begins to add the songs to the iTunes library.

If you want time to think about which songs you want from each CD, then you can tell iTunes to download only the song *titles,* and then give you a few minutes to ponder your selections. To do that, choose iTunes→Preferences→ General (Mac) or Edit→Preferences→General (Windows). Use the When you insert a CD: pop-up menu to choose Show CD.

From now on, if you don't want the entire album, you can exclude the dud songs by turning off their checkmarks. Then click Import CD in the bottom-right corner of the screen.

 Tip You can ⌘-click (Mac) or Ctrl-click (Windows) any box to turn *all* the checkboxes on or off. This technique is ideal when you want only one or two songs in the list. First, turn all the checkboxes off, and then turn just those two back on again.

In that same Preferences box, you can also click Import Settings to choose the *format* (file type) and *bit rate* (amount of audio data compressed into that format) for your imported tracks. The factory setting is the AAC format at 128 kilobits per second.

Most people think these settings make for fine-sounding music files, but you can change your settings to, for example, MP3, which is another format that lets you cram big music into a small space. Upping the bit rate from 128 kbps to 256 kbps makes for richer-sounding music files—which also happen to take up more room because the files are bigger (and the iPhone's "hard drive" doesn't hold as much as your computer's). The choice is yours.

As the import process starts, iTunes moves down the list of checked songs, ripping each one to a file in your Home→Music→iTunes→iTunes Music folder (Mac) or Documents→Music→iTunes→iTunes Media→Music folder (Windows). An orange squiggle next to a song name means that the track is currently converting. Feel free to switch into other programs, answer email, surf the Web, and do other work while the ripping is under way.

Once the importing is finished, each imported song bears a green checkmark, and iTunes signals its success with a melodious flourish. Now you have some brand-new files in your iTunes library.

 Tip If you always want *all* the songs on that stack of CDs next to your computer, then change the iTunes CD import preferences to Import CD and Eject to save yourself some clicking. When you insert a CD, iTunes imports it and spits it out, ready for the next one.

Download Podcasts

The iTunes Store houses thousands upon thousands of *podcasts,* those free audio (and video!) recordings put out by everyone from big TV networks to a guy in his barn with a microphone.

To explore podcasts, click the Podcasts tab at the top of the store's window. Now you can browse shows by category, search for podcast names by keyword, or click around until you find something that sounds good.

Many podcasters produce regular installments of their shows, releasing new episodes onto the Internet when they're ready. You can have iTunes keep a look out for fresh editions of your favorite podcasts and automatically download them for you, where you can find them in the Podcasts area in the iTunes Source list. All you have to do is *subscribe* to the podcast, which takes a couple of clicks in the store.

If you want to try out a podcast, click the price button (Free) near its title to download just that one show. If you like it (or know that you're going to like it before you even download the first episode), then there's also a Subscribe button that signs you up to receive all future episodes.

You play a podcast just like any other file in iTunes: Double-click the file name in the iTunes window and use the playback controls in the upper-left corner. On the iPhone, podcasts show up in their own list.

Buy audiobooks

Some people like the sound of a good book, and iTunes has plenty to offer; click the Audiobooks tab at the top of the Store window. You can find verbal versions of the latest best sellers here, usually priced lower than the hardback version of the book—which would be four times the size of your iPhone anyway.

If iTunes doesn't offer the audiobook you're interested in, you can find a larger collection (over 50,000 of them) at Audible.com. This Web store sells all kinds of audio books, plus recorded periodicals like *The New York Times* and radio shows. To purchase Audible's wares, though, you need to go to the Web site and create an Audible account.

If you use Windows, then you can download from Audible.com a little program called Audible Download Manager, which catapults your Audible downloads into iTunes for you. On the Mac, Audible files land in iTunes automatically when you buy them.

And when those files do land in iTunes, you can play them on your computer or send them over to the iPhone with a quick sync.

Playlists

A *playlist* is a list of songs you've decided should go together. It can be any group of songs arranged in any order, all according to your whims. For example, if you're having a party, you can make a playlist from the current Top 40 and dance music in your music library. Some people may question your taste if you, say, alternate tracks from *La Bohème* with Queen's *A Night at the Opera,* but hey—it's your playlist.

To create a playlist, press ⌘-N (Mac) or Ctrl+N (Windows). Or choose File→New Playlist, or click the ✚ button below the Source list.

A freshly minted playlist starts out with the impersonal name "Untitled Playlist." Fortunately, the renaming rectangle is open and highlighted. Just type a better name: *Cardio Workout, Shoe-Shopping Tunes, Hits of the Highland Lute,* or whatever you want to call it. As you add them, your playlists alphabetize themselves in the Source window.

Once you've created this new playlist, you're ready to add your songs or videos. The quickest way is to drag their names directly onto the playlist's icon.

 Tip Instead of making an empty playlist and then dragging songs into it, you can work the other way. You can scroll through a big list of songs, selecting tracks as you go by ⌘-clicking (on the Mac) or Ctrl-clicking (in Windows)—and then, when you're finished, choose File→New Playlist From Selection. All the songs you selected immediately appear on a brand new playlist.

When you drag a song title onto a playlist, you're not making a copy of the song. In essence, you're creating an *alias* or *shortcut* of the original, which means you can have the same song on several different playlists.

iTunes even starts you out with some playlists of its own devising, like "Top 25 Most Played" and "Purchased" (a convenient place to find all your iTunes Store goodies listed in one place).

 Tip You can also create playlists right on the phone; see page 114.

Editing and Deleting Playlists

A playlist is easy to change. Here's what you can do with just a little light mousework:

- **Change the order of songs on the playlist.** Click at the top of the first column in the playlist window (the one with the numbers next to the songs) and drag song titles up or down within the playlist window to reorder them.

- **Add new songs to the playlist.** Tiptoe through your iTunes library and drag more songs into a playlist.

#	Name	Artist
1	☑ Tortured, Tangled Hearts	Dixie Chicks
2	☑ Boxed In (live)	Ian Bennett & the Brothers of Sol
3	☑ The Night They Drove Old Dixie Down	Joan Baez
4	☑ Village Green Preservation Society	The Kinks
5	☑ Gee Baby, Ain't I Good To You	Oscar Peterson
6	☑ Ode To A Butterfly	Nickel Creek
7	☑ Ring of Fire	Lucy Kaplansky
8	☑ Shut Up And Kiss Me	Mary Chapin Carpenter
9	☑ Then Came Lo Mein	Robert Earl Keen

- **Delete songs from the playlist.** If your playlist needs pruning, or that banjo tune just doesn't fit in with the brass-band tracks, you can ditch it quickly: Click the song in the playlist window and then hit Delete or Backspace to get rid of it. When iTunes asks you to confirm your decision, click Yes.

  Deleting a song from a playlist doesn't delete it from your music library— it just removes the title from your *playlist*. (Pressing Delete or Backspace when the Library Music icon is selected gets rid of the song for good.)

- **Delete the whole playlist.** To delete an entire playlist, click it in the Source list and press Delete (Backspace). Again, this zaps only the playlist itself, not all the songs you had in it. (Those are still in your computer's iTunes folder.)

 Tip If you want to see how many playlists a certain song appears on, Ctrl-click (Mac) or right-click (Mac or PC) the track's name; from the shortcut menu, choose "Show in Playlist."

Authorizing Computers

Before the iTunes Store moved to not-copy-protected songs, music fans had to suffer through the hostility of computer authorization. Since you may still have some of those older, protected songs, here's the scoop.

When you create an account in iTunes (a requirement of owning an iPhone), you automatically *authorize* that computer to play copy-protected songs from the iTunes Store. Authorization is Apple's way of making sure you don't go playing those music tracks on more than five computers, which would greatly displease the record companies.

You can copy those older songs onto a maximum of four other computers. To authorize each one to play music from your account, choose Store→Authorize Computer. (Don't worry; you just have to do this once per machine.)

When you've maxed out your limit and can't authorize any more computers, you may need to *deauthorize* one. On the computer you wish to demote, choose Store→Deauthorize Computer.

 Note As noted above, most songs on iTunes today bear the little + sign, meaning "iTunes Plus." They have slightly higher audio quality—and they're *not* copy protected. You can play them on any player that recognizes AAC files.

Then again, you can't go nuts, uploading them all over the Internet. Your name and email address are embedded in the file and quite visible to anyone (including any Apple lawyer) who chooses the track, chooses File→Get Info, and clicks the Summary **tab.**

TV, Movies, and Movie Rentals

iTunes hasn't been just about music for years. Nowadays, you can also buy TV episodes ($2 apiece, no ads), movies, and music videos. You can also *rent* movies from iTunes for $3 to $5 apiece. That is, once you download a movie, you have 30 days to start watching—and once you start, you have 24 hours to finish before it turns into a pumpkin (actually, it deletes itself from your computer and phone).

You have to do your renting and buying using the iTunes software on your Mac or PC—the direct-to-phone video downloading era hasn't yet dawned.

But once it's on your computer, you can sync this stuff to the iPhone by following the steps later in this chapter.

When you get right down to it, the iPhone is pretty much the same idea as a Palm Pilot: It's a pocket-sized data bucket that lets you carry around the most useful subset of the information on your Mac or PC. In the iPhone's case, that's music, photos, movies, ebooks, calendars, your address book, email settings, ringtones, and Web bookmarks.

Automatic Syncing

Transferring data between the iPhone and the computer is called *synchroniza-tion*. Syncing is sometimes a one-way street, and sometimes it's bidirectional, as you'll find out in a moment.

This section covers the ins and outs—or, rather, the backs and forths—of iPhone syncing over a USB cable. (Syncing wirelessly, over the airwaves, is a treat reserved for MobileMe and Microsoft Exchange people, as described in Chapters 13 and 14.)

So how do you sync? You connect the iPhone to the computer. That's it. As long as the cable is plugged into your computer's USB port, iTunes opens automatically, and the synchronization begins. iTunes controls all iPhone syn-chronization, acting as a software bridge between phone and computer.

 Note Your photo-editing program (like iPhoto or Photoshop Elements) probably springs open every time you connect the iPhone, too. See page 332 if that bugs you.

When the iPhone and the computer are communicating, the iTunes window and the iPhone screen both say, "Sync in progress."

Unlike an iPod, which gets very angry (and can potentially scramble your data) if you interrupt while its "Do not disconnect" screen is up, the iPhone is much more understanding about interruptions. If you need to use the iPhone for a moment, just drag your finger across the "slide to cancel" slider on the screen. The sync pauses. When you reconnect the phone to the cable, the sync intelligently resumes.

In fact, if someone dares to call you while you're in mid-sync, the iPhone can-cels the session *itself* so you can pick up the call. Just reconnect it to the com-puter when you're done chatting so it can finish syncing.

Now, ordinarily, the iPhone-iTunes relationship is automatic and complete. An automatic sync takes care of all of these details:

- **Contacts, calendars, and Web bookmarks.** These get copied in both directions. That is, after a sync your computer and phone contain exactly the same information.

  So if you entered an appointment on the iPhone, it gets copied to your computer—and vice versa. If you edited the same contact or appointment on both machines at once while they were apart, your computer now displays the two conflicting records and asks you which one "wins."

- **Music, apps, TV, movies, ringtones, and ebooks you bought using iTunes on your computer; photos from your computer; and email account information.** All of this gets copied in one direction: computer→phone.

- **Photos and videos taken with the iPhone's camera; music, apps, and ebooks you bought right from the phone.** All of this gets copied the other way: phone→computer.

- **A complete backup.** iTunes also takes it upon itself to back up *everything else* on your iPhone: settings, text messages, call history, and so on. (Details on this backup business are on page 338.)

 Tip If you're in a hurry, you can skip the time-consuming backup portion of the sync. Just click the ✖ at the top of the iTunes window whenever it says "Backing up." iTunes gets the message and skips right ahead to the next phase of the sync— transferring contacts, calendars, music, and so on.

Manual Syncing

OK, but what if you don't *want* iTunes to fire up and start syncing every time you connect your iPhone? What if, for example, you want to change the assortment of music and video that's about to get copied to it? Or what if you just don't like matters being taken out of your hands, just because it reminds you too much of robot overlords?

In that case, you can stop the autosyncing in any of three ways:

- **Interrupt a sync in progress.** Click the ✖ button in the iTunes status window until the syncing stops.

- **Stop iTunes from syncing the iPhone just this time.** As you plug in the iPhone's cable, hold down the Shift+Ctrl keys (Windows) or the ⌘-Option keys (Mac) until the iPhone pops up in the iTunes window. Now you can see what's on the iPhone and change what will be synced to it—but no syncing takes place until you command it.

- **Stop iTunes from autosyncing any iPhone, ever.** In iTunes, choose Edit→Preferences (Windows) or iTunes→Preferences (Mac). Click the Devices tab and turn on Prevent iPods, iPhones, and iPads from syncing automatically. You can still trigger a sync on command when the iPhone is wired up—by clicking the Sync button.

Once you've made iTunes stop syncing automatically, you've disabled what many people consider the greatest feature of the iPhone: its magical self-updating with the stuff on your computer.

Still, you must have turned off autosyncing for a reason. And one of those reasons might be that you want to control what gets copied onto it. Maybe you're in a hurry to leave for the airport, and you don't have time to sit there for an hour while six downloaded movies get copied to the phone. Maybe you have 50 gigabytes of music but only 16 gigs of iPhone storage.

In any case, here are the two ways you can sync manually:

- **Use the tabs in iTunes.** With the iPhone connected, you can specify exactly what you want copied to it—which songs, which TV shows, which apps, and so on—using the various tabs in iTunes, as described on the following pages. Once you've made your selections, click the Summary tab, and then click Apply. (The Apply button says Sync instead if you haven't actually changed any settings.)

- **Drag files onto the iPhone icon.** Yes, this sneaky little trick is what insiders might recognize as the iPod Paradigm. Once your iPhone is cabled into your computer, you can click its icon and then turn on Manually manage music and videos (on the Summary screen). Click Apply.

  Now, you can drag songs and videos directly onto the iPhone's icon to copy them there. Wilder yet, you can bypass iTunes *entirely* by dragging music and video files *from your computer's desktop* onto the iPhone's icon. That's handy when you've just inherited or downloaded a bunch of song files, converted a DVD to the iPhone's video format, or whatever.

  Just two notes of warning here. First, unlike a true iPod, the iPhone accommodates dragged material from a *single* computer only.

Second, if you ever turn off this option, all those manually dragged songs and videos will disappear from your iPhone at the next sync opportunity.

> **Tip** Also on the Summary tab, you'll find the baffling little option called Sync only checked songs and videos. This is a global override—a last-ditch "keep the embarrassing songs off my iPhone" option.
>
> When this option is turned on, iTunes consults the tiny checkboxes next to every single song and video in your iTunes library. If you turn off a song's checkbox, it will not get synced to your iPhone, no matter what—even if you use the Music tab to sync All songs or playlists, or explicitly turn on a playlist that contains this song. If the song's or video's checkbox isn't checked in your Library list, then it will be left behind on your computer.

12 Tabs to Glory

Once your iPhone is cabled up to the computer's USB port, click its icon in the iTunes Source list. The middle part of the iTunes window now reveals a horizontal row of file-folder tabs, representing the categories of stuff you can sync to your iPhone.

Here's what each one tells you:

- **Summary.** This screen gives basic stats on your iPhone, like its serial number, capacity, and phone number. Buttons in the middle let you check for iPhone software updates or restore it to its out-of-the-box state. Checkboxes at the bottom of the screen let you set up manual syncing, as described previously.

- **Info.** The settings here control the syncing of your contacts, calendars, email account settings, and bookmarks.

- **Apps.** Those useful and not-useful-but-totally-fun-anyway little programs from the iPhone App Store get synced up here (Chapter 7).

- **Ringtones.** Any ringtones that you've bought from the iTunes Store or made yourself (Chapter 4) appear here; you can specify which ones you want synced to the iPhone.

- **Music.** You can opt to sync all your songs, music videos, and playlists here—or, if your collection is more than the iPhone can store, just some of them.

- **Movies, TV Shows.** You can choose both movies and TV shows from the iTunes Store for syncing here, along with other compatible video files in your library.

- **Podcasts.** This screen lets you sync all—or just selected—podcasts. You can even opt to get only the episodes you haven't heard yet.

- **iTunes U.** Free educational podcasts and lectures from universities.

- **Books.** Ebooks and PDF documents you want to read in the iBooks app.

- **Photos.** Here you can get iPhone-friendly versions of your pictures copied over from a folder on your hard drive—or from a photo-management program like Photoshop Elements, Photoshop Album, or iPhoto.

- **Nike + iPod.** See Chapter 4 for details.

At the bottom of the screen, a colorful map shows you the amount and types of files: Audio, Video, Photos, Apps, Books, and Other (for your personal data). More importantly, it also shows you how much room you have left, so you won't get overzealous in trying to load the thing up.

The following pages cover each of these tabs, in sequence, and detail how to sync each kind of iPhone-friendly material.

This discussion assumes that you've (a) connected your iPhone to the computer with its USB cable, and (b) clicked the iPhone's icon in the Source list at the left side of the iTunes window.

Info Tab (Contacts, Calendars, Settings)

On this tab, you're offered the chance to copy some distinctly non-entertainment data over to your iPhone: your computer's calendar, address book, email settings, notes, and Web bookmarks. The PalmPilot-type stuff (Rolodex, date book) is extremely useful to have with you, and the settings and bookmarks save you a lot of tedious setup on the iPhone.

 Note If you're a subscriber to Apple's data-in-the-clouds MobileMe service, then you won't see the controls described on the following pages. That's because MobileMe, not iTunes, handles synchronization with the iPhone. Instead, all you see is a message to the effect that, for example, "Your calendars are being pushed to your iPhone over the air from MobileMe."

Syncing Notes

Any notes you create on the iPhone can synchronize with the notes in Mail, Outlook (in Windows), or in the Notes folders of Gmail, Yahoo Mail, or AOL; see page 227 for details. If you're lucky, turning on the Sync notes checkbox is all there is to it. If you're not, try the suggestions at *http://bit.ly/hKPkl*.

Syncing Contacts

If you've been adding to your address book for years in a program like Microsoft Outlook or Mac OS X's Address Book, then you're just a sync away from porting all that accumulated data right over to your iPhone. Once there, phone numbers and email addresses show up as links, so you can reach out and tap someone.

Here's how to sync up your contacts with the iPhone. The steps depend on which program you keep them in.

- **Outlook 2003 and 2007.** Turn on Sync contacts with: and, from the pop-up menu, choose Outlook. Finally, click Apply.

 Note that some of the more obscure fields Outlook lets you use, like Radio and Telex, won't show up on the iPhone. All the major data points do, however, including name, email address, and (most importantly) phone number.

Tip Having weird syncing issues with Outlook's contacts and calendars? In iTunes, go to Edit→Preferences→Syncing and click Reset Sync History. This function doesn't wipe out the data you've synced, just the Windows memory of it. The next time you sync the iPhone, it'll be like the very first time.

- **Outlook Express.** Microsoft's free email app for Windows XP stores your contacts in a file called the Windows Address Book. To sync it with your iPhone, turn on Sync contacts from:, choose Windows Address Book from the pop-up menu, and then click Apply.

- **Windows Live Mail.** Windows Live Mail, a free download for Windows 7 (and called Windows Mail in Windows Vista), is essentially a renamed version of Outlook Express. You set it up to sync with the iPhone's Contacts program just as described—except in iTunes, choose Windows Contacts, rather than Windows Address Book, before clicking Apply.

- **Yahoo Address Book.** The Yahoo Address Book is the address book component of a free Yahoo Mail account. It's therefore an *online* address book, which has certain advantages—like your ability to access it from any computer on the Internet.

  To sync with it, turn on Sync contacts from: and then choose Yahoo Address Book from the pop-up menu. (On the Mac, just turn on Yahoo Address Book; no menu is needed.)

  Since Yahoo is an *online* address book, you need an Internet connection and your Yahoo ID and password to sync it with the iPhone. Click Configure, and then type your Yahoo ID and password. When finished, click OK. Now click Apply to get syncing.

Because it's online, syncing your Yahoo address book has a couple of other quirks.

First, Yahoo Address Book, ever the thoughtful program, lets you remember both birthdays and anniversaries in a data field. The iPhone, however, grabs only the birthday part, leaving you to remember the anniversary dates yourself. Just don't forget your own!

Furthermore, any custom labels you slap on phone entries on the iPhone side get synced into the Other field when they get to Yahoo. It seems Yahoo is just not as creative as you are when it comes to labeling things.

Finally, Yahoo Address Book doesn't delete contacts during a sync. So if you whack somebody on the iPhone, you still have to log into Yahoo and take 'em out there, too.

- **Google Contacts.** The addresses from your Gmail, Google Mail, and Google Apps accounts can sync up to the iPhone as well. Turn on Sync contacts from: and then choose Google Contacts from the pop-up menu. (On the Mac, just turn on Google Contacts; no menu is needed.) Agree to the legal disclaimer about iTunes snatching data.

  Since Google Contacts are kept on the Web, you need an Internet connection and your Gmail/Google ID and password to sync your contacts with the iPhone. In the password box that pops up (click Configure on the Info screen if it doesn't), type your Gmail name and password. When finished, click OK. Now click Apply to get syncing.

  Only one contact per email address gets synced, so if you have multiple contacts with the same address, someone will get left out of the syncing party. Google has a page of troubleshooting tips and info for other Contacts-related questions at *www.google.com/support/contactsync*.

- **Mac OS X Address Book.** Apple products generally love one another, and the built-in contact keeper that comes with Mac OS X is a breeze to sync up with your iPhone. Turn on Sync contacts from: and then pick Address Book from the pop-up menu.

  If you've gathered sets of people together as *groups* in your address book, then you can also transfer *them* to the iPhone by turning on Selected groups and then checking the ones you want. When finished, click Apply to sync things up.

- **Entourage 2004 and 2008.** Entourage, the email program in Microsoft Office for the Mac, also plays nice with the iPhone, as long as you introduce it properly first.

In Entourage, choose Entourage→Preferences. Under General Preferences, choose Sync Services. Turn on Synchronize contacts with Address Book and .Mac.

Click OK, and then plug the iPhone into the Mac. Click the iPhone's icon in the iTunes Source list, and then click the Info tab. Turn on Sync contacts from: and, from the pop-up menu, choose Address Book. Finally, click Apply to sync.

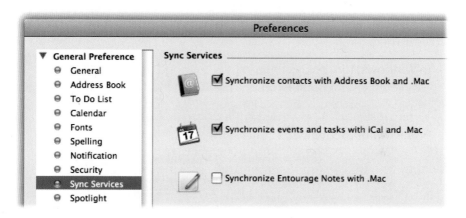

- **Other programs.** Even if you keep your contacts in a Jurassic-era program like Palm Desktop, you may still be able to get them into the iPhone/iTunes sync dance. If you can export your contacts as vCards (a contacts-exchange format with the extension .vcf), then you can import them into the Windows Address Book or the Mac's Address Book.

In Palm Desktop 4.1 for the Mac, for instance, choose File→Export→ Addresses, select vCard for the export format, and then click OK. Export the file to your desktop, open the Mac Address Book, and then *import* the same file.

It's trickier on the PC version of Palm Desktop 4.1, since you can export only one contact at a time. But a handy little freeware program called Palm2iPod can do it all for you. It's available from this book's "Missing CD" page at *www.missingmanuals.com*. Chapura's $20 PocketCopy program is another option at *www.chapura.com/pocketcopy.php*.

Now you can sync to your heart's delight.

Syncing Bookmarks

Bookmarks—those helpful shortcuts that save you countless hours of mis-typing Web site addresses—are a reflection of your personality, because they tend to be sites that are important to *you*. Fortunately, they can make the trip to your iPhone, too. In fact, any bookmarks you create on the iPhone can also be copied back to your computer; it's a two-way street.

iTunes can transfer your bookmarks from Internet Explorer or Safari (Windows), or from Safari on a Mac. In iTunes, on the Info tab, scroll down past Contacts and Calendars and Mail Accounts until you get to the section called Web Browser. Then:

- **In Windows,** turn on Sync bookmarks from: and then choose either Safari or Internet Explorer from the pop-up menu. Click Apply to sync.

- **On the Mac,** turn on Sync Safari bookmarks and click Apply.

And what if Firefox is your preferred browser? You can still get those favorites moved over to the iPhone, thanks to an ingenious free Firefox plug-in called the Firefox Sync Add-on. It's available at *www.mozilla.com/en-US/firefox/sync/*, or you can just Google it.

Best of all, the Sync Add-on doesn't just copy your bookmarks to the phone—it creates a live two-way wireless sync between your computer and your phone. Bookmarks, yes, but also your History list and even your open tabs. Go, Google!

Actually, *most* other browsers can export their bookmarks. You can use that option to export your bookmarks file to your desktop and then use Safari's File→Import Bookmarks command to pull it from there.

Syncing Your Calendar

With its snazzy-looking calendar program tidily synced with your computer, the iPhone can keep you on schedule—and even remind you when you have to call a few people.

Out of the box, the iPhone's calendar works with Outlook 2003 and later for Windows, and with iCal and Entourage on the Mac.

The iPhone's calendar program isn't especially full-featured, however. For example, it doesn't have its own built-in to-do lists (which ought to be something on *Apple's* to-do list, come to think of it). The iPhone can display your calendar's color-coded categories (Work, Social, and so on), but it can't *create* categories. Otherwise, though, it's very pretty, and it does generally keep you on track.

Here again, setting up the sync depends on the calendar program you're using on your computer.

 Note If you have Windows Vista or Windows 7, then you have a built-in calendar program—Windows Live Calendar—but no way to sync it with the iPhone. The reason, according to Apple, is that Microsoft has not made public the format of its calendar program.

- **Outlook Calendar (Windows).** In the Calendars area of the Info tab, turn on Sync calendars from Outlook.

  You can also choose how many days' worth of old events you want to have on your iPhone, since you probably rarely need to reference, say, your calendar from 2002. Turn on Do not sync events older than ____ days, and then specify the number of days' worth of old appointments you want to have on hand.

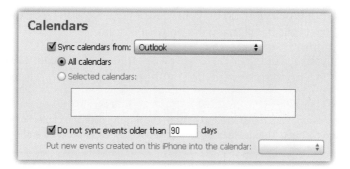

  Events you add on the iPhone get carried back to Outlook when you reconnect to the computer and sync up.

- **iCal (Macintosh).** Mac OS X comes with a nimble little datebook called iCal, which syncs right up with the iPhone. To use it, on the Info tab's Calendars area, turn on Sync iCal calendars.

  If you have several different *calendars* (color-coded categories) in iCal—Work, Home, Book Club, and so on—then you can turn on Selected calendars and choose the ones you want to copy to the iPhone. See page 200 for details on using the categories once they're on the phone.

  Near the bottom of the calendar-sync preferences, there's a place to indicate how far back you want to sync old events.

  Once you get all your calendar preferences set up the way you like, click Apply to get your schedule in sync.

- **Entourage (Mac).** Entourage can sync its calendar events with the iPhone, too. Start by opening Entourage, and then choose Entourage→Preferences. Under General Preferences, choose Sync Services, and then turn on Synchronize events and tasks with iCal and MobileMe. Click OK, and then plug the iPhone into the computer.

  Click the iPhone icon in the iTunes source list, and then, on the Info tab, turn on Sync iCal calendars. Click the Apply button to sync.

Syncing Email Settings

Teaching a new computer of *any* sort to get and send your email can be stressful; the job entails plugging in all sorts of user-hostile information bits called things like the SMTP Server Address and Uses SSL. Presumably, though, you've got your email working on your Mac or PC—wouldn't it be great if you didn't have to duplicate all that work on your iPhone?

That's exactly what iTunes can do for you. It can transfer the *account setup information* to the iPhone so it's ready to start hunting for messages immediately.

 Note No mail *messages* are transferred to or from the iPhone over the cable. For that sort of magic, you need MobileMe or Exchange service. (See Chapters 13 and 14.)

It can do that—*if*, that is, your current email program is Mail or Entourage (on the Mac) or Outlook or Outlook Express (in Windows).

On the iTunes Info tab, scroll down to Mail Accounts. The next step varies by operating system:

- **Windows.** Turn on Sync selected mail accounts from: and, from the shortcut menu, choose Outlook or Outlook Express.

- **Macintosh.** Turn on Sync selected Mail accounts.

Finally, if your email program collects messages from multiple accounts, then turn on the checkboxes of the accounts you want to see on your iPhone. Click Apply to start syncing.

 This business of transferring email settings doesn't always go smoothly. Mac fans have learned, for example, that Mail transfers settings more successfully than Entourage. And Windows Vista people have discovered that even though Windows Mail is just a renamed, updated version of Outlook Express, iTunes isn't especially friendly with it.

The Apps Tab

On this tab, you get a convenient duplicate of your iPhone's Home screens. You can drag app icons around, create and manage folders, shift Home screens into a different order, and otherwise organize your Home life much faster than you'd be able to do on the phone itself (because you have a mouse, a keyboard, and a big screen). Details are on page 177.

At the left side, there's a list of all the iPhone programs you've got on your computer, including programs you just bought in that two-hour shopping frenzy in the App Store. The list also shows all the apps you bought on the iPhone that have since been transferred into iTunes as a backup.

If you don't want to sync *all* those programs at the moment—maybe you want to leave off the Crash Bandicoot game until the weekend because you know you'll never get any work done if you add it on Tuesday—click Sync Apps. Then turn on the checkboxes for the programs you want to load onto the iPhone right now.

Any programs you leave unchecked will be *removed* from the iPhone when you sync. (Of course, you can always reinstall them by turning their checkboxes back on before the next sync.)

The Ringtones Tab

Once you click the Ringtones tab in iTunes, checkboxes await, corresponding to the ringtones you've bought from Apple or made through various do-it-yourself craft projects (Chapter 4). Be sure to sync over any ringtones you've assigned to your frequent callers so the iPhone can alert you with a personalized audio cue like Pink's rendition of "Tell Me Something Good" when they call you up.

The Music Tab

To copy over the music and audiobooks you want to take along on your phone, click the Music tab. Next, turn on Sync Music. Now you need to decide *what* music to put on your phone.

- If you have a big iPhone and a small music library, you can opt to sync Entire music library with one click.

- If you have a big music collection and a small iPhone, you'll have to take only *some* of it along for the iPhone ride. In that case, click Selected playlists, artists, and genres. In the lists below, turn on the checkboxes for the playlists, artists, and music genres you want to transfer. (These are cumulative. If there's no Electric Light Orchestra in any of your selected playlists, but you turn on ELO in the Artists list, you'll get all of your ELO anyway.)

 Tip Playlists make it fast and easy to sync whole batches of tunes over to your iPhone. But don't forget that you can add individual songs, too, even if they're not in any playlist. Just turn on Manually manage music and videos. Now you can drag individual songs and videos from your iTunes library onto the iPhone icon to install them there.

If you've got music videos, you'll see that they get their own checkbox. As for audiobooks, they already live in their own self-titled playlists. Click the appropriate checkbox to include them in your sync.

Making It All Fit

Sooner or later, everybody has to confront the fact that a current iPhone holds only 8, 16, or 32 gigabytes of music and video. (Actually less, because the operating system itself eats up over a gigabyte.) That's enough for around 2,000, 4,000, or 8,000 average-length songs—assuming you don't put any video or photos on there.

Your multimedia stash is probably bigger than that. If you just turn on all Sync All checkboxes, then you'll get an error message telling you that it won't all fit on the iPhone.

One way to solve the problem is to tiptoe through the Music, Podcasts, Photos, Apps, Books, and Videos tabs, turning off checkboxes and trying to sync until the "too much" error message goes away.

If you don't have quite so much time, turn on Automatically fill free space with songs. It makes iTunes use a little artificial Genius intelligence to load up your phone automatically, using your most played and most recent music as a guide. (It does not, in fact, fill the phone completely; it leaves a few hundred megabytes for safety—so that you can download more stuff on the road, for example.)

Another helpful approach is to use the *smart playlist,* a music playlist that assembles itself based on criteria that you supply. For example:

❶ **In iTunes, click Music in the Source list; then choose File→New Smart Playlist.** The Smart Playlist dialog box appears.

❷ **Specify the category.** Use the pop-up menus to choose, for example, a musical genre, or songs you've played recently, or *haven't* played recently, or that you've rated highly.

❸ **Turn on the "Limit to" checkbox, and set up the constraints.** For example, you could limit the amount of music in this playlist to 2 gigabytes, chosen at random. That way, every time you sync, you'll get a fresh, random supply of songs on your iPhone, with enough room left for some videos.

❹ **Click OK.** The new Smart Playlist appears in your Source list, where you can rename it.

Click it to look it over, if you like. Then, on the Music tab, choose this playlist for syncing to the iPhone.

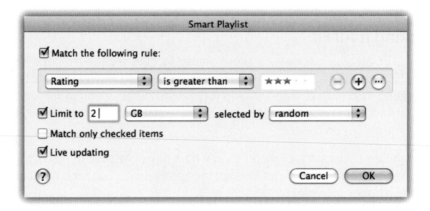

The Movies & TV Shows Tabs

When it assumes the role of an iPod, one of the things the iPhone does best is play video on its gorgeous, glossy screen. TV shows and movies you've bought or rented from the iTunes Store look especially nice, since they're formatted with iPods in mind. (And if you started watching a rented movie on your computer, the iPhone begins playing it right from where you left off.)

Syncing TV shows and movies works just like syncing music or podcasts. You can have iTunes copy all your stuff to the iPhone, but video fills up your storage awfully fast. That's why you can turn on the checkboxes of just the individual movies or shows you want—or, using the Automatically include pop-up menu, request only the most recent, or the most recent ones you haven't seen yet.

Remember that if you've rented a movie from the iTunes Store and started watching it, you have less than 24 hours left to finish before it turns into a pumpkin.

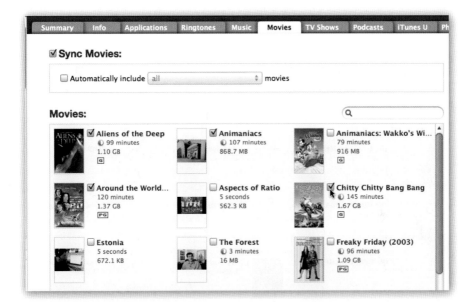

The Podcasts & iTunes U Tabs

One of the great joys of iTunes is the way it gives you access, in the iTunes Store, to thousands of free amateur and professional *podcasts* (basically, downloadable radio or TV shows), including free college lectures and videos in the iTunes U category.

Here, you can choose to sync all podcast episodes, selected shows, all unplayed episodes—or just a certain number of episodes per sync. Individual checkboxes let you choose *which* podcast series get to come along for the ride, so you can sync to suit your mood at the time.

The Books Tab

Here are the thumbnails of your audiobooks and your ebooks—those you've bought from Apple, those you've downloaded for free from the Web, and those you've dragged right into iTunes from your desktop (PDF files, for example; see page 236). You can ask iTunes to send them all to your phone, or only the ones whose checkboxes you turn on.

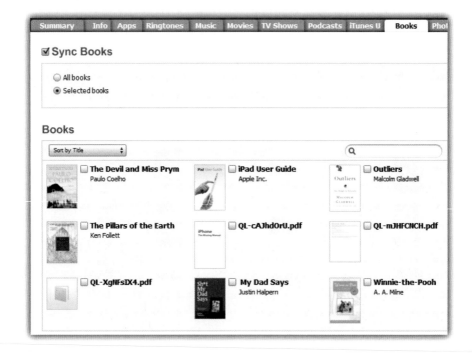

The Photos Tab (Computer→iPhone)

Why corner people with your wallet to show them your kid's baby pictures, when you can whip out your iPhone and dazzle them with a finger-tapping slideshow?

iTunes can sync the photos from your hard drive onto the iPhone. If you use a compatible photo-management program, you can even select individual albums of images that you've already assembled on your computer. Here are your photo-filling options for the iPhone:

- **Photoshop Elements 3.0 or later** for Windows.

- **Photoshop Album 2.0 or later** for Windows.

- **iPhoto 4.0.3 or later** on the Mac.

- **Aperture,** Apple's high-end program for photography pros.

- **Any folder of photos on your hard drive,** like My Pictures (in Windows), Pictures (on the Mac), or any folder you like.

The common JPEG files generated by just about every digital camera work fine for iPhone photos. The GIF and PNG files used by Web pages work, too.

 Note You can sync photos from only one computer. If you later attempt to snag some snaps from a second machine, iTunes warns you that you must first erase all the images that came from the *original* computer.

When you're ready to sync your photos, click the Photos tab in iTunes. Turn on Sync photos from, and then indicate where you'd like to sync them *from* (Photoshop Elements, iPhoto, or whatever).

If you want only *some* of the albums from your photo-shoebox software, then click Selected albums, events, and faces. Then turn on the checkboxes of the albums, events, and faces you want synced. (The Faces option is available only if you're syncing from iPhone or Aperture on the Mac, and only if you've used the Faces feature, which groups your photos according to who's in them.)

Once you make your selections and click Apply, the program computes for a very long time, "optimizing" copies of your photos to make them look great on the iPhone (for example, downsizing them from 10-megapixel overkill to something more appropriate for a 0.6-megapixel screen), and then ports them over.

After the sync is complete, you'll be able to wave your iPhone around, and people will *beg* to see your photos.

Syncing Photos and Videos (iPhone→Computer)

The previous discussion describes copying photos in only one direction: computer→iPhone. But here's one of those rare instances when you can actually *create* data on the iPhone so that you can later transfer it to the computer:

photos and videos that you take with the iPhone's own camera. You can rest easy, knowing that they can be copied back to your computer for safekeeping with only one click.

Now, it's important to understand that *iTunes is not involved* in this process. It doesn't know anything about photos or videos coming *from* the iPhone; its job is just to copy pictures *to* the iPhone.

So what's handling the iPhone→computer transfer? Your operating system. It sees the iPhone as though it's a digital camera and suggests importing them just as it would from a camera's memory card.

Here's how it goes: Plug the iPhone into the computer with the USB cable. What you'll see is probably something like this:

- **On the Mac.** iPhoto opens. This free photo-organizing/editing software comes on every Mac. Shortly after it notices that the iPhone is on the premises, it goes into Import mode. Click Import All, or select some thumbnails from the iPhone, and then click Import Selected.

  After the transfer (or before it, in older iPhoto versions), click Delete Photos if you'd like the iPhone's cameraphone memory cleared out after the transfer. (And yes, both photos and videos get imported together.)

- **In Windows.** When you attach a camera (or an iPhone), a dialog box pops up that asks how you want its contents handled. It lists any photo-management program you might have installed (Picasa, Photoshop Elements, Photoshop Album, and so on), as well as Windows' own camera-management software (Scanner and Camera Wizard in Windows XP; using Windows in Vista or Windows 7).

  Click the program you want to handle importing the iPhone pictures and videos. You'll probably also want to turn on Always do this for this device, so it'll happen automatically the next time.

Shutting Down the Importing Process

Then again, some iPhone owners would rather *not* see some lumbering photo-management program firing itself up every time they connect the phone. You, too, might wish there were a way to *stop* iPhoto or Windows from bugging you every time you connect the iPhone. That, too, is easy enough to change—if you know where to look.

- **Windows XP.** With the iPhone connected, choose Start→My Computer. Right-click the iPhone's icon. From the shortcut menu, choose Properties. Click the Events tab; next, click Take no action. Click OK.

- **Windows Vista, Windows 7.** When the AutoPlay dialog box appears, click Set AutoPlay defaults in Control Panel. (Or, if the AutoPlay dialog box is no longer on the screen, choose Start→Control Panel→AutoPlay.)

  Scroll all the way to the bottom until you see the iPhone icon. From the pop-up menu, choose Take no action. Click Save.

- **Macintosh.** Open iPhoto. Choose iPhoto→Preferences. Where it says Connecting camera opens:, choose No application. Close the window.

From now on, no photo-importing message will appear when you plug in the iPhone. (You can always import its photos manually, of course.)

Windows Vista, Windows 7

Windows XP

One iPhone, Multiple Computers

In general, Apple likes to keep things simple. Everything it ever says about the iPhone suggests that you can sync only *one* iPhone with *one* computer.

That's not really true, however. You can actually sync the same iPhone with *multiple* Macs or PCs.

And why would you want to do that? So you can fill it up with material from different places: music and video from a Mac at home; contacts, calendar, ebooks, and iPhone applications from your Windows PC at work; and maybe even the photos from your laptop.

iTunes derives these goodies from different sources to begin with—pictures from your photo program, addresses and appointments from your contacts and calendar programs, music and video from iTunes. So all you have to do is set up the tabs of each computer's copy of iTunes to sync *only* certain kinds of material.

On the Mac, for example, you'd turn on only the Sync checkboxes for the Music, Podcasts, and Video tabs. Sync away.

Next, take the iPhone to the office; on your PC, turn on the Sync checkboxes only on the Info, Books, and Apps tabs. Sync away once more.

Then on the laptop, turn off Sync on all tabs except Photos.

And off you go. Each time you connect the iPhone to one of the computers, it syncs that data set according to the preferences set in that copy of iTunes.

One Computer, Multiple iPhones

It's fine to sync multiple iPhones with a single computer, too. iTunes cheerfully fills each one up, and backs each one up, as they come. In fact, if you open the Preferences box (in the iTunes menu on the Mac, the Edit menu on Windows), the Devices tab shows a list of all the iPhones (and iPads, and iPod Touches) that iTunes is tracking.

If you use Windows, however, here's a note of warning: You have to use the same sync settings for everyone's phones.

If, for example, you try to switch your Contacts syncing from Google to Outlook Express, an iTunes dialog box informs you that your changes will affect everyone else syncing iPods and iPhones on the PC. (If you really want every family member happy, have each person sign in with his own Windows user account and copy of iTunes.)

Conflicts

If you use only one machine at a time, you'll never have *conflicts*. You'll never change your dentist appointment to 3:00 p.m. on the iPhone but change it to 4:00 p.m. on your computer, between syncs. Or you'll never edit a phone number in Contacts simultaneously in two different ways on the two different machines. One machine would always be the "hot potato."

In the real world, though, conflicts occasionally happen. Fortunately, iTunes is pretty smart about handling them. In fact, you can set it up to warn you if more than, say, 5 percent of the address book or calendar is now different from what's on your computer.

In Windows, you set up this alert in iTunes at Edit→Preferences→Syncing. On the Mac, go to your Applications folder. Open the iSync program; choose iSync→Preferences.

The same preference screen also gives you access to the Reset Sync History button, which wipes out the computer's record of your data-sync sessions (but not the data itself). This can be useful if your iPhone just won't sync right and you want to start clean.

If, when encountering the conflict warning, you don't know what could possibly be that different in your contacts file, click Show Details. You're shown a list of all the contacts that will be affected if you go through with the change. Better yet, you get a Before and After button for each one, so you can see the discrepancies up close. That way, you can make an informed decision to sync or not to sync (that is, cancel).

Many conflict problems are not especially drastic. If iTunes discovers that, since the last sync, you've edited a single phone number or appointment in two different ways (once each on the iPhone and your computer), it lets you know with a message box.

You're offered two buttons:

- **Review Later.** This button actually means, "The computer's version wins for now. I'll ask you again the next time you sync."

- **Review Now.** You're shown the two changes, side by side, in a window. Click the one you think seems more authoritative; that's the one that will wind up prevailing on both machines. Then click Done.

Of course, the computer has to sync one more time to apply the change you've indicated. On the Mac, you're offered buttons that say Sync Now or

Sync Later; in Windows, the buttons say Sync Now or Cancel (meaning "Not now"). In both cases, you should click Sync Now to avoid confusion.

 Tip If you edit two *different* phone numbers on a single person's card—like a cellphone number on the PC and a fax number on the iPhone—that doesn't count as a conflict. Both machines will inherit both phone numbers.

iTunes considers it a conflict, and asks you to settle it, only when two changes were made to the *same* phone number.

One-Way Emergency Sync

In general, the iPhone's ability to handle bidirectional syncs is a blessing. It means that whenever you modify the information on one of your beloved machines, you won't have to duplicate that effort on the other one.

It can also get hairy. Depending on what merging, fussing, and button-clicking you do, it's possible to make a mess of your iPhone's address book or calendar. You could fill it with duplicate entries, or the wrong entries, or entries from a computer that you didn't intend to merge in there.

Fortunately, as a last resort, iTunes offers a *forced one-way sync* option, which makes your computer's version of things the official one. Everything on the iPhone gets replaced by the computer's version, just this once. At least you'll know exactly where all that information came from.

To do an emergency one-way sync, plug the iPhone into the computer with the USB cable. Click its icon in iTunes. On the Info tab, scroll all the way to the bottom, until you see the Advanced area. There it is: Replace the information on this iPhone, complete with checkboxes for the five things that iTunes can completely replace on the phone: Contacts, Calendars, Bookmarks, Notes, or Mail Accounts. Click Apply to start minty fresh.

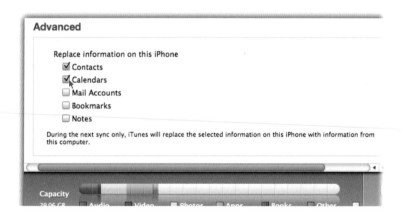

Backing Up the iPhone

You've spent all this time tweaking preferences, massaging settings, and getting everything just so on your brand-new iPhone. Wouldn't it be great if you could *back up* all that work so that if something bad happens to the phone, you wouldn't have to start from scratch?

With iTunes, you can. You get a backup every time the iPhone syncs with iTunes. The backup also happens before you install a new iPhone firmware version from Apple. iTunes also offers to do a backup before you use the Restore option described on the next page. iTunes backs up everything it doesn't already have a copy of: stuff you've downloaded to the phone (music, ebooks, apps, and so on), plus less visible things, like your iPhone's mail and network settings, your call history, contact favorites, notes, text messages, and other personal preferences that are hard or impossible to recreate.

Using That Backup

So the day has come when you really need to *use* that backup of your iPhone. Maybe it's become unstable, and it's crashing all over. Or maybe you just lost the dang thing, and you wish your replacement iPhone could have all of your old info and settings on it. Here's how to save the day (and your data):

❶ Connect the iPhone to the computer you normally use to sync with.

❷ When the iPhone pops up in the iTunes source list, click the Summary tab.

❸ Take a deep breath and click Restore. A message announces that after iTunes wipes your iPhone clean and installs a fresh version of the iPhone firmware, you can restore your personal data.

❹ Take iTunes up on its offer to restore all your settings and stuff from the backup. If you see multiple backup files listed from other iPhones (or an iPod Touch), be sure to pick the backup file for *your* phone. Let the backup restore your phone settings and info. Then resync all your music, videos, and podcasts. Exhale.

> **Tip** For the truly paranoid, there's nothing like a *backup* of your backup. Yes, you can actually back up the iTunes backup file, maybe on a flash drive for safekeeping. On a Mac, look in Home→Library→Application Support→MobileSync→Backup. In Windows XP, go to the C: drive→ Documents and Settings→Username→Application Data→Apple Computer→MobileSync→Backup. For Windows Vista or Windows 7, visit C: drive →User→App Data (hidden folder)→Roaming →Apple Computer→MobileSync→Backup.
>
> If you get in a situation where you need to restore your iPhone through iTunes on a different computer (say, if your old machine croaked), install iTunes on it and slip this backup file into the same folder on the new computer. Then follow the steps on page 339 to restore your data to the iPhone.

Deleting a Backup File

Want to delete the existing iPhone backup and start over completely from a little place called Square One? Go to the iTunes preferences (Edit→Preferences in Windows or iTunes→Preferences on the Mac) and click the Devices tab.

Click the dated backup file you don't want and hit Remove Backup. Then connect your iPhone and do one of the things described on page 338 to make yourself a new backup.

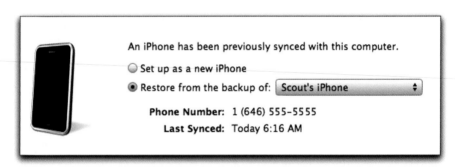

13 | MobileMe

Ever since the original Palm Pilot came along in 1996, the world has been captivated by the idea of having a pocket-sized satellite computer. Imagine having your whole address book and calendar on a tiny computer in your pocket!

Which is all fine, except for one thing: To bring that pocket-sized computer up to date, you have to connect it to your big computer with a cable. Worse, while you're away from your desk, your electronic datebook and Rolodex could be changing in different ways on your various machines as you and your family or coworkers make changes.

MobileMe, Apple's $100-a-year suite of Internet services, solves that problem rather neatly. It keeps your iPhone updated *constantly* with changes that are made to your Macs, PCs, or both. In fact, it keeps them *all* synced with one another: your Windows machine at work, your Macs at home, your spouse's iPod Touch, your kid's iPad, and, of course, your iPhone.

Make a change on your Mac, and watch it appear on your iPhone and your PC. Add a new friend to the address book in Outlook Express in Windows XP, and it appears in Windows Contacts on your Vista PC. Change an appointment in iCal on the kitchen Mac, and know that it will wirelessly wing its way onto your traveling spouse's iPhone four states away.

Not just your address book and calendar, either—*all your email* remains in sync (if you use the *yourname@me.com* address that comes with the service). And your Web bookmarks are the same everywhere, too.

In addition to your gadgets, there's another place you can view and edit your vital information: online, at *www.me.com*. That's a very handy feature when you're on the road somewhere, borrowing a PC.

There's a lot of other good stuff that comes with a MobileMe account. For example, you can upload pictures and movies to one of the best gallery sites on the Web. Stunning slideshows greet your visitors; your audience can, at your option, even download your photo files at full resolution for printing. You also get an iDisk, a virtual, multigigabyte hard drive where you can park, back up, or transfer files that are too big to send by email.

This chapter, though, concerns what MobileMe can do for you, the iPhone owner—including the awesome Find My iPhone, a feature you'll wish were on every cellphone ever made.

The Setup

MobileMe can keep your computer's mail, address book, and calendar in sync only if you use certain compatible programs:

- **Macintosh.** You have to use the built-in Mail, Address Book, and iCal programs.

- **Windows Vista or 7.** You can use Outlook (mail, address book, and calendar), Windows Live Mail (mail), and Windows Contacts (address book).

- **Windows XP.** MobileMe works with Outlook and Outlook Express.

No matter which kind of computer you have, it's *really important* to sync your iPhone with iTunes before you begin your MobileMe experiment. Check your computer's address book and calendar programs, for example, to make sure your data from the iPhone has indeed landed there.

To complete your setup in Windows, open the new MobileMe Preferences icon in your Control Panel. (It got deposited there when you installed iTunes.)

Then follow the steps at *www.apple.com/mobileme/setup/iphone/pc.html* and *www.apple.com/mobileme/setup/pc.*

To complete your setup on the Mac, open System Preferences, click MobileMe, and then follow the steps at *www.apple.com/mobileme/setup/iphone/mac.html* and *www.apple.com/mobileme/setup/mac.*

Finally, to set up your iPhone, start on the Home screen. Tap Settings→Fetch New Data; make sure it says Push, meaning that changes MobileMe picks up from other sources (Macs, PCs, or the Web) will be automatically beamed down to your phone.

Then, again from the main Settings page, tap Mail, Contacts, Calendars. If you don't see the name of your MobileMe account, then tap Add Account and fill in your name and password.

Next, tap the new MobileMe account name and turn on the kinds of data you want updated wirelessly (Mail, Contacts, Calendars, Bookmarks), and then tap Sync.

At this point, the copy of your data on the Web (the master information) *wipes out* what's currently on the iPhone. Of course, since you've recently synced the iPhone to your computer, the result should be…no change at all.

How It Works

From now on, the Web and your iPhone are in *instant* synchronization. If you make a change to your address book, calendar, bookmarks, or email on the iPhone, you'll find that the copies of those items at Me.com are updated in seconds, and vice versa.

That's true even with email: If you delete a piece of mail on your iPhone, or file it into a folder, you'll find that same message deleted or filed at Me.com. If you reply to a message on the iPhone, you'll find the response in the Sent Mail folder online, and vice versa.

Now then, what about your computers? They're part of the loop, too. Any change you make on *any* device (Mac, PC, iPhone, iPad, iPod Touch, Web site), to any kind of data (calendar, contacts, email, bookmarks), appears very soon on all the other machines you've set up.

In short, MobileMe is great for keeping (for example) your computers at home and at work in sync, or your desktop and your laptop—or all of them with your iPhone.

> **Note:** Avoid editing calendar appointments or address-book entries on your computer *while* a sync is going on (as indicated by the whirling arrows on the Mac menu bar or the Windows system tray). The changes you make won't get picked up by your other machines.

MobileMe on the iPhone

Once you've turned on MobileMe on the iPhone, everything is pretty much automatic. Just a few things to be aware of:

- **Turning off "push."** "Push" email, contacts, and calendar means that your iPhone is updated instantly, automatically, wirelessly, whenever changes are made to your email, address book, or calendar on the Web or on one of your computers.

    Push means never having to check for updates, but it also means faster battery drain. At Settings→Mail, Contacts, Calendars→Fetch New Data, you can turn the push feature *off* to save battery life when you're desperate. Now your iPhone checks for updates only on a schedule—every 15 minutes, every hour, or whatever you specify in the Fetch section here. (Except for Web bookmarks. They're always pushed, no matter what your setting here.)

Or, perhaps wisest of all, you can choose Manually. Now the iPhone updates the data in each program—Mail, Calendar, or Contacts—only when you *open* that program.

 Tip You can also specify push or fetch (on a schedule) settings for each *type* of data individually. You can make the calendar push, but the email fetch, and so on. To find these controls, tap Settings→Mail, Contacts, Calendars→Fetch New Data→Advanced.

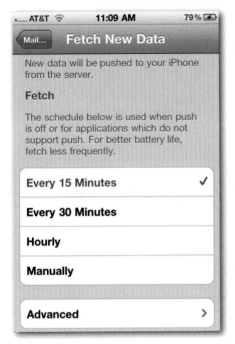 

- **Conflict Resolution.** What happens when you change an address book entry on one machine, and someone makes a *different* change to the same person's entry on another machine? How does MobileMe decide which change "wins"?

  Easy: It asks you. On your computer, a message alerts you to the conflict and offers you the chance to pick a "winner" right now, by comparing the conflicting entries and clicking the one you want.

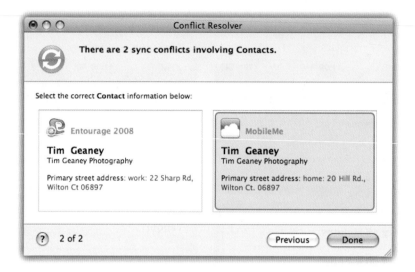

MobileMe Photos and Videos

The online photo gallery of Me.com is one of its juiciest features. It means any photos or movies you've uploaded (or published from iPhoto on the Mac, or sent straight from the iPhone) are available to anyone in the world, right on the Web. (Or anyone to whom you've provided the password, if you so desire.)

Uploading Straight from the iPhone

You can send photos and videos to your online gallery straight from the iPhone, wirelessly—an amazing, futuristic feature that's a blessing to photo-bloggers, photojournalists, and photo-lovers of all kinds.

The steps appear on page 152.

It's worth noting, though, that some useful options are lurking in each gallery when you visit it using your computer. Using your computer, log into *www. me.com*. Click the little cloud icon in the upper left to view the icons of the different MobileMe features; click the Gallery icon to view your photo galleries.

In the list at left, click the name of an album (gallery). Then click the Settings button, identified by the cursor on page 342.

Now you're looking at the master Settings box for this album. There are some very cool options here that aren't available from other Web gallery services. One of them is Downloading of photos, movies or entire album, which lets your audience download full-resolution, printable copies of your photos; full-length videos; or even a zipped-up, self-contained package of *all* the album's photos. You can also turn on Uploading of photos or movies via web browser, which means other people can submit their *own* photos and videos to your album—great after a social event.

You can even turn on Adding of photos via email or iPhone. When you turn that on, you'll be shown an email address that people can use to submit new photos right to the gallery—even from their phones.

When you're finished, click Publish.

Viewing Galleries on the iPhone

If you try to call up a MobileMe gallery on the iPhone itself, you get the peculiar little screen shown at left below. It's telling you that you need an app for that—a special MobileMe Gallery app. Tap Install Gallery App to go download it.

From now on, when you want to view your online albums, open your Gallery. It offers a tidy list of all your albums, with quick access and beautiful slide-shows—right on the iPhone (previous page, right). There's even a little ✉ icon that lets you email a link to a particularly excellent shot.

Find My iPhone

If you have MobileMe and an iPhone, then you've got a piece of real magic at your disposal: the ingeniously named Find My iPhone. The bottom line: If you ever lose your iPhone, you have a fighting chance at getting it back.

You can make the iPhone beep loudly for 2 minutes—even if the ringer switch is off, and even if the phone is asleep—so you can figure out what couch cushion it's under, or what jacket pocket you left it in. You can also make a message pop up on the screen; if you actually left the iPhone in a taxi or on some restaurant table, you can use this feature plead for its return.

If an ethical person finds your phone, you might get it back. If it's a greedy person who says, "Hey, cool! A free iPhone!" then maybe you can bombard him with so many of these messages that he gives it back in exasperation.

If not, and if you're worried about some stranger seeing all your private email and listening to your most private pop songs, you can either lock the phone with a password (yes, by remote control) or even avail yourself of one more amazing last-ditch feature: Remote Wipe.

That means *erasing your iPhone by remote control,* from wherever you happen to be. The evil thief can do nothing but stare in amazement as the phone suddenly erases itself, winding up completely empty.

(If you ever get the phone back, you can just sync with iTunes, and presto! Your stuff is back on the phone—at least everything since your last sync.)

The Setup

To get started, from the Home screen, tap Settings→Mail, Contacts, Calendars. Tap the name of your Me.com account. Turn on Find My iPhone.

That's it; your phone is now ready for some remote-control magic.

The Action

If the worst should come to pass and you can't find your phone, go to any computer and call up *www.me.com*. Log in with your MobileMe name and password.

Click the cloud icon at upper left; in the list of MobileMe features, click Find My iPhone. If you're asked for your password again, type it; Apple wants to make sure it's really, *really* you who's messing around with your account settings.

Finally, in the panel on the left side, click the name of your iPhone.

Immediately, the Web site updates to show you, on a map, the current location of your iPhone. (It doesn't have to be turned on, but it does have to have power.) The location process can take a couple of minutes. You can zoom into or out of the map, or click Satellite to see an overhead photo of the area, or click Hybrid to see the photo with street names superimposed.

If just knowing where the thing *is* isn't enough to satisfy you, click the little pushpin that represents your phone, and try one of these three buttons:

- **Display Message or Play Sound.** Click this button, type a message, and then click Send. Instantly, that message appears on the iPhone's screen, wherever it is, no matter what app was running—even if it was asleep. Whoever's using it can't miss it, can't even do anything without dismissing the message.

Tip If you turn on Play a sound for 2 minutes, then the phone will also start dinging and vibrating—a great option if the iPhone hasn't been so much *stolen* as *misplaced* in your own home or office. (Unfortunately, the volume of the dinging is determined by the current ring-volume setting; if it's turned down, you might not hear much.)

When it's all over, Apple sends an email confirmation to your @me.com address.

- **Lock.** What if you worry about the security of your phone's info, but you don't want to erase it completely, and just want to throw a low-level veil of casual protection over the thing? Easy: Just lock it by remote control. The Lock button lets you make up a four-digit passcode (which overrides the one you already had on the phone, if any). Without it, the sleazy crook can't get into your phone without erasing it.

- **Remote Wipe.** This is the last-ditch security option described earlier, for when your immediate concern isn't so much the phone as all the private stuff that's on it. Click this button, confirm the dire warning box, and click Erase All Data. By remote control, you've just erased everything from your iPhone, wherever it may be. (Fortunately, if it's ever returned, you can just sync it with iTunes and get everything back—everything since your last sync.)

Once you've wiped the phone, you can no longer find it or send messages to it using Find My iPhone.

There's an app for this,too. Download the Find My iPhone app from the App Store. It lets you do everything described above from another iPhone, in a tidy, simple control panel.

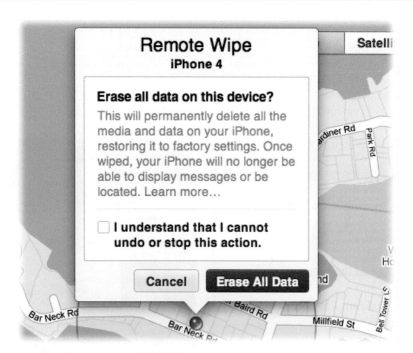

iDisk

The iDisk is yet another cool MobileMe feature. It's essentially an external hard drive—really, *really* external. In fact, it's on the Internet.

But you can bring its icon to your Mac or PC screen and load it up with files—which are then accessible from any *other* computer. And now, thanks to the iDisk app, even from your iPhone.

Grab the iDisk app from the iTunes Store. When you open it and log in, you see a list of everything you've ever put onto your iDisk.

Some of this stuff you can open right on the phone—pictures, movies, PDF documents, Word documents, PowerPoint files, Excel spreadsheets, and so on—and some of it you can't.

But the cool part is that you can email any of it, right from the phone. You're stuck on a plane on the runway in Raleigh, and your boss in Boston needs the Franklin file ASAP? No problem. You can forward it along right from the iDisk app, even if it's some huge 250-megabyte file that would never fit in an email—and even if it's a file type the iPhone can't open, as shown below.

To do that, tap the file you want to pass along (below, left). On the Details screen that appears (below, right), tap the 🔊 button. Tap Share & Email Link. An outgoing email message appears; address it, add a note if you like, and then tap Send.

Your recipients won't get an attachment; instead, they'll get a link they can click to download the file directly from your MobileMe account. Fast, easy, and incredibly convenient.

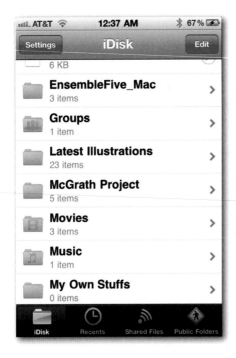

14

The Corporate iPhone

N o, the chapter name "The Corporate iPhone" is not an oxymoron. Yes, in its younger days, people thought of the iPhone as a *personal* device, meant for consumers and not for corporations. But somebody at Apple must have gotten sick of hearing, "Well, the iPhone is cool, but it's no BlackBerry." These days, the iPhone is nipping at the BlackBerry's heels. The iPhone, especially in iOS 4, now has the security and compatibility features your corporate technical overlords require.

Even better, the iPhone can talk to Microsoft Exchange ActiveSync servers, staples of corporate computer departments that, among other things, keep smartphones wirelessly updated with the calendar, contacts, and email back at the office. (Yes, it sounds a lot like MobileMe. Which is probably why Apple's MobileMe slogan was, "Exchange for the rest of us.")

The Perks

This chapter is intended for you, the iPhone owner—not for the highly paid, well-trained, exceedingly friendly IT (information technology) managers at your company.

Your first task is to convince them that your iPhone is now secure and compatible enough to welcome into the company's network. Here's some information you can use:

- **Microsoft Exchange ActiveSync.** Exchange ActiveSync is the technology that keeps smartphones wirelessly synced with the data on the mother ship's computers. The iPhone now works with Exchange ActiveSync, so it can remain in wireless contact with your company's Exchange servers exactly like BlackBerries and Windows Mobile phones do.

(*Exchange ActiveSync* is not to be confused with regular old *ActiveSync,* which is a much older technology that's designed to update smartphones and palmtops over a cable.)

Your email, address book, and calendar appointments are now sent wirelessly to your iPhone so it's always kept current—and they're sent in a way that those evil rival firms can't intercept. (It uses 128-bit encrypted SSL, if you must know.)

 Tip That's the same encryption used by Outlook Web Access (OWA), which lets employees check their email, calendar, and contacts from any Web browser. In other words, if your IT administrators are willing to let you access your data using OWA, they should also be willing to let you access it with the iPhone.

- **Mass setup.** Using a free software program for Mac or Windows called the iPhone Configuration Utility, your company's network geeks can set up a bunch of iPhones all at once.

  This program generates iPhone *profiles* (.mobileconfig files): canned iPhone setups that determine all WiFi, network, password, email, and VPN settings.

  The IT manager can email this file to you, or post it on a secure Web page; either way, you can just open that file on your iPhone, and presto—you're all configured and set up. And the IT manager never has to handle the phones individually.

  Said manager can now send you new custom apps wirelessly, without your having to sync up to iTunes.

- **Security.** In the event of the unthinkable—you lose your iPhone, or it gets stolen, and vital company secrets are now "in the wild," susceptible to discovery by your company's rivals—network administrators have a handy tool at their disposal. They can erase your entire iPhone by remote control, even though they have no idea where it is or who has it. (As page 315 makes clear, MobileMe members can do this on a personal iPhone, too.)

  The iPhone can connect to wireless networks using the latest, super-secure connections (WPA Enterprise and WPA2 Enterprise), which are highly resistant to hacker attacks. And when you're using virtual private networking, as described at the end of this chapter, you can use a very secure VPN protocol called IPSec. That's what most companies use for secure, encrypted remote access to the corporate network. Juniper and Cisco VPN apps are available, too.

Speaking of security: Not only does iOS 4 let you create much tougher-to-crack passwords than the feeble four-digit passwords of time gone by, but this password now encrypts all email, email attachments, and the data of any apps that are written to take advantage of this feature.

 This Data Protection feature isn't available on the 3G or original iPhones. It requires an iPhone with 32 GB of memory or more. And it requires doing a full Restore from an iTunes backup.

- **Fewer tech-support calls.** Finally, don't forget to point out to the IT staff how rarely you'll need to call them for tech support. It's pretty clear the iPhone is easier to figure out than, ahem, certain rival smartphones.

And what's in it for you? Complete synchronization of your email, address book, and calendar with what's on your PC at work. Send an email from your iPhone, find it in the Sent folder of Outlook at the office. And so on.

You can also accept invitations to meetings on your iPhone that are sent your way by coworkers; if you accept, they're added to your calendar automatically, just as on your PC. You can also search the company's master address book, right from your iPhone.

The biggest perk for you, though, is just getting permission to *use* an iPhone as your company-issued phone.

Setup

Once you've convinced the IT squad of the iPhone's work-worthiness, they can set up things on their end by consulting Apple's free, downloadable setup guide: the infamous *iPhone OS Enterprise Deployment Guide.* (It incorporates Apple's individual, smaller guides for setting up Microsoft Exchange, Cisco IPSec VPN, IMAP email, and Device Configuration profiles.)

This guide is filled with handy tips, like: "On the Front-End Server, verify that a server certificate is installed and enable SSL for the Exchange ActiveSync virtual directory (require basic SSL authentication)."

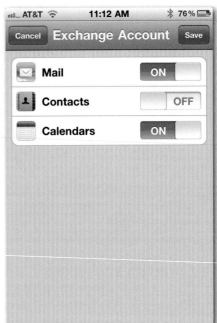

In any case, you (or they) can download the deployment guide from this site: *www.apple.com/support/iphone/enterprise.*

At that point, they must grant you and your iPhone permission to access the company's Exchange server using Exchange ActiveSync. Fortunately, if you're already allowed to use Outlook Web Access, then you probably have permission to connect with your iPhone, too.

The steps for *you,* the lowly worker bee, to set up your iPhone for accessing your company's Exchange ActiveSync server are much simpler.

First, set up your iPhone with your corporate email account, if that hasn't been done for you. Tap Settings→Mail, Contacts, Calendars→Add Account→Microsoft Exchange. Fill in your work email address, user name, and password as they were provided to you by your company's IT person. The Username box is the only potentially tricky spot.

Sometimes, your user name is just the first part of your email address—so if your email address is *smithy@worldwidewidgets.com*, then your user name is simply *smithy.*

In other companies, though, you may also need to know your *Windows domain* and stick that in front of the user name, in the format *domain\user name* (for example, *wwwidgets\smithy*). In some companies, this is exactly how you log into your PC at work or into Outlook Web Access. If you aren't sure, try your user name by itself first; if that doesn't work, then try *domain\ user name.* And if *that* doesn't work, then you'll probably have to ask your IT people for the info.

Incidentally, what's in the Description field doesn't matter. It can be whatever you want to call this particular email account ("Gol-durned Work Stuff," for example).

When you're finished plugging in these details, tap Next at the top of the screen.

If your company is using Exchange 2007 or later, that should be all there is to it. You're now presented with the list of corporate information that the iPhone can sync itself with: Email, Contacts, and Calendars. This is your opportunity to turn *off* any of these things if you don't particularly care to have them sent to your iPhone. (You can always change your mind in Settings.)

However, if your company uses Exchange 2003 (or 2007/2010 with AutoDiscovery turned off—they'll know what that means), you're now asked to provide the *server* address. It's often the same address you'd use to get to the Web version of your Outlook account, like *owa.widgetsworldwide.com*. But if in doubt, here again, your company techie should be able to assist. Only then do you get to the screen where you choose which kinds of data to sync.

And that's it. Your iPhone will shortly bloom with the familiar sight of your office email stash, calendar appointments, and contacts.

Life on the Corporate Network

Once your iPhone is set up, you should be in wireless corporate heaven.

- **Email.** Your corporate email account shows up among whatever other email accounts you've set up (Chapter 11); you can view it in the new unified Inbox, if you like. In fact, you can now have *multiple* Exchange accounts on the same phone. And not only is your email "pushed" to the phone (it arrives as it's sent, without your having to explicitly *check* for messages), but it's also synced with what you see on your computer at work. If you send, receive, delete, flag, or file any messages on your iPhone, you'll find them sent, received, deleted, flagged, or filed on your computer at the office. And vice versa.

  All the iPhone email niceties described in Chapter 11 are available to your corporate mail: opening attachments, rotating and zooming into them, and so on. Your iPhone can even play back your office voicemail, presuming your company has one of those unified messaging systems that send out WAV audio file versions of your messages via email.

  Oh—and when you're addressing an outgoing message, the iPhone's autocomplete feature consults *both* your built-in iPhone address book *and* the corporate directory (on the Exchange server) simultaneously.

- **Contacts.** In the address book, you gain a new superpower: You can search your company's master name directory right from the iPhone. That's great when you need to track down, say, the art director in your Singapore branch.

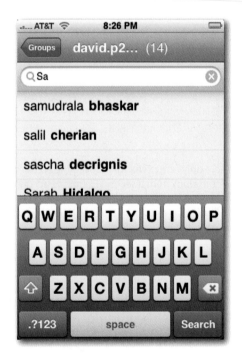

To perform this search, tap Contacts on the Home screen. Tap the Groups button in the upper-left corner. On the Groups screen, a new section appears that mere mortal iPhone owners never see: Directories. Just beneath it, tap the name of your Exchange account ("Gol-durned Work Stuff," for example).

On the following screen, start typing the name of the person you're looking up; the resulting matches appear as you type. (Or type the whole name, and then tap Search.)

In the list of results, tap the name you want. That person's Info screen appears so you can tap to dial a number or compose a preaddressed email message. (You can't send a text message to someone in the corporate phone book, however.)

- **Calendar.** Your iPhone's calendar is wirelessly kept in sync with the master calendar back at the office. If you're on the road and your minions make changes to your schedule in Outlook, you'll know about it; you'll see the change on your iPhone's calendar.

  There are some other changes to your calendar, too, as you'll find out in a moment.

 Tip Don't forget that you can save battery power, syncing time, and mental clutter by limiting how much *old* calendar stuff gets synced to your iPhone. (How often do you really look back on your calendar to see what happened more than a month ago?) Page 386 has the details.

Exchange + Your Stuff

The iPhone can display calendar and contact information from multiple sources at once—your Exchange calendar/address book and your own personal data, for example. (Be grateful. It wasn't always this way.)

Here's how it works: Open your iPhone calendar. Tap the Calendars button at the top left.

Now you're looking at the complete list of calendar *categories*. Here's what you might find there:

- **All Calendars.** This button, at the very top, takes you to your *single, unified* calendar, showing all appointments from your Exchange account,

MobileMe, maybe your Google or Yahoo calendars, and your Mac's or PC's calendar program. No wonder you've been feeling so busy.

- **All [your MobileMe name].** Tap this one to see all your MobileMe categories on the same calendar (Social, School, Kids, and so on).

- **Google calendar [or another CalDAV subscription].** Tap this one to see all the events listed on some Internet-based calendar to which you've subscribed.

- **[Your Exchange account name.]** Tap this button to see only your work calendar. (You may see subcategories, if your company uses them, listed under the Exchange heading, bearing color-coded dots.)

- **Home, Personal, Social....** Tap one of the individual category names to see *only* that category of your MobileMe, Exchange, or personal calendar.

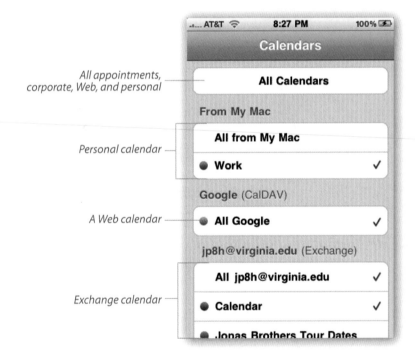

All appointments, corporate, Web, and personal

Personal calendar

A Web calendar

Exchange calendar

You can pull off a similar stunt in Contacts. Whenever you're looking at your list of contacts, you can tap the Groups button (top left of the screen). Here, once again, you can tap All Contacts to see a combined address book—or you can look over only your MobileMe contacts, your Exchange contacts, your personal contacts, and so on. Or tap [group name] to view only the people in your tennis circle, book club, or whatever (if you've created groups); or [your Exchange account name] to search only the company listings.

Invitations

If you've spent much time in the world of Microsoft Outlook (that is, corporate America), then you already know about *invitations.* These are electronic invitations that coworkers send you directly from Outlook. When you get one of these invitations by email, you can click Accept, Decline, or Tentative.

If you click Accept, then the meeting gets dropped onto the proper date in your Outlook calendar, and your name gets added to the list of attendees maintained by the person who invited you. If you click Tentative, then the meeting is flagged *that* way, on both your calendar and the sender's.

Exchange meeting invitations on the iPhone show up in *four places,* just to make sure you don't miss them:

- **In your face.** An incoming invitation pops up as a translucent alert, no matter what you're doing. Tap Close to get rid of it or View to open its Info screen. That's where you can read what it's about, who else is coming, and where it's taking place.

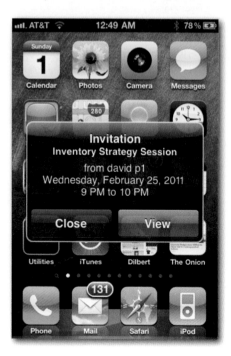
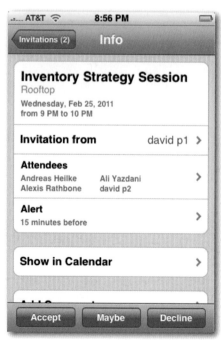

Here's also where you can tap Accept, Maybe, or Decline. ("Maybe" = Outlook's "Tentative.")

 Tip If you scroll down the Info screen, you'll see Add Comments. If you tap here and type a response, it will be automatically emailed to the meeting leader when you tap one of the response buttons (Accept, Maybe, Decline). (Otherwise, the leader gets an empty email message, containing only your response to the invitation.)

Tapping Decline deletes the invitation from every corner of your iPhone, although it will sit in your Mail program's Trash for a while in case you change your mind.

- **On your Home screen.** The Calendar icon on your Home screen sprouts a red, circled number, indicating how many invites you haven't yet looked at.

- **In email.** Invitations also appear as attachments to messages in your corporate email account, just as they would if you were using Outlook. Tap the name of the attachment to open the invitation Info window.

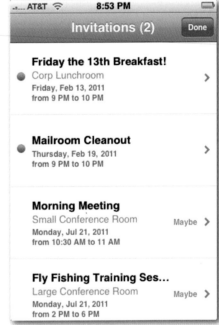

- **In Calendar.** When your iPhone is connected to your company's Exchange calendars, there's a twist: An Inbox button appears at the lower-right corner of your Calendar program.

  When an invite (or several) is waiting for you, a red, circled number appears on this icon, letting you know you've got waiting invitations to attend to (and telling you how many). Tap the Inbox icon to see the Invitations list, which summarizes all invitations you've accepted, maybe'd, or not responded to yet.

 Tip Invitations you haven't dealt with also show up on the Calendar's list view or day view with a dotted outline. That's the iPhone's clever visual way of showing you just how severely your workday will be ruined if you accept this meeting.

You can also *generate* invitations. When you're filling out the Info form for a new appointment, you get a new field that doesn't appear on a non-Exchange iPhone—Invitees. Tap there to enter the email addresses of the people you'd like to invite.

Your invitation will show up in whatever calendar programs they use, and they'll never know you didn't send it from some corporate copy of Microsoft Outlook.

A Word on Troubleshooting

If you're having trouble with your Exchange syncing and can't find any steps that work, ask your Exchange administrators to make sure that ActiveSync's settings are correct on their end. You've heard the old saying that in 99 percent of computer troubleshooting, the problem lies between the keyboard and the chair? The other 1 percent of the time, it's between the *administrator's* keyboard and the chair.

> **Tip** You can access your company's SharePoint sites, too. That's a Microsoft document-collaboration feature that's also a common part of corporate online life.
>
> The iPhone's browser can access these sites; it can also open Word, Excel, PowerPoint, and PDF documents you find there. Handy indeed!

Virtual Private Networking (VPN)

The typical corporate network is guarded by a team of steely-eyed administrators for whom Job One is preventing access by unauthorized visitors. They perform this job primarily with the aid of a super-secure firewall that seals off the company's network from the Internet.

So how can you tap into the network from the road? Only one solution is both secure and cheap: the *virtual private network,* or VPN. Running a VPN lets you create a super-secure "tunnel" from your iPhone, across the Internet, and straight into your corporate network. All data passing through this tunnel is heavily encrypted. To the Internet eavesdropper, it looks like so much undecipherable gobbledygook.

VPN is, however, a corporate tool, run by corporate nerds. Your company's tech staff can tell you whether or not there's a VPN server set up for you to use.

If they do have one, then you'll need to know the type of server it is. The iPhone can connect to VPN servers that speak *PPTP* (Point-to-Point Tunneling Protocol) and *L2TP/IPSec* (Layer 2 Tunneling Protocol over the IP Security Protocol), both relatives of the PPP language spoken by modems. Most corporate VPN servers work with at least one of these protocols.

The iPhone can also connect to Cisco servers, which are among the most popular systems in corporate America, and with a special app, Juniper's Junos Pulse servers, too.

To set up your VPN connection, visit Settings→General→Network→VPN. Tap the On/Off switch to make the VPN configuration screen pop up. Tap L2TP, PPTP, or IPSec (that's the Cisco one), depending on which kind of server your company uses (ask the network administrator).

The most critical bits of information to fill in are these:

- **Server.** The Internet address of your VPN server (for example, *vpn.ferrets-r-us.com*).

- **Account; Password.** Here's your user account name and password, as supplied by the IT guys.

- **Secret.** If your office offers L2TP connections, then you'll need yet another password called a Shared Secret to ensure that the server you're connecting to is really the server you intend to connect to.

Once you know everything is in place, the iPhone can connect to the corporate network and fetch your corporate mail. You don't have to do anything special on your end; everything works just as described in this chapter.

VPN on Demand

If you like to access your corporate email or internal Web site a few times a day, having to enter your name-and-password credentials over and over again can get old fast. Fortunately, iOS 4 offers a huge time-saving assist with its introduction of *VPN on Demand.*

That is, you just open up Safari and tap the corporate bookmark; the iPhone creates the VPN channel automatically, behind the scenes, and connects.

There's nothing you have to do, or even anything you *can* do, to make this feature work; your company's network nerds have to turn this feature on at their end.

They'll create a *configuration profile* that you'll install on your iPhone. It includes the VPN server settings, an electronic security certificate, and a list of domains and URLs that will automatically turn on the iPhone's VPN feature.

From now on, whenever you open Safari and try to visit a Web page that's behind the company's firewall, the iPhone makes the VPN connection for you automatically. You're spared the hassle of entering a user name or password.

When your iPhone goes to sleep, it terminates the VPN connection, both for security purposes and to save battery power.

 Clearly, eliminating the VPN sign-in process also weakens the security that the VPN was invented for in the first place. Therefore, you'd be well advised—and probably required by your IT guys—to use the iPhone's password feature (page 376), so some evil corporate spy (or teenage thug) can't just steal your iPhone and start snooping through your corporate servers.

15 Settings

Your iPhone is a full-blown computer—well, at least a half-blown one. And like any good computer, it's customizable. The Settings application, right there on your Home screen, is like the Control Panel in Windows, or System Preferences on the Mac. It's a tweaking center that affects every aspect of the iPhone: the screen, ringtones, email, Web connection, and so on.

You scroll the Settings list as you would any iPhone list: by dragging your finger up or down the screen.

Most of the items on the Settings page are doorways to other screens, where you make the actual changes. When you're finished inspecting or changing the preference settings, you can return to the main Settings screen by tapping the Settings button in the upper-left corner—or just pressing the Home button.

In this book, you can read about the iPhone's preference settings in the appropriate spots—wherever they're relevant. But so you'll also have it all in one place, here's an item-by-item walkthrough of the Settings application.

Airplane Mode

As you're probably aware, you're not allowed to use cellphones on airplanes. According to legend (if not science), a cellphone's radio can interfere with a plane's navigation equipment.

But the iPhone does a lot more than make calls. Are you supposed to deprive yourself of all the music, videos, movies, and email that you could be using in flight, just because cellphones are forbidden?

Nope. Just turn on Airplane mode by tapping the Off button at the top of the Settings list (so the orange On button appears). Now it's safe (and permitted) to use the iPhone in flight—at least after takeoff, when you hear the announcement about "approved electronics"—because the cellular and WiFi features of the iPhone are turned off completely. You can't make calls or get online, but you can do anything else in the iPhone's bag of nonwireless tricks.

WiFi

WiFi—wireless Internet networking—is one of the iPhone's best features. This item in Settings opens the WiFi Networks screen, where you'll find three useful controls:

- **WiFi On/Off.** If you don't plan to use WiFi, turning it off gets you a lot more life out of each battery charge. Tap anywhere on this On/Off slider to change its status.

 Note: Turning on Airplane mode automatically turns off the WiFi antenna—but you can turn WiFi back on. That's handy when you're in one of those rare, amazing airplanes with WiFi on board.

- **Choose a Network.** Here you'll find a list of all nearby WiFi networks that the iPhone can "see," complete with a signal-strength indicator and a padlock icon if a password is required. An Other item lets you access WiFi networks that are invisible and secret unless you know their names. See Chapter 9 for details on using WiFi with the iPhone.

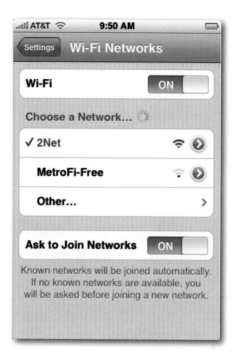

- **Ask to Join Networks.** If this option is On, then whenever you attempt to get online (to check email or the Web, for example), the iPhone sniffs around to find a WiFi network. If it finds one you haven't used before, the iPhone invites you, with a small dialog box, to hop onto it.

So why would you ever want to turn this feature off? To avoid getting bombarded with invitations to join WiFi networks, which can happen in heavily populated areas, and to save battery power. (The phone will still hop automatically onto hot spots it's joined in the past.)

Carrier

If you see this panel at all, then you're doubly lucky. First, you're enjoying a trip overseas; second, you have a choice of cellphone carriers who have roaming agreements with AT&T. Tap your favorite and prepare to pay some serious roaming fees.

Notifications

This Settings panel, new in iOS 4, lists all the apps that think they have the right to nag for your attention. Flight-tracking programs alert you that there's an hour before takeoff. Social-networking programs ping you when someone's trying to reach you. Games let you know when it's your move (in a game against someone else online). Instant-messaging apps ding to let you know that you have a new message. It can add up to a lot of interruption.

On this panel, you can tap an app's name one to see three On/Off switches for it: Sounds (alert noises), Alerts (blue text balloons that appear in front of whatever you're doing, and even wake the phone if necessary), and Badges (the circled number that you see on, for example, your Mail app icon, telling you how many new messages you have). By turning certain things off, you can reduce that feeling of sensory overload from your phone.

Sounds

Here's a more traditional cellphone settings screen: the place where you choose a ringtone sound for incoming calls.

- **Silent Vibrate, Ring Vibrate.** Like any self-respecting cellphone, the iPhone has a Vibrate mode—a little shudder in your pocket that might get your attention when you can't hear the ringing. As you can see, there are two On/Off controls for the vibration: one for when the phone is in Silent mode (page 18), and one for when the ringer's on.

- **Ring Volume.** The slider here controls the volume of the phone's ringing. Of course, it's usually faster to adjust the ring volume by pressing the up/down buttons on the left edge whenever you're not on a call.

- **Ringtone.** Tap this row to view the iPhone's list of 25 built-in ringtones, plus any new ones you've added yourself (see Chapter 4). Tap a ring sound to hear it. After you've tapped one you like, confirm your choice by tapping at the top of the screen. You've just selected your *default* (standard) ringtone. Tap Sounds to return to the Sounds screen.

 Note Of course, you can choose a different ringtone for each person in your phone book (page 63). You can also set up a "vibrate, then ring" effect (page 105).

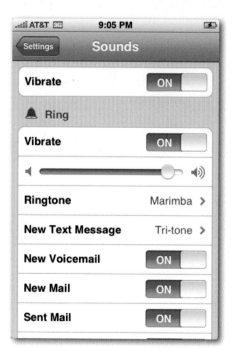

- **New Text Message, New Voicemail, New Mail, Sent Mail...** These On/ Off switches let you silence the little sounds the iPhone plays to celebrate various events: the arrival of new voicemail, text messages, or mail; the successful sending of an outgoing email message; calendar events arriving; locking the iPhone by tapping the Sleep/Wake switch on the top of the phone; and typing on the virtual keyboard. (Note that you can choose a ringtone for the arrival of new text messages—or None.)

Brightness

Ordinarily, the iPhone controls its own screen brightness. An ambient-light sensor hidden behind the smoked glass at the top of the iPhone's face samples the room brightness each time you wake the phone and adjusts the brightness automatically: brighter in bright rooms, dimmer in darker ones.

When you prefer more manual control, here's what you can do:

- **Brightness slider.** Drag the handle on this slider, or just tap on the slider, to control the screen brightness manually, keeping in mind that more brightness means shorter battery life.

  If Auto-Brightness is turned on, then the changes you make here are relative to the iPhone's self-chosen brightness. In other words, if you goose the brightness by 20 percent, then the screen will always be 20 percent brighter than the iPhone would have chosen for itself.

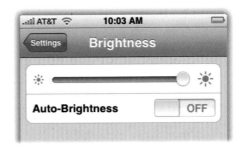

- **Auto-Brightness On/Off.** Tap anywhere on this switch to disable the ambient-light sensor completely. Now the brightness of the screen is under complete manual control.

Wallpaper

Wallpaper can mean either the photo on the Unlock screen (what you see when you wake the iPhone up), or the background picture on your Home screen. On this panel, you can change the image used for either one. Page 148 has step-by-step instructions.

General

The General pages offer a *huge,* motley assortment of settings governing the behavior of the virtual keyboard, the Bluetooth transmitter, the iPhone's little-known password-protection feature, and about six trillion other things.

- **About.** Tapping this item opens a page for the statistics nut. Here you can find out how many songs your iPhone holds; how much storage your iPhone has; techie details like the iPhone's software and firmware versions, serial number, model, WiFi and Bluetooth addresses; and so on. (It's kind of cool to see how many applications you've installed.)

- **Usage.** The first option here, Battery Percentage, is an iPhone feature that wound up on this screen for no apparent reason; still, it's nice. Turn it On to see your battery gauge with a numeric percentage readout (for example, "89%").

  The Usage readout shows, in hours and minutes, how much time you've spent using all iPhone functions since the last time it was charged up (although it's not broken down by activity, alas). Standby is how much time the iPhone has spent in sleep mode, awaiting calls.

  The two statistics under Call Time tell you how much time you've spent talking on the iPhone, broken down by Current Period (that is, this AT&T billing month) and in the iPhone's entire Lifetime. That's right, folks: For what's probably the first time in history, a cellphone actually keeps track of your minutes, to help you avoid exceeding the number you've signed up for (and therefore racking up 45-cent overage minutes).

  Finally, the Sent and Received tallies indicate how much you've used the Internet, expressed as kilobytes or megabytes of data, including email messages and Web-page material. These are extremely important statistics, because your iPhone plan is probably capped at 250 megabytes or 2 gigabytes a month. (There's no longer an AT&T unlimited-data plan, although people who had this plan before the new capped-data plans were introduced have been allowed to keep it.)

If you exceed your monthly maximum, you're instantly charged another $15 or $10 for another chunk of data. So keeping an eye on these statistics is a very good idea.

The Reset Statistics button, of course, sets all these counters back to zero.

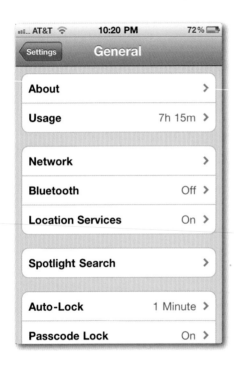 

- **Network.** Tap Network to open a screen containing five items.

  One is Enable 3G, which lets you turn off the iPhone's 3G radio when you'd rather have battery life than high Internet speed; see Chapter 9.

  Another is Cellular Data, new in iOS 4. It's a reaction to AT&T's capped-monthly-data plans, described above. For example, if you see that you've already used up 248 of your monthly 250-meg allotment, you might want to turn your Internet features off for a couple of days to make sure you don't go over the limit. Your smartphone becomes a dumbphone, suitable for making calls but not getting online, but at least you won't trigger that $15 overage fee. (You can still get online in a WiFi hot spot.)

Then there's Data Roaming, which refers to the iPhone's ability to get online when you're outside AT&T's U.S. network. Unless you're particularly wealthy, leave this item turned off. Otherwise, you might run up unexpectedly massive AT&T charges (like $5,000 for two weeks) when you're overseas because your iPhone continues to check for new mail every few minutes.

Up next: Internet Tethering, the On/Off switch for the iPhone' new ability to act as an Internet antenna for your laptop; see page 250.

The next is VPN, for virtual private networking. A VPN is a secure, encrypted tunnel that carries the data from one computer, across the Internet, and into a company's computers; see page 364.

The final item on the Network page is Wi-Fi, which is an exact duplicate of the WiFi controls described on page 368.

- **Bluetooth.** Here's the On/Off switch for the iPhone's Bluetooth transmitter, which is required to communicate with a Bluetooth earpiece, keyboard, laptop (for tethering), or hands-free system in a car. When you turn the switch on, you're offered the chance to pair the iPhone with other Bluetooth equipment; the paired gadgets are listed here for ease of connecting and disconnecting.

- **Location Services.** Almost everybody loves how the iPhone can determine where you are on a map, geotag your photos, find the closest ATM, tell your friends where you're hanging out, and so on. A few people, however, appreciate being able to turn *off* the iPhone's location circuits. Either they imagine that shadowy agencies can somehow tap in and track their comings and goings, or they just want to save some battery power.

  This screen lists every app that uses your location information, and lets you turn off this feature on a per-app basis. (The little ➹ icon indicates which apps have actually *used* your location data in the past 24 hours.)

- **Spotlight Search.** New in iOS 4: You can control which kinds of things Spotlight finds when it searches your phone. Tap to turn off the kinds of data you don't want it to search: Mail, Notes, Calendar, whatever.

 Tip You can also drag these categories into a new order, using the little ☰ as a handle. Why? Because that's the order that things will appear in the results list when you actually perform a search. If you mainly search your text messages, for example, by all means drag Messages to the top of the list, so they'll appear first.

- **Auto-Lock.** As you may have noticed, the iPhone locks itself after a few minutes of inactivity on your part. In locked mode, the iPhone ignores screen taps.

  All cellphones (and iPods) offer locked mode. On this machine, however, locking is especially important because the screen is so big. Reaching into your pocket for a toothpick or a ticket stub could, at least theoretically, fire up some iPhone program or even dial a call from the confines of your pocket.

  On the Auto-Lock screen, you can change the interval of inactivity before the auto-lock occurs (1 minute, 2 minutes, and so on), or you can tap Never. In that case, the iPhone locks only when you send it to sleep.

- **Passcode Lock.** Here, you can make up a password that you have to enter whenever you wake up the iPhone. If you don't know the password, you can't use the iPhone. It's designed to keep your stuff private from other people in the house or the office, or to protect your information in case you lose the iPhone.

  To begin, tap to turn Simple Passcode off, if you like. This is a new iOS 4 feature. It specifies what kind of password you want to use. If Simple Passcode is on, then you'll have a four-digit number, as in years past—convenient, but not so impossible to guess. If you turn it off, you'll be allowed to make up a full-blown, long, complicated, alphanumeric one.

  Now tap Turn Passcode On. You're asked to type in the password you want, either on the number keypad (for Simple Passcodes) or the alphabet keyboard. You're asked to do it again to make sure you didn't make a typo.)

 Note: Don't kid around with this passcode. It's a much more serious deal than the iPod passcode. If you forget the iPhone code, you'll have to restore your iPhone (page 339), which wipes out everything on it. You've still got most of the data on your computer, of course (music, video, contacts, calendar), but you may lose text messages, mail, and so on.

Once you confirm your password, you return to the Passcode Lock screen. Here you have a few more options.

For example, the Require Passcode option lets you specify how quickly the password is requested before locking somebody out: immediately after the iPhone wakes or 1, 15, 30, 60, or 240 minutes later. (Those options are a convenience to you, so you can quickly check your calendar or missed messages without having to enter the passcode—while still protecting your data from, for example, evildoers who pick up your iPhone while you're out getting coffee.)

The On/Off switch for Voice Dial is here, too. Remember, you can voice-dial even when the phone is locked; if you're concerned enough about security to want a passcode, then you might not want a thief blindly voice-dialing your colleagues. If you turn Voice Dial off, then pressing the Home button still produces the Voice Controls screen, but you can't actually dial; the phone says only, "Voice dialing disabled."

Finally, here is Erase Data—an option that's scary and reassuring at the same time. When this option is on, then if someone makes 10 guesses at your passcode, your iPhone erases itself. It's assuming that some lowlife burglar is trying to crack into it to have a look at all your personal data.

This option, a pertinent one for professional people, presents potent protection from patient password guessers.

 Note Even when the phone is locked and the password unguessable, a tiny blue Emergency Call button still appears on the unlock screen. It's there just in case you've been conked on the head by a vase, you can't remember your own password, and you need to call 911.

- **Restrictions.** "Restrictions" means "parental controls." (Apple called it Restrictions instead so as not to turn off potential corporate customers. Can't you just hear it? "Parental controls? This thing is for *consumers!?*")

  Anyway, if you tap Enable Restrictions, then you're asked to make up a four-digit password (not the same as the passcode described above) that permits only you, the all-knowing parent, to make changes to these settings. (Or you, the corporate IT administrator who's doling out iPhones to the white-collar drones.)

  Once you've changed the settings described below, the only way to change them again (when your kid turns 18, for example) is to return to the Restrictions page and correctly enter the password. That's also the only way to turn off the entire Restrictions feature (tap Disable Restrictions and correctly enter the password). To turn it back on, you'll have to make up a password all over again.

  Once Restrictions is turned on, you can put up data blockades in a number of different categories.

  For starters, you can turn off access to iPhone features that locked-down corporations might not want their employees—or parents might not want their children—to use, either because they're considered security holes or time drains: Safari (can't use the Web at all), YouTube, iTunes, the Camera, the ability to go Installing Apps, or the Location feature.

Most of these restrictions work by *removing icons altogether* from the iPhone's Home screen: Safari, YouTube, iTunes, Camera, and Installing Apps (that is, the App Store). (When the switch says Off, the corresponding icon has been taken off the Home screen, and can't be found even by Spotlight searches.)

At the bottom of the screen, you'll find the Allowed Content options— better known as parental controls. Here you can spare your children's sensitive eyes and ears by blocking inappropriate material.

In-App Purchases permits you to buy new material (game levels, book chapters, and so on) from within an app that you've already bought. In other words, even if you've shut down access to your offspring's ability to install new apps, as described above, this loophole remains. That's why it has its own Off switch.

Ratings are a big deal; they determine the effectiveness of the parental controls described below. Since every country has its own rating schemes (for movies, TV shows, games, raunchy song lyrics, and so on), you use the Ratings For control to tell the iPhone which country's rating system you want to use.

Once that's done, you can use the Music & Podcasts, Movies, TV Shows, and Apps controls to specify what your kid is allowed to watch, play, and listen to. For example, you can tap Movies and then tap PG-13; any movies rated "higher," like R or NC-17, won't play on the iPhone now. (And if your sneaky offspring try to buy these naughty songs, movies, or TV shows wirelessly from the iTunes Store, they'll discover that the Buy button is dimmed and unavailable.)

Tap Explicit to prevent the iPhone from playing songs that have naughty language in the lyrics. (This works only on songs bought from the iTunes store.)

- **Home (iPhone 3G only).** The iPhone's hub-like software structure—a Home screen that leads to all other functions—is simple but not always efficient; you can't jump directly to another feature without passing through the Home screen first. The Home options, however, let you jump *directly* from your current program to one of five frequently used screens. In each case, you teleport by *pressing the Home button twice quickly:*

Search opens the Spotlight search window. It's probably not a great idea to waste the quick double-press Home shortcut on this, because Search *already* has a shortcut: a slow double-press on the Home button.

Phone Favorites takes you directly to the speed-dial list in the Phone program. Since one of the iPhone's most important uses is as, well, a phone, it makes sense that you might want a direct line to this screen, bypassing the Home screen.

Camera is a great option if you use the iPhone for taking photos much.

iPod takes you into the iPod module to view the "Now Playing" screen for whatever's playing at the moment. This option (and the next) are intended for situations where you started music playback and then ducked into a different iPhone program to listen while you work—and now you want to change songs, pause, or whatever.

If you turn on both iPod and iPod Controls, then pressing the Home button twice leaves you in the program you're already in but makes a miniature playback-control console appear so you can pause, adjust the volume, or change tracks with a minimum of interruption.

(If you leave this preference set to Home, then pressing the Home button twice doesn't do anything special. You go Home as usual.)

Finally, at the bottom of this screen, you'll find the Search Results option. It controls what kinds of things Spotlight looks for.

 Note On the iPhone 3GS and iPhone 4, of course, double-pressing the Home button has a completely different function: It opens the task switcher. That's why the Home settings appear only on the iPhone 3G, which isn't fast enough for multitasking.

- **Date & Time.** At the top of this screen, you'll see an option to turn on 24-hour time, also known as military time, in which you see "1700" instead of "5:00 p.m." (You'll see this change everywhere times appear, including at the top edge of the screen.)

  Set Automatically refers to the iPhone's built-in clock. If this item is turned on, then the iPhone finds out what time it is from an atomic clock out on the Internet. If not, then you have to set the clock yourself. (Turning this option off makes two more rows of controls appear automatically: a Time Zone option so you can specify your time zone and Set Date & Time, which opens a "number spinner" so you can set the clock.)

- **Keyboard.** Here you can turn off some of the very best features of the iPhone's virtual keyboard. (All these shortcuts are described in Chapter 2.)

  It's hard to imagine why you wouldn't want any of these tools working for you and saving you time and keystrokes, but here you go: Auto-

Correction is where the iPhone suggests spelling corrections as you type. Auto-Capitalization is where the iPhone thoughtfully capitalizes the first letter of every new sentence for you. Enable Caps Lock is the On/Off switch for the Caps Lock feature, in which a fast double-tap on the Shift key turns on Caps Lock. Finally, "." Shortcut turns on or off the "type two spaces to make a period" shortcut for the ends of sentences.

Below those options is International Keyboards. Tap it to view the 46 keyboard layouts and languages the iPhone offers for your typing pleasure. See page 40 for details on how you rotate among them.

 There are some crazy new keyboard options in iOS 4. For example, you can add a new keyboard, like English UK, and then tap its name to change its layout independently for the software keyboard (on-screen); you can also specify the layout of a wireless Bluetooth keyboard that you've attached.

- **International.** The iPhone: It's not just for Americans anymore. The Language screen lets you choose a language for the iPhone's menus and messages; Voice Control determines what language the iPhone listens for when you utter spoken commands. The Keyboards item here opens the same keyboard-choosing screen described above. And Region Format controls how the iPhone displays dates, times, and currency. (For example, in the U.S., Christmas is on 12/25; in Europe, it's 25/12.)

- **Accessibility.** These options, on the iPhone 3GS and iPhone 4, are intended for people with visual or hearing impairments, but they might come in handy now and then for almost anyone. They include VoiceOver (the iPhone speaks anything you touch), Zoom (magnifies the screen), Large Text (blows up tiny text in Contacts, Mail, Messages, and Notes), White on Black (arguably easier to read), Mono Audio (for people who are deaf in one ear), and Speak Auto-Text (pronounces any word the iPhone suggests as you type). All these features are described in Chapter 4, and the triple-click shortcut is covered on page 18.

- **Reset.** On the Reset screen, you'll find six ways to erase your tracks. Reset All Settings takes all the iPhone's settings back to the way they were when it came from Apple. Your data, music, and videos remain in place, but the settings you've changed all go back to their factory settings.

Erase All Content and Settings is the one you want when you sell your iPhone, or when you're captured by the enemy and want to make sure they will learn nothing from you or your iPhone.

Note This feature takes awhile to complete—and that's a good thing. The iPhone doesn't just delete your data; it also overwrites the newly erased memory with gibberish to make sure the bad guys can't see any of your deleted info, even with special hacking tools.

Reset Network Settings makes the iPhone forget all the memorized WiFi networks it currently autorecognizes.

Reset Keyboard Dictionary has to do with the iPhone's autocorrection feature, which kicks in whenever you're trying to input text. Ordinarily, every time you type something the iPhone doesn't recognize—some name or foreign word, for example—and you don't accept the iPhone's suggestion, it adds the word you typed to its dictionary so it doesn't bother you with a suggestion again the next time. If you think you've entered too many words that aren't legitimate terms, you can delete from its little brain all the new words you've "taught" it.

Reset Home Screen Layout undoes any icon-moving you've done on the Home screen. It also consolidates all your Home-screen icons, fitting them, 20 per page, onto as few screens as possible.

Finally, Reset Location Warnings refers to the "OK to use location services?" warning that appears whenever an iPhone program, like Maps or Camera, tries to figure out where you are. This button makes the iPhone forget all your responses to those permission boxes. In other words, you'll be asked permission all over again the first time you use each of those programs.

Mail, Contacts, Calendars

There's a lotta stuff going on in one place here. Breathe deeply; take it slow.

Accounts

Your email accounts are listed here; this is also where you set up new ones. See page 278 for details.

Fetch New Data

More than ever, the iPhone is a real-time window into the data stream of your life. Whatever changes are made to your calendar, address book, or email back on your computer at home (or at the office) can magically show up on your iPhone, seconds later, even though you're across the country.

That's the beauty of "push" email, contacts, and calendars. You get push email if you have a free Yahoo Mail account. You get all three if you've signed up for a MobileMe account (Chapter 13), or if your company uses Microsoft Exchange (Chapter 14).

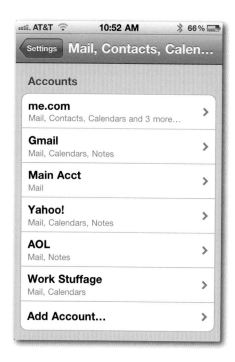
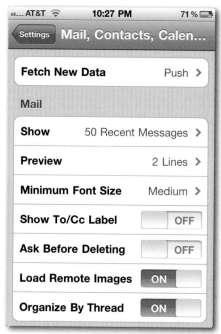

Having an iPhone that's updated with these critical life details in real time is amazingly useful, but there are several reasons why you might want to use the Off button here. Turning off the push feature saves battery power, saves you money when you're traveling abroad (where every "roaming" Internet use can run up your AT&T bill), and spares you the constant "new mail" jingle when you're trying to concentrate (or sleep).

 Tip If you tap Advanced, you can specify either push (real-time syncing over the air) or fetch (checking on a schedule) for each type of program—Mail, Contacts, and Calendars—for each account you have.

And what if you don't have a push email service, or if you turn it off? In that case, your iPhone can still do a pretty decent job of keeping you up to date. It can check your email every 15 minutes, every half-hour, every hour, or only on command (Manually). That's the decision you make in the Fetch panel here. (Keep in mind that more frequent checking means shorter battery life.)

 Tip The iPhone always checks email each time you open the Mail program, regardless of your setting here. If you have a push service like MobileMe or Exchange, it also checks for changes to your schedule or address book each time you open Calendar or Contacts—again, no matter what your setting here.

Mail

Here you set up your email account information, specify how often you want the iPhone to check for new messages, change the font size for email, and more.

- **Show.** Using this option, you can limit how much mail the Mail program shows you, from the most recent 25 messages to the most recent 200. This feature doesn't stop you from getting and seeing all your mail—you can always tap Download More in the Mail program—but it may help to prevent the sinking feeling of Email Overload.

 Note The number you specify here also controls how many messages sit in your Sent, Drafts, and Trash folders before being deleted. On Exchange accounts, you're offered a different control here—not how many messages to retain, but how many *days' worth* of mail.

- **Preview.** It's cool that the iPhone shows you the first few lines of text in every message. Here you can specify how many lines of text appear. More means you can skim your inbound mail without having to open many of them; less means more messages fit without scrolling.

- **Minimum Font Size.** Anyone with fading vision—and those of us over 40 know who we are—will appreciate this option. It lets you scale the type size of your email from Small to Giant.

- **Show To/Cc Label.** If you turn this option on, a tiny, light-gray logo appears next to many of the messages in your inbox. The **To** logo indicates that this message was addressed directly to you; the **Cc** logo means you were merely "copied" on a message primarily intended for someone else.

If there's no logo at all, then the message is in some other category. Maybe it came from a mailing list, or it's an email blast (a BCC), or the message is from you, or it's a bounced message.

- **Ask Before Deleting.** Ordinarily, you can delete a message quickly and easily (page 288). But if you'd prefer to see an "Are you sure?" confirmation box before the message disappears, then turn this option on.

 Note The confirmation box appears only when you're deleting an open message—not when you delete one from the list of messages.

- **Load Remote Images.** Spammers, the vile undercrust of lowlife society, have a famous trick. When they send you email that includes a picture, they don't actually paste the picture into the message. Instead, they include a "bug"—a piece of code that instructs your email program to *fetch* the missing graphic from the Internet. Why? Because that gives the spammer the ability to track who has actually opened the junk mail, making their email addresses much more valuable for reselling to other spammers.

  That's a long explanation for a simple feature: If you turn this option off, then the iPhone does not fetch "bug" image files at all. You're not flagged as a sucker by the spammers. You'll see empty squares in the email where the images ought to be. (Graphics sent by normal people and legitimate companies are generally pasted right into the email, so they'll still show up just fine.)

- **Always Bcc Myself.** If this option is on, then you'll get a secret copy of any message you send.

- **Signature.** A signature is a bit of text that gets stamped at the bottom of your outgoing email messages. Here's where you can change yours.

- **Default account.** Your iPhone can manage an unlimited number of email accounts. Here, tap the account you want to be your *default*—the one that's used when you create a new message from another program, like when you're sending a photo or tapping an email link in Safari.

Contacts

Contacts is a first-class citizen with an icon of its own on the Home screen, so it gets its own little set of options in Settings.

- **Sort Order, Display Order.** The question is: How do you want the names in your Contacts list sorted—by first name or last name?

  Note that you can have them *sorted* one way, but *displayed* another way. This table shows how a very short Contacts list would appear, using each of the four combinations of settings:

	Display "Last, First"	Display "First, Last"
Sort order "First, Last"	O'Furniture, Patty Minella, Sal Peace, Warren	Patty O'Furniture Sal Minella Warren Peace
Sort order "Last, First"	Minella, Sal O'Furniture, Patty Peace, Warren	Sal Minella Patty O'Furniture Warren Peace

As you can see, not all of these combinations make sense.

- **Import SIM Contacts.** If you come to the iPhone from another, lesser GSM phone, then your phone book may be stored on its little SIM card (page 8) instead of in the phone itself. In that case, you don't have to retype all those names and numbers to bring them into your iPhone. This button can do the job for you. (The results may not be pretty. For example, some phones store all address-book data in CAPITAL LETTERS.)

Calendar

Your iPhone's calendar can be updated by remote control, wirelessly, through the air, either by your company (via Exchange, Chapter 14) or by somebody at home using your computer (via MobileMe, Chapter 13).

- **New Invitation Alerts.** Part of that wireless joy is receiving invitations to meetings, which coworkers can shoot to you from Outlook—wirelessly, when you're thousands of miles apart. Very cool.

  Unless, that is, you're getting a lot of these invitations, and it's beginning to drive you a little nuts. In that case, turn New Invitation Alerts off.

- **Sync.** If you're like most people, you refer to your calendar more often to see what events are *coming up* than what you've already lived through. Ordinarily, therefore, the iPhone saves you some syncing time and storage space by updating only relatively recent events on your iPhone calendar. It doesn't bother with events that are older than 2 weeks, or 6 months, or whatever you choose here. (Or you can turn on All Events if you want your entire life, past and future, synced each time—storage and wait time be damned.)

- **Time Zone Support.** Now, here's a mind-teaser for you world travelers. If an important event is scheduled for 6:30 p.m. New York time, and you're in California, how should that event appear on your calendar? Should it appear as 3:30 p.m. (that is, your local time)? Or should it remain stuck at 6:30 (East Coast time)?

It's not an idle question, because it also affects reminders and alarms.

Out of the box, Time Zone Support is turned on.

That is, everything stays on the calendar just the way you entered it, even as you travel from time zone to time zone.

If you turn Time Zone Support off, then the iPhone automatically translates all your appointments into the local time. If you scheduled a reminder to record a TV movie at 8:00 p.m. New York time, and you fly to California, the reminder will pop up at 5:00 p.m. local time. The iPhone actually learns (from the local cell towers) what time zone it's in, changes its own clock automatically, and literally slides appointments around on your calendar. Handy—but dangerous if you forget what you've done.

 If Time Zone Support is turned on, you can still make it shift your appointments to the local time—by setting the time zone manually. You do that by tapping Time Zone on this screen. (Of course, this control's real purpose is for you to establish the "home" time zone, so the iPhone knows those calendar appointments' *real* times.)

- **Default Calendar.** This option lets you answer the question: "When I add a new appointment to my calendar on the iPhone, which *calendar* (category) should it belong to?" You can choose Home, Work, Kids, or whatever category you use most often.

Phone

These settings have to do with your address book, call management, and other phone-related preferences.

- **My Number.** Here's where you can see your iPhone's own phone number. You can even edit it, if necessary (just how it appears—you're not actually changing your phone number).

- **International Assist.** When this option is turned on, and when you're dialing from another country, the iPhone automatically adds the proper country codes when dialing U.S. numbers.

- **Call Forwarding.** Tap to open the Call Forwarding screen, where you can turn this feature on or off. See page 99 for details.

- **Call Waiting.** Call Waiting, of course, is the feature that produces an audible beep when you're on a phone call to let you know that someone else is calling you. (Page 98 has details on how to handle such a traffic jam.)

  If call waiting is turned off, then such incoming calls go directly to voicemail.

- **Show My Caller ID.** Ordinarily, other people can see who's calling even before they answer the phone, thanks to the Caller ID display on their cellphones or some land-line phones. If you'd feel more private by hiding your own number, so people don't know who's calling until they answer your call, then turn this feature off.

- **TTY.** A TTY (teletype) machine lets people with hearing or speaking difficulties use a telephone—by typing back and forth, or sometimes with the assistance of a human TTY operator who transcribes what the other person is saying. When you turn this iPhone option on, you can use the iPhone with a TTY machine, if you buy the little $20 iPhone TTY adapter from Apple.

- **SIM PIN.** As noted on page 8, your SIM card stores all your account information. SIM cards are especially desirable overseas, because in most countries, you can pop yours into any old phone and have working service. If you're worried about yours getting stolen or lost, turn this option on. You'll be asked to enter a passcode.

  Then, if some bad guy ever tries to put your SIM card into another phone, he'll be asked for the password. Without the password, the card (and the phone) won't make calls.

 Tip And if the evildoer guesses wrong three times, the words "PIN LOCKED" appear on the screen and the SIM card is locked forever. You'll have to get another one from AT&T. So don't forget the password.

- **AT&T Services.** This choice opens up a cheat sheet of handy numeric codes that, when dialed, play the voice of a robot providing useful information about your account. For example, *225# lets you know the latest status of your bill, *646# lets you know how many airtime minutes you've used so far this month, and so on.

 Tip The AT&T My Account button at the bottom of the screen opens up your account page on the Web, for further details on your cellphone billing and features.

Safari

Here's everything you ever wanted to adjust in the Web browser but didn't know how to ask.

- **Search Engine.** Your choice here determines who does your searching from the Search bar: Google, Bing, or Yahoo.

- **AutoFill.** Safari's AutoFill feature (page 216) saves you tedious typing by filling in your passwords, name, address, and phone numbers on Web forms automatically (just for the sites you want). Here's the On/Off switch.

- **Fraud Warning.** *Phishing* is the latest scheme to separate you from your money. You get an email message that purports to be from your bank, or eBay, or PayPal. Apparently there's a problem with your account! So you click the provided link for the account-verification Web page—which, behind the scenes, is a fake. The bad guy's computers collect your name and password as you "log in." This Safari feature is supposed to display a big warning box when you atempt to visit one of these phony sites.

- **JavaScript.** JavaScript is a programming language whose bits of code frequently liven up Web pages. If you suspect some bit of code is choking Safari, however, you can turn off its ability to decode JavaScript here.

- **Block Pop-ups.** In general, you want this turned on. You really don't want pop-up ad windows ruining your surfing session. Now and again, though, pop-up windows are actually useful. When you're buying concert tickets, for example, a pop-up window might show the location of the seats. In that situation, you can turn this option off.

- **Accept Cookies.** As described on page 275, these options let you limit how many cookies (Web preference files) are deposited on your iPhone.

- **Databases.** Safari now recognizes HTML5, a Web technology that lets Web sites store data on your phone, for accessing even when you're not online (like your Gmail stash). Here, you can see which Web apps have created these databases on your phone, and delete them if necessary.

- **Clear History.** Like any Web browser, Safari keeps a list of Web sites you've visited recently to make it easier for you to revisit them: the History list. And like any browser, Safari therefore exposes your tracks to any suspicious spouse or crackpot colleague who feels like investigating what you've been up to. If you're nervous about that prospect, tap Clear History to erase your tracks.

- **Clear Cookies**, similarly, deletes all the cookies that Web sites have deposited on your "hard drive."

- **Clear Cache.** See page 276.

- **Developer.** This item lets you turn on the Debug Console, which is an information strip at the top of the Safari screen. It's intended to display errors, warnings, tips, and logs for HTML, JavaScript, and CSS—solely for the benefit of people who are designing and debugging Web pages or Web apps for the iPhone.

Messages

This panel offers two neat text-message options that govern text messages (SMS), described in Chapter 4:

- **Show Preview** means that when a text message arrives, it wakes up your phone and shows itself. Which is great, as long as the message isn't private and the phone isn't lying on the table where everyone can see it. If you turn this option off, you'll see who the message is from, but not the actual text of the message (until you tap View).

- **Repeat Alert.** If someone sends you a text message but you don't read it, the iPhone will remind you a couple more times that you have an unread text message. If you really want to ignore that message and you don't want to be nagged about it, turn this option off.

- **Group Messaging, Character Count.** These two new options are described on page 94.

iPod

On this panel, you can adjust four famous iPod playback features:

- **Shake to Shuffle.** C'mon…you wouldn't really turn off this fun feature, would you? It's the one that makes the iPod module skip to another song when you shake the iPhone hard (although only when you're in the iPod app itself and the screen is on). Oh well; here's the On/Off switch.

- **Sound Check** is a familiar iPod feature that attempts to create a standard baseline volume level for the different songs in your library, so you don't crank up the volume to hear one song and then get your eardrums turned to liquid by the next due to differences in CD mastering. Here's the On/Off switch.

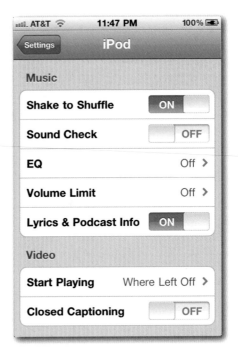

- **EQ.** EQ is equalization—the art of fiddling with specific frequencies in your music to bring out highs, lows, midrange, or whatever, to suit certain types of music and certain musical tastes. This screen offers a scrolling list of predesigned EQ "envelopes" designed for different situations: Bass Booster, Hip-Hop, Small Speakers, Spoken Word, Treble Reducer, and so on. You can also choose Off if you want the music to play just the way the record company released it.

Be aware, however, that EQ uses up your battery faster.

- **Volume Limit.** It's well established that listening to loud music for a long time can damage your hearing. It's also well established that parents worry about this phenomenon. So all iPods, and the iPhone, include an optional maximum-volume control. The idea is that if you give your kid an iPhone (wow, what a generous parent!), you can set a maximum volume level, using the slider on this screen.

  You can also prevent your kid from bypassing your good intentions and dragging the slider right back to maximum. Just tap Lock Volume Limit; you'll be asked for a four-digit password. (The password isn't especially hard to bypass.)

 Needless to say, the risk of hearing damage exists only when you're wearing earbuds. Music pumped through the tiny speaker wouldn't damage a gnat's hearing.

- **Video.** When you play a video you've seen before, you can have it begin either from Where Left Off or From Beginning. You can also opt to see dialogue subtitles (Closed Captioning), when available (which is almost never).

- **TV Out.** Apple's $50 TV cables let you play your iPhone's videos on an actual TV set. You can use these options to control the format of the video signal the iPhone sends: Widescreen (on or off) or TV Signal (NTSC, the U.S. video signal, or PAL, the European standard).

Photos

All the options here govern the behavior of the photo slideshows described on page 146.

- **Play Each Slide For.** How long do you want each photo to remain on the screen? You can choose 2, 3, 5, 10, or 20 seconds. (Hint: 2 is plenty, 3 at most. Anything more than that will bore your audience silly.)

- **Transition.** These options are visual effects between slides: various crossfades, wipes, and other transitions.

- **Repeat, Shuffle.** These options work just as they do for music. Repeat makes the slideshow loop endlessly; Shuffle plays the slides in random order.

Store

This panel offers just two buttons. View Account takes you to the Web, where you can look over your Apple account information, including credit-card details. Tap Sign Out when, for example, a friend wants to use her own iTunes account to buy something on your iPhone. As a gift, maybe.

App Preferences

If you've indulged in a few new programs (or a few hundred) from the App Store (Chapter 7), then you may well find some additional listings in Settings. This is where downloaded programs may install setting screens of their own. For example, here's where you can edit your screen name and password for the AIM chat program, change how many days' worth of news you want the NY Times Reader to display, and so on.

Appendixes

A Setup and Signup

In its first year of existence, the iPhone was remarkable (among other ways) in that you didn't *activate* it (sign up for service) in the cellphone store, with a salesperson breathing down your neck. You did it at home, on your computer, in iTunes, where you could take all the time you needed to read about the plans and choose the one you wanted.

That all changed with the iPhone 3G in 2008. These days, you sign up in the cellphone store, with a salesperson breathing down your neck.

This appendix covers the AT&T plans you might sign up for, plus how to upgrade an existing iPhone's software to iOS 4.

Activation

Activation means signing up for a plan, turning on the service, and either finding out your new phone number or transferring your old number to the iPhone.

A non-activated iPhone isn't altogether useless. It's still a very nice iPod—in fact, it's pretty much an iPod Touch. But without a two-year AT&T contract, the iPhone 4 costs $600 or $700 (for the 16- and 32-gig models)—so if an iPod Touch is what you want, then you should just buy an iPod Touch and save a lot of money.

Incidentally, the iPhone is a *locked* GSM phone, meaning that it works *only* with an AT&T account. As of 2010, it won't work with Verizon, Sprint, T-Mobile, or any other carrier, and you can't insert the SIM card (page 8) from a non-AT&T phone and expect it to work.

Yes, hackers have succeeded in unlocking the iPhone so it can be used on other cell companies' networks; their primary motivation for doing so was to be able to use it in countries where the iPhone hasn't been available. But now that the iPhone is sold legitimately in 90 countries (and counting), there may be less reason to go that questionable route.

All right then: Here you are in the AT&T store, or about to head to one. Here are some of the issues you'll face and the decisions you'll have to make:

- **Transferring your old number.** You can bring your old cellphone or home phone number to your new iPhone. Your friends and coworkers can keep dialing your old number—but your iPhone will ring instead of the old phone.

  It usually takes under an hour for a cellphone-number transfer to take place, but it may take several hours. During that time, you can make calls on the iPhone, but you can't receive them.

 Note Transferring a landline number can take several *days.*

- **Select your monthly AT&T plans.** Signing up for cellphone service involves more red tape than a government contract. In essence, you have to choose *three* plans: one for voice calls (required), one for Internet service (required), and one for text messages (optional).

  For voice calls, most people sign up for the $40 monthly plan, which offers 450 weekday calling minutes. But there's a 900-minute plan for $60, and an unlimited calling plan for $70.

  All the voice plans offer *rollover minutes,* a feature no other carrier offers. That is, if you don't use up all your monthly minutes this month, the unused ones are automatically added to your allotment for next month, and so on. All plans offer unlimited free calls to other AT&T phones.

  All but the cheapest plan also offer unlimited calls on nights and weekends. (On that plan, you get 5,000 night/weekend minutes, which is actually pretty close to "unlimited.")

  Next, you have to choose an Internet data plan for your iPhone's email, Web, and app-downloading pleasure. You have a choice of two. *DataPlus* costs $15 a month and gives you 200 megabytes' worth of data transfer.

  Of course, who has any idea what "200 megabytes' worth of data transfer" is? AT&T says that that's 1,000 email messages without attachments, plus 150 that do have attachments, plus 400 Web-page views, plus posting 50 photos on Facebook and similar sites, plus watching 20 minutes of video from sites like YouTube or Hulu. If you use more than 200 megabytes, you're automatically billed $15 more that month for another 200.

DataPro costs $25 a month and gives you 10 times as much data. Data-Pro also entitles you to use your iPhone for tethering—that is, the phone acts a as an Internet antenna for your laptop—for $20 more. Details on tethering appear on page 250.

If your Internet activities break down differently, then use the sliders at *www.att.com/datacalculator* to see what your typical activity would consume.

In each case, AT&T sends you three free text messages and email alerts as you approach your monthly limit (at 65, 90, and 100 percent of your maximum). You can also check your data use by calling *DATA#, or by using a free iPhone app. Yes, it's a pain to have to worry about data limits, but at least monitoring them is fairly easy.

 Note These capped data plans are required if you're signing up for your first AT&T phone. If you had the old $30 unlimited-data plan, you can keep it if you want. (Of course, you won't be able to take advantage of the tethering feature.) It might be good insurance against the data-heavy cellphone features of the future—because if you give up your unlimited-data plan by switching to one of the less expensive ones, you can never get it back.

None of these includes any text messages. For those, you'll have to pay $5 more for 200 messages, $15 for 1,500, or $20 for unlimited messages. Of course, you can always pay à la carte, too: 20 cents for each message sent or received.

 Tip The choice you make here isn't etched in stone. You can change your plan at any time. At *www.wireless.att.com*, you can log in with your iPhone number and make up a password. Click My Account, and then click Change Rate Plan to view your options.

All iPhone plans require a two-year commitment and a $36 "activation fee" (ha!).

As you budget for your plan, keep in mind that, as with any cellphone, you'll also be paying taxes as high as 22 percent, depending on your state. Ouch.

Once you get the phone home, hook it up to iTunes. (You'll be told, as though you didn't know by now, that you need iTunes 9.2 or later.) Now you can specify what you want copied onto the phone. Turn to Chapter 12 for details.

AT&T Fringe Cases

For most people, the plans described above are all they'll ever need. There are, however, plenty of oddball cases—business plans, family plans, pay-as-you-go plans—that might be worth considering. For example:

- **Business plans.** If you're using a corporate iPhone, you have the same decisions to make—you have to choose a voice plan and a data plan. In this case, the two data plans (for 200 MB or 2 GB of data a month) are $25 or $40. Tethering, once again, is $20 on top of the more expensive data plan. Those prices are more expensive than the regular iPhone plan—because, as AT&T sees it, "Business customers tend to be heavier users of data than consumers." (Plausible? You decide.)

- **Upgrading from an original iPhone.** If you have an existing iPhone, and its 2-year contract would have expired before the end of 2010, then you can get the iPhone 4 for the new-customer price ($200 or $300), or the iPhone 3GS for $100. Just bring your old iPhone to the store and get the new one activated. You can give the old phone to another family member, sell it, put it up on eBay, whatever you like.

  If you have an iPhone 3GS but want the newer iPhone 4, however, things might get sticky. If you've had the 3GS for under about 18 months, you may have to pay a $200 premium. That's to reimburse AT&T for your subsidized iPhone 3G. The gory details, if you care to read them, are here: *http://nyti.ms/9d8O9C.*

- **Family plans.** The iPhone can be part of an AT&T family plan. It works just like any other phone: For $10 more per month per person, it shares a pool of minutes with other phones belonging to the same family. (It still has to have its own Internet data plan, though.)

Upgrading an Older iPhone

There's not much involved in bringing the iOS 4 software to your existing iPhone 3G or 3GS. One day—probably a long time ago, at this point—iTunes alerts you that a free upgrade is available. You click Update. When it's all over, your new iPhone has all the new features of iOS 4: folders, multitasking, camera zoom, wallpaper, unified email Inbox, and so on. And all your old data is put back onto it.

There's not much to it. Basically, just keep clicking the blue buttons in the lower-right corners of the progress screens: Next, OK, Continue, and so on.

And then, suddenly, it's all over. The iPhone is reborn.

 Note An upgraded iPhone 3G can be a very sluggish phone indeed. Do some reading online before proceeding to see if Apple has addressed the problem.

B

Accessorizing the iPhone

Like the iPods that came before it, the iPhone is inspiring a torrent of accessories that seems to intensify with every passing month. Stylish cases, speakers, docks, cables—the list goes on.

This appendix gives you a tiny representative sampling. It also points you in the right direction so you can find iPhone accessories that look good, sound good, and most importantly—fit.

Proper Shopping for the iPhone

This is the most important thing to remember when you're looking for iPhone hardware: *Not all iPod and iPhone accessories are created equal.* (Or, as Yoda might say: *Created equal, not all iPod and iPhone accessories are.*)

For example:

- The iPhone 4 is shaped differently from the iPhone 3G and 3GS. Form-fitting cases, sockets, and accessories designed for the older models don't fit the newer one.

- The iPhone is also a phone, with components inside that can cause static and interference when used with external speakers (which have their own electronic innards). So accessories for the *iPod* may not work.

To help you identify products that are compatible with the iPhone, Apple has its own "Works with iPhone" logo program. As the company puts it, products bearing the logo are "electronic accessories designed to connect specifically to iPhone and certified by the developer to meet Apple performance standards."

Getting stuff with the "Works with iPhone" logo should save you the grief that comes with "Buying the Wrong Thing."

Some good places to look:

- **Apple's iPhone Accessories page.** Here are all of Apple's own, official white plastic cables, the optional iPhone dock adapters, and power plugs, alongside tons of iPhone-friendly products from other manufacturers. Click the link for iPhone Accessories on the main store page to see the goods—and ratings from other customers. *http://store.apple.com*

- **Incase.** Incase has been turning out handsome iPod cases practically since the little white MP3 player took the first spin of its scroll wheel. Somehow, they had iPhone cases and other accessories in stock before the first iPhone hit the street. *www.goincase.com*

- **iPhoneAccessories.com.** The site's name says it all—and the site itself pretty much *sells* it all if you're looking for iPhone stuff. You can find cables, cases, speakers, headphones, and more from all the major iPhone accessory manufacturers, along with frequent clearance sales. *www.iphoneaccessories.com*

- **Griffin Technology.** Cables, cases, and many audio accessories. *www.griffintechnology.com*

- **Belkin.** From acrylic cases to sporty armbands, Belkin markets several iPhone items, including an adapter for the headphone port on the original iPhone. *www.belkin.com*

- **EverythingiCafe.** If it works with an iPhone, you can probably find it here by clicking the Store tab: cleaning cloths, screen protectors, Bluetooth headsets, cases, and on and on. It's not just a shopping center; user forums, reviews, and news make the site live up to its all-encompassing name. *http://store.everythingicafe.com*

If you're looking for specific categories of products, say a not-too-geeky belt case or a Bluetooth headset for hands-free dialing, the next few pages give you an idea of what's out there.

Protecting Your iPhone

It should be called the iPhone Paradox: People buy the thinnest, sleekest, shiniest, most gorgeous smartphone in existence—and then bury it in an ugly, fat, thick carrying case. There's just something so wrong about that.

On the other hand, this thing is made of a layer of breakable glass on both the front and the back; the instinct to protect it is perfectly understandable. Two types of accessories in particular can bring an extra layer of protection (and peace of mind): cases and screen protectors.

Cases

When you shop for a case, consider how you use your iPhone. Into sports and activity? A brightly colored rubberized covering that lets you dial without taking it out of the case might work best. Using it as you stroll around the office all day? Consider a leather holster-style case with a belt clip. Some examples:

- **Apple Bumper Case.** Made from "durable rubber" and "molded plastic", the Bumper Case is Apple's answer to the iPhone case issue (and also its antenna issue; see page 4). The bumpers come in six (bright) colors: black, white, blue, orange, green, and pink. ($30; *www.apple.com*)

- **Case-Mate I.D. Credit Card Case.** This case is the perfect accessory for a night out on the town: The case's built-in slot can fit two credit card size items (like an ID and a credit card). A bonus: It comes with a free screen protection kit. ($35; *www.case-mate.com*)

- **Speck Products Fitted Case.** This form-fit two-piece hardshell case offers the best of both worlds: fashion and protection. And the case's original fabric-wrapped patterns afford the iPhone some serious style points. ($30; *www.speckproducts.com*)

- **Sena Case UltraSlim Leather Case.** The UltraSlim Leather Case is one of the thinnest cases on the market—perfect for the minimalist crowd. Available in an eccentric eighteen different color combinations, the UltraSlim offers high-quality luxury for an affordable price. ($30; *www.senacases.com*)

Screen Protectors

People who've used stylus-based Palms, Pocket PCs, or smartphones are big fans of screen protectors—thin sheets of sticky plastic that lie smoothly over the glass to provide a protective barrier.

- **ZAGG invisibleSHIELD.** Designed to protect both the front and back of your iPhone, this screen-protector has a formidable pedigree: Its thin polyurethane film was originally created for the military to protect the leading edge of helicopter blades. ZAGG also sells its invisibleSHIELD for only the back, only the front, and only the sides (where it works as a "Death Grip" fix!) ($10-$25; *www.zagg.com*)

- **Fusion of Ideas Stealth Armor.** Like ZAGG, Fusion of Ideas offers some pretty great screen protection, especially with its "nano-fusion technology" protective screen films. And if you're not in the mood for boring old clear, the company offers some fun, unconventional faux-texture alternatives like leather, tungsten, carbon fiber, and brushed aluminum. ($15-$35; *www.fusionofideas.com*)

Making the iPhone Heard

Your iPhone comes with a pair of wired, mike-equipped earbuds and a not-very-powerful external speaker. If you want a bump up from this factory equipment, you can find plenty of other options. For example:

- **foxL v2.** This compact sound system belts out music far more powerfully than you might think by looking at it. The foxL 2 works over Bluetooth, so you don't have to leave your beloved iDevice chained to the confines of your hi-fi. Better yet, the Bluetooth doubles as a speakerphone. The system runs on a lithium-ion "Bass Battery" that's rechargeable via USB or a wall charger, so it should last you awhile, too. ($200; *www.soundmatters.com*)

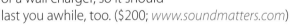

- **V-MODA Remix Remote.** Because these earbuds come with four pairs of silicon ear fittings in both clear and black, you'll be able to create a better-fitting earbud that seals in the music and blocks out background noise. The earbuds also come with a built-in three-button remote, which packs an omnidirectional

microphone. A control button lets you make and take calls. The V-MODAs should last you awhile, too—the cables are reinforced with Kevlar—and a two-year warranty. ($100; *www.v-moda.com*)

- **BlueAnt S4 True Handsfree Bluetooth Speakerphone.** The iPhone's speakerphone isn't all that loud, even when it's cranked up all the way—and you still have to take a hand off the steering wheel to pick up a call. With the BlueAnt S4, you can pair up your iPhone, clip it to the car's sun visor, and just say "OK" to pick up incoming calls the next time the phone rings. Or let the speakerphone's Bluetooth transmitter play music right from your iPhone, or give turn-by-turn directions using your favorite navigation app, without any extra cables. ($100; *www.myblueant. com*)

- **Aliph Jawbone Icon Bluetooth Headset.** CNET's highest-rated headset ever, the Jawbone Icon, almost looks like something out of the prop department on a sci-fi movie. But there's good stuff inside, including noise-cancellation circuitry to help eliminate wind and background chatter for improved call clarity. ($100; *www.jawbone.com*)

Power to the iPhone

Every year, the newest iPhone isn't even out for more than a day before people start complaining about the battery life. If you're on the road for hours and away from your charger, here are a few products designed to boost your battery and keep that iPhone running as long as you are.

- **Exogear ExoLife Battery Case.** It's an iPhone case! No, it's a backup battery! Wait, it's both. Exogear's form-fitting lithium polymer battery (housed in a sleek polycarbonate hardshell case) adds 5 hours of talk time and 5 hours of Internet time when you're on the go and connected to AT&T's 3G network. A pass-through USB port lets you charge and sync the iPhone without having to extract it from the case, and you can also charge the phone and the case at the same time. Available in both black and white. ($90; *www. exogear.com*)

- **Richard Solo 1800 Battery.** Snap-on batteries like this one may add a couple of inches onto the end of your iPhone, but they also add on extra hours of useful battery time. The Solo 1800 can recharge a completely dead iPhone and still have juice left over. The kit comes with a wall charger, a dual USB car charger, and a retractable USB cable so that you can charge it in the wall, in your car, or from your computer. ($70; *www.richardsolo.com*)

- **Griffin iTrip FM Transmitter.** This gadget transmits music from your iPhone to your car's built-in stereo system. And while you're blissing out in gridlock, it also charges the iPhone through the car's power port. The iTrip automatically scans the car's FM radio dial for an available frequency. Once it finds some empty airspace, the iTrip's screen displays the frequency to use so you can pipe your iPhone's tunes or podcasts right through the dashboard speakers. ($50; *www.griffintechnology.com*)

> Inventive and exciting iPhone products are coming out all over the place. If you don't have time to keep up, let the gadget blogs do it for you. A few to hit regularly if you want to see the latest in cool: Gizmodo (*www.gizmodo.com*), Engadget (*www.engadget.com*), and Crave (*news.cnet.com/crave*). And for a thorough examination of just about every major iPhone and iPod accessory hitting the shelves, don't miss the news and reviews over at iLounge (*www.ilounge.com*).

Snap-On Accessories

It seems as if iPhone add-ons, like apps and dongles (snap-on hardware accessories) are advancing just as fast as the iPhone itself. Two wild examples:

- **Square Payment System and Card Reader.** Suppose you're at your buddy's house, and you want to buy an old PowerBook that's sitting there in his garage—but you don't have any cash on you. In the new Square world, that's no big deal. The Square is a tiny white snap-on credit-card reader for the iPhone. It lets anyone—even ordinary people—process credit cards, even for small amounts. Once you're paid, Square automatically deposits the dough into your bank account (after assessing a small fee, of course). The little reader plugs right into the iPhone's headphone jack. Receipts arrive instantly via email or mobile phone and can include a photo of the item, a photo of the buyer, and the buyer's signature. (*www.squareup.com*)

- **RedEye mini.** Imagine being able to control your entire home entertainment system, TV, stereo, cable box and Blu-ray player with something the size of the index finger you're using to change the channels. ThinkFlood's RedEye mini dongle does just that. Its infrared blaster can control just about any other device that receives standard infrared signals. No real setup required: Plug the RedEye mini into your iPhone's headphone jack, and run the free RedEye application. The RedEye mini comes backed by ThinkFlood's online infrared code database, so you can control devices even if you don't have the original remote at hand. ($50; *www.thinkflood.com*)

Double-Dipping: iPod Accessories

The "Works with iPhone" logo ensures happy shopping, but your existing iPod gear *might* play nice with iPhone. If you're game, keep the following advice in mind.

Most speakers that connect through the 30-pin port on the bottom of modern iPods also fit the iPhone. You may need one of Apple's Universal Dock adapters—a white plastic booster seat that makes most iPod models sit securely in speaker docks—for a good fit.

One thing to remember, though: electronic interference. If you forget, the iPhone will remind you. If it senses you're seating it in a non–"Works with iPhone" speaker system, you'll see a message suggesting that you put it in Airplane mode. Doing so takes care of the interference, but it also prevents you from making or getting phone calls. You can blow past the warning and keep Airplane mode off, but you may get some unwanted static blasts with your music.

Troubleshooting & Maintenance

The iPhone is a computer, and you know what that means: Things can go wrong. This particular computer, though, is not quite like a Mac or a PC. It runs a spin-off of the Mac OS X operating system, but that doesn't mean you can apply the same troubleshooting techniques.

Therefore, let this chapter be your guide when things go wrong.

First Rule: Install the Updates

There's an old saying: "Never buy version 1.0 of anything." In the iPhone's case, the saying could be: "Never buy version 4.0 of anything."

The very first version (or major revision) of anything has bugs, glitches, and things the programmers didn't have time to finish they way they would have liked. The iPhone is no exception.

The beauty of this phone, though, is that Apple can send it fixes, patches, and even new features through software updates. One day you'll connect the phone to your computer for charging or syncing, and—bam!—there'll be a note from iTunes that new iPhone software is available.

So the first rule of trouble-free iPhoning is to accept these updates when they're offered. With each new software blob, Apple removes another few dozen tiny glitches.

Remember that within the first two months of the original iPhone's life, software updates 1.0.1 and 1.0.2 came down the pike, offering louder volume, security fixes, bug fixes, and many other subtle improvements. The big-ticket updates, bringing more actual features, came tumbling after (1.1.1 through 1.1.4). The same thing happened with the 2.0 and 3.0 cycles—and now that iOS 4 is here, you can expect a similar flurry of fixes to follow.

Reset: Six Degrees of Desperation

The iPhone runs actual programs, and as actual programs do, they actually crash. Sometimes, the program you're working in simply vanishes and you find yourself back at the Home screen. Just reopen the program and get on with your life.

If the program you're in just doesn't seem to be working right—it's frozen or acting weird, for example—then one of these six resetting techniques usually clears things right up.

 Note Proceed down this list in order! Start with the easy ones.

- **Force-quit the program.** On an iPhone, you're never aware that you're launching and exiting programs. They're always just *there*, like TV channels, when you switch to them. But if a program locks up or acts glitchy, you can *force* it to quit.

   To do that, hold down the Sleep switch until the slide to power off message appears. Then hold down the Home button for 10 seconds, or until the frozen program quits. The next time you open the troublesome program from the Home screen, it should be back in business.

 Note These steps have changed since the first couple of iPhone generations.

- **Turn the phone off and on again.** If it seems something more serious has gone wrong, then hold down the Sleep switch for a few seconds. When the screen says, slide to power off, confirm by swiping. The iPhone shuts off completely.

   Turn it back on by pressing the Sleep switch for a second or two.

- **Force-restart the phone.** If you haven't been able to force-quit the program, and you can't shut the phone off either, you might have to force a restart. To do that, hold both the Home button and the Sleep switch for 10 seconds. Keep holding, even if the screen goes black or you see the "power off" slider appear. Don't release until you see the Apple logo appear, meaning that the phone is restarting.

- **Reset the phone's settings.** Relax. This procedure doesn't erase any of your data—only the phone's settings. From the Home screen, tap Settings→General→Reset→Reset All Settings.

- **Erase the whole phone.** From the Home screen, tap Settings→ General→Reset→Erase All Content and Settings. Now, *this* option zaps all your stuff—*all* of it. Music, videos, email, settings, apps, all gone, and all overwritten with random 1's and 0's to make sure it's completely unre-coverable. Clearly, you're getting into last resorts here. Of course, you can now sync with iTunes to copy all that stuff back onto your iPhone.

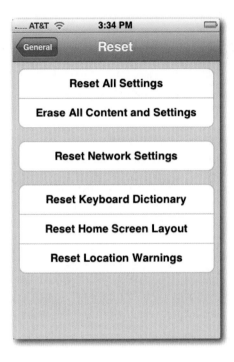

- **Restore the phone.** If none of these steps seem to solve the phone's glitchiness, it might be time for the Nuclear Option: erasing it completely, resetting both hardware and software back to factory-fresh condition.

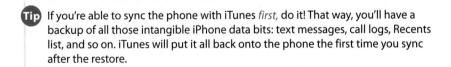

Tip If you're able to sync the phone with iTunes *first,* do it! That way, you'll have a backup of all those intangible iPhone data bits: text messages, call logs, Recents list, and so on. iTunes will put it all back onto the phone the first time you sync after the restore.

To restore the phone, connect it to your computer. In iTunes, click the iPhone icon and then, on the Summary tab, click Restore.

The first order of business: iTunes offers to make a backup of your iPhone (all of its phone settings, text messages, and so on—see page 338) before proceeding. Accepting this invitation is an excellent idea. Click Back Up.

When it's all over, you can sync your life right back onto the iPhone—this time, if the technology gods are smiling, with better success.

What Else to Try

If the phone is still glitchy, try to remember what changes you made to it recently. Did you install some new App Store program, add a new video, mess around with your calendar?

It's worth fishing through iTunes, turning off checkboxes, hunting for the recently changed items, and resyncing, in hopes of figuring out what's causing the flakiness.

iPhone Doesn't Turn On

Usually, the problem is that the battery's dead. Just plugging it into the USB cord or USB charger doesn't bring it to life immediately, either; a completely dead iPhone doesn't wake up until it's been charging for about 10 minutes. It pops on automatically when it has enough juice to do so.

If you don't think that's the trouble, then try the resetting tactics on the previous pages.

Doesn't Show Up in iTunes

If the iPhone's icon doesn't appear in the Source list at the left side of the iTunes window, you've got yourself a real problem. You won't be able to load it up with music, videos, or photos, and you won't be able to sync it with your computer. That's a bad thing.

- **The USB factor.** Trace the connection from the iPhone, to its cradle (if you're using one), to the USB cable, to the computer, making sure everything is seated. Also, don't plug the USB cable into a USB jack on your keyboard, and don't plug it into an unpowered USB hub. Believe it or not, just trying a different USB jack on your computer often solves the problem.

- **The iPhone factor.** Try turning the phone off and on again. Make sure its battery is at least partway charged; if not, wait 10 minutes, until it's sucked in enough power from the USB cable to revive itself.

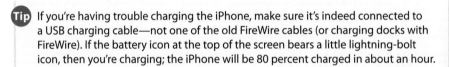

Tip If you're having trouble charging the iPhone, make sure it's indeed connected to a USB charging cable—not one of the old FireWire cables (or charging docks with FireWire). If the battery icon at the top of the screen bears a little lightning-bolt icon, then you're charging; the iPhone will be 80 percent charged in about an hour.

But if the red part of the battery icon on the iPhone screen flashes three times and the screen goes black, then the iPhone is not getting power and won't charge.

- **The iTunes factor.** The iPhone requires iTunes version 9.2 or later. Download and install the latest. No success? Then reinstall it.

Phone and Internet Problems

What can go wrong with the phone part of the iPhone? Let us count the ways.

- **Can't make calls.** First off, do you have enough AT&T cellular signal to make a call? Check your signal-strength bars. Even if you have one or two, flakiness is par for the course, although one bar in a 3G area is much better than one bar in a non-3G area. Try going outside, standing near a window, or moving to a major city (kidding).

  Also, make sure Airplane mode isn't turned on (page 250). Try calling somebody else, to make sure the problem isn't with the number you're dialing.

In areas where everyone is using phones at once (airports, conferences, New York, San Francisco), consider turning off 3G (page 249). Often, you'll have a better chance of connecting using the older AT&T network.

Finally, be aware of the Death Grip (page 4). Nestling the lower-left corner of the phone in the palm of your left hand can lower the signal strength (unless your phone is in a case or has a "bumper").

If nothing else works, try the resetting techniques described at the beginning of this chapter.

- **Can't get on the Internet.** Remember, the iPhone can get online in three ways: via a WiFi hot spot, via AT&T's 3G network, and via AT&T's much slower EDGE network. If you're not in a hot spot *and* you don't have an AT&T signal—that is, if there's no .ıll, E, or 3G icon at the top of the screen—then you can't get online at all.

- **Can't send text messages.** Make sure the recipient's phone number in Contacts has an area code—and, of course, that you've signed up for a texting plan. Make sure you haven't turned on Show Subject Line (page 94) and forgotten to fill out the body of the message.

Email Problems

Getting your email settings right the first time isn't easy. There are all kinds of tweaky codes and addresses that you have to enter—if they weren't properly synced over from your computer, that is.

If email isn't working, here are some steps to try:

- Sometimes, there's nothing for it but to call your Internet provider (or whoever's supplying the email account) and ask for help. Often, the settings you use at home won't work when you're using a mobile gadget like the iPhone. Open Settings→Mail, Contacts, Calendars and tap your email account's name to view the Settings screen.

- If you're getting a "user not recognized" error, you may have typed your password wrong. (It's easy to do, since the iPhone converts each character you type into a • symbol about a second after you type it.) Delete the password in Settings and re-enter it.

- If you're having trouble connecting to your company's Exchange server, see the end of Chapter 14.

- Oh—and it probably goes without saying, but remember that you can't get email if you can't get online, and you can't get online unless you have a WiFi or cellular signal.

Messages Are Disappearing

Strange but true: Unbeknownst to just about everyone but Apple programmers, there's a hidden setting that controls how many messages are allowed to pile up in your Sent, Drafts, and Trash email folders. And it comes set to 25 messages each.

If any more messages go into those three folders, then the earlier ones are auto-deleted from the iPhone (although not from the server on the Internet). The idea is to keep your email stash on the phone manageable, but if you're not prepared, it can be somewhat alarming to discover that messages have vanished on their own.

To see this setting, tap Settings→Mail, Contacts, Calendars; under Mail, you can adjust the Show item to say 25, 50, 75, 100, or 200 Recent Messages. This feature is intended to keep the number of messages in your *Inbox* to a reasonable number; most people don't realize, however, that it also applies to the Sent, Drafts, and Trash folders in all your POP and IMAP email accounts.

Can't Send Email

It's happened to thousands of people. You set up your POP email account, and everything looks good. But although you can *receive* mail, you can't *send* it. You create an outgoing message; you tap Send. The whirlygig "I'm thinking" cursor spins and spins, but the iPhone never sends the message.

The cause is very technical, but here's a nicely oversimplified explanation.

When you send a piece of postal mail, you might drop it off at the post office. It's then sent over to the *addressee's* post office in another town and delivered from there.

In a high-tech sort of way, the same thing happens with email. When you send a message, it goes first to your Internet provider's *email server* (central mail computer). It's then sent to the *addressee's* mail server, and the addressee's email program picks it up from there.

But spammers and spyware writers became an increasing nuisance, especially people who wrote *zombies*—spyware on your computer that churns out spam without your knowledge. So the big ISPs (Internet service providers) began fighting back in two ways—both of which can block outgoing mail from your iPhone, too. Here's how you can use this information to your advantage:

- **Use port 587.** *Ports* are invisible "channels" from a computer to the Internet. One conducts email, one conducts Web activity, and so on. Most computers send email out on port 25.

  In an effort to block zombie spam, though, the big ISPs have rigged their networks so that mail you send from port 25 can go to only one place: the ISPs' own mail servers. (Most zombies attempt to send mail directly to the *addressees'* mail servers, so they're effectively blocked.) Your iPhone tries to send mail on port 25—and it gets blocked.

  The solution? Choose a different port. From the Home screen, tap Settings→Mail, Contacts, Calendars. Tap the name of your POP account. Scroll down to the Outgoing Mail Server. Tap the address there to edit it. Finally, tap On to open the SMTP screen.

  At the bottom of this screen, you'll find the Server Port box. Change it to say *587*.

  Try sending mail again. If it's still not sending, try changing that Server Port to *465*.

- **Use AT&T's mail server.** When you're home, your computer is connected directly, via cable modem or DSL, to the Internet provider's network. It knows you and trusts you.

  But when you're out and about, using AT&T's cellular network (Chapter 9), your Internet provider doesn't recognize you. Your email is originating *outside* your ISP's network—and it gets blocked. For all the ISP knows, you're a spammer.

  Your ISP may have a special mail-server address that's just for people to use while they're traveling. But the simpler solution may just be to use AT&T's *own* mail-server address.

  Once again, from the Home screen, tap Settings→Mail, Contacts, Calendars. Tap the name of your POP account. Scroll down to the Outgoing Mail Server. Tap the address there to edit it.

  Here you'll discover that you can set up backup mail-server addresses. If the first one is blocked or down, the iPhone will automatically try the next one in the list.

  You'll notice that the AT&T SMTP server is listed here already. (If you tap it, you find out that its actual address is *cwmx.com,* which, at one time, stood for Cingular Wireless Mail Exchange.)

If you're like thousands of people, that simple change means you can now send messages when you're on AT&T's network, and not just receive them.

 Tip If you're having trouble connecting to your company's Exchange mail, see Chapter 14.

Problems That Aren't Really Problems

There's a difference between "things not working as they were designed to" and "things not working the way I'd *like* them to." Here are a few examples:

- **Rotation sensor doesn't work.** As you know, the screen image is supposed to rotate into horizontal mode when you turn the iPhone itself. But this feature works only in certain programs, like Safari, Mail, Notes, the iPod music-playback mode, and when viewing photos or email attachments.

  Furthermore, the iPhone has to be more or less upright when you turn it. It can't be flat on a table, for example. The orientation sensor relies on gravity to tell it which way you're holding the phone.

  Finally, if the display isn't rotating the way you'd like it to, it may be that you've turned on the new rotation lock. If so, you'll see the ⟲ icon at the top of the screen. See page 17 for the details.

- **The phone volume is low—even the speakerphone.** Actually, the recent iPhone models have surprisingly loud, clear audio volume, so something must be wacky. With all due respect, did you remove the plastic film from your brand-new iPhone? (This plastic, intended to be on the phone only during shipping, covers up the earpiece.)

 Tip The speaker volume is a lot better when it's pointed at you, either on a table or with your hand cupped around the bottom of the phone to direct the sound.

iPod Problems

The iPhone is a great iPod, but even here, things can go wrong.

- **Can't hear anything.** Are the earbuds plugged in? They automatically cut the sound coming from the iPhone's built-in speaker.

  Is the volume up? Press the Up volume key on the side of the phone. Also make sure that the music is, in fact, supposed to be playing (and isn't on Pause).

- **Can't sync music or video files to the iPhone.** They may be in a format the iPhone doesn't understand, like WMA, MPEG-1, MPEG-2, or Audible Format 1.

  Convert them first to something the iPhone does understand, like AAC; Apple Lossless; MP3'WAV; Audible Formats 2, 3, or 4; AIFF (these are all audio formats); H.264; or MPEG-4 (video formats).

- **Something's not playing or syncing right.** It's technically possible for some corrupted or incompatible music, photo, or video file to jam up the entire syncing or playback process. In iTunes, experiment with playlists and videos, turning off checkboxes until you figure out which one is causing the problem.

Warranty and Repair

The iPhone comes with a one-year warranty. If you buy an AppleCare contract ($70), you're covered for a second year.

 Tip AT&T tech support is free for both years of your contract. They handle questions about your iPhone's phone features.

If, during the coverage period, anything goes wrong that's not your fault, Apple will fix it free. You can either take the phone to an Apple Store, which is often the fastest route, or call 800-APL-CARE (800-275-2273) to arrange shipping back to Apple. In general, you'll get the fixed phone back in three business days.

Sync the phone before it goes in for repair. The repair process generally erases the phone completely—Apple very often simply hands you a new (or refurbished) iPhone instead of your original. In fact, if you're worried that someone at Apple might snoop around, you might want to erase the phone *first*. (Use the Restore option—page 339.)

Also, don't forget to remove your SIM card (page 8) before you send in your broken iPhone—and to put it back in when you get the phone. Don't leave it in the loaner phone. AT&T can help you get a new card if you lose your original, but it's a hassle.

While your phone is in the shop, you can sign up for a loaner iPhone to use in the meantime for $30. Apple will ship it to you, or you can pick one up at the Apple Store. Just sync this loaner phone with iTunes, and presto—all your stuff is right back on it.

You can keep this service phone until seven days after you get your fixed phone back.

Out-of-Warranty Repairs

Once the year or two has gone by, or if you damage your iPhone in a way that's not covered by the warranty (backing your car over it comes to mind), Apple charges $200 to repair an iPhone (they usually just replace it).

The Battery Replacement Program

Why did Apple seal the battery inside the iPhone, anyway? Everyone knows lithium-ion batteries don't last forever. After 300 or 400 charges, the iPhone battery begins to hold less charge (perhaps 80 percent of the original). After a certain point, the phone will need a new battery. How come you can't change it yourself, as on any normal cellphone?

Conspiracy theorists have all kinds of ideas: It's a plot to generate service fees. It's a plot to make you buy a new phone. It's Steve Jobs' design aesthetic on crack.

The truth is more mundane: A user-replaceable battery takes up a lot more space inside the phone. It requires a plastic compartment that shields the guts of the phone from you and your fingers; it requires a removable door; and it needs springs or clips to hold the battery in place. (As an eco-bonus, Apple properly disposes of the old batteries, which consumers might not do on their own.)

In any case, you can't change the battery yourself. If the phone is out of warranty, you must send it to Apple (or take it to an Apple Store) for an $85 battery-replacement job.

Where to Go From Here

At this point, the iPhone is such a phenomenon that there's no shortage of resources for getting more help, news, tips, and information. Here are a few examples:

- **Apple's Official iPhone User Guide.** No, it doesn't come with the iPhone. But yes, there is an actual downloadable PDF user's manual. *http://manuals.info.apple.com/en/iPhone_User_Guide.pdf*

- **Apple's Official iPhone Help Web Site.** There's a lot going on here: online tips, tricks, and tutorials; highlighted troubleshooting topics; downloadable PDF help documents; and, above all, an enormous, seething treasure trove of discussion boards, where ordinary iPhone owners complain and solve one another's problems. *www.apple.com/support/iphone/*

- **Apple's Service Site.** If the thing is really, truly broken, this site lists all the dates, prices, and expectations for getting your iPhone repaired. Includes details on getting a replacement unit to use while yours is in the shop. *www.apple.com/support/iphone/service/faq/*

- **iPhoneBlog.** News, tips, tricks, all in a blog format (daily posts, with comments). *www.TiPb.com/*

- **iLounge.** Another great blog-format site. Available in an iPhone format so you can read it right on the device. *www.iLounge.com/*

- **MacRumors/iPhone.** Blog-format news; accessory blurbs; help discussions; iPhone wallpaper. *www.macrumors.com/iphone/*

- **iPhoneAtlas.** Discussion, news, applications, how-tos. *www.iphoneatlas.com*

- **Gizmodo.** Snarky, funny, sometimes raunchy—the commercial bloggers' take on the iPhone. *www.gizmodo.com/iphone*

Index